Archetype, Culture, and the Individual in Education

In *Archetype, Culture, and the Individual in Education: The Three Pedagogical Narratives*, Clifford Mayes presents a unique approach to understanding how Jungian principles can inform pedagogical theory and practice. In a time when what the educational historian Lawrence Cremin called the 'military-industrial-*educational* complex' and its standardized education are running roughshod over the psyche and spirit of students, Mayes deploys depth psychology, especially the work of Jung, to advance an archetypal approach to teaching and learning.

Mayes demonstrates how catastrophic it is to students when the classroom is governed by forces that objectify the individual in a paralysing strangle-hold. He argues that one's life-narrative is significantly impacted by one's narrative as a learner; thus, schooling that commodifies learning and turns the student into an object has neuroticizing effects that will spread throughout that student's entire life. In Part I, Mayes explores the interaction between archetypes and various types of time—ultimately focusing on the individual but always mediated by 'the cultural unconscious'. In Parts II and III, he brings together education with (post-)Jungian and (post-)Freudian psychology, examining transference/countertransference in the classroom; the Jungian idea of 'the shadow' applied to educational processes; Jung's unique vision of 'the symbol' and its importance for educational theory; and Jung's 'transcendent function' as a prime educational modality. Mayes concludes by looking to the future of archetypal pedagogy.

This groundbreaking work in the emerging field of Jungian pedagogy is invaluable reading in Jungian Studies, depth psychological theory, educational theory, and for teachers and psychotherapists.

Clifford Mayes, now an independent scholar, was, until his recent retirement, a professor of educational psychology at Brigham Young University. He holds two doctorates: The Cultural Foundations of Education (University of Utah) and Clinical Psychology (Southern California University for Professional Studies). As the founder of archetypal pedagogy, Professor Mayes continues working to expand that field.

'In this sparkling and erudite book that illuminates narrative and so much else, Mayes brings together philosophy, Shakespeare, the Gospels, educational theory, cultural history and above all, Jungian psychology in the service of what education needs to be. Here is a brilliantly persuasive way forward for a humane and rejuvenating teaching and learning to show us the way in the crises of our times. *Archetype, Culture, and the Individual in Education* is a blessed book and a spiritual-intellectual support for every teacher and learner.'

Susan Rowland, PhD, Chair, Engaged Humanities and the Creative Life, Pacifica Graduate Institute, and author of *Jung as a Writer*

'Mayes presents a beautifully articulated psychospiritual theory of teaching and learning. It has the power to animate the design of lessons, classroom teaching, and even to show how schools and other educational systems could ideally operate to promote the emotional and intellectual well-being of all students. And though deeply theoretical, this work provides a robust argument and a practical basis for accomplishing this goal. Mayes' theory of teaching melds narrative theory and archetypal theory into a pedagogy that, if embraced in teacher education, would lead to the development of a new generation of amazing and influential teachers.'

Stefinee Pinnegar, PhD, Acting Dean of The Invisible College, author of *Learning from Research on Teaching*, and the editor of *Advances in Research on Teaching*

Archetype, Culture, and the Individual in Education

The Three Pedagogical Narratives

Clifford Mayes

Routledge
Taylor & Francis Group

LONDON AND NEW YORK

First published 2020
by Routledge
2 Park Square, Milton Park, Abingdon, Oxon OX14 4RN

and by Routledge
52 Vanderbilt Avenue, New York, NY 10017

Routledge is an imprint of the Taylor & Francis Group, an informa business

© 2020 Clifford Mayes

British Library Cataloguing-in-Publication Data
A catalogue record for this book is available from the British Library

Library of Congress Cataloging-in-Publication Data
A catalog record has been requested for this book

ISBN: 978-1-138-38968-7 (hbk)
ISBN: 978-1-138-38969-4 (pbk)
ISBN: 978-0-429-42375-8 (ebk)

Typeset in Times New Roman
by Newgen Publishing UK

To Evelyn, my wife, and Elizabeth, my daughter

Contents

Acknowledgements

My discussions with my students at Pacifica Graduate Institute in 'Jung in Context' and 'Introduction to Depth Psychology' around sections from the manuscript, which I invited them to critique, were enlightening and impactful. Daniel Culbertson, Ben Edwards, Kyle Jankowski, Vanessa Jankowski, Kevin Kell, Dr Donald Marks, and Susan Persing were extremely helpful.

I have been reading Jung for almost 50 years. Dr Pamela Blackwell, a sister and mentor, has read him longer. Although a clinician of the rarest abilities, her intuitive understanding of Jung's work rivals any scholar's theoretical formulations of it, and I have been blessed for 27 years to benefit from that. For this, and for so much else, thank you, Pam.

Dr Lance Owens, physician, a leading figure in the Jungian study of the Kabbalah, and Gnostic Christian priest, was very generous to me during a difficult transition in my life for no other reason than that he is so kind, and he has influenced my thinking greatly for the simple reason that he is so brilliant.

Fr David Mayer (*Societas Verbi Divini*) has been a spiritual advisor since I met him 37 years ago at Nanzan University in Nagoya, Japan, where we both taught. As a literary scholar, Fr Mayer's comments and criticisms regarding my work have made me a better researcher and writer. As a physician of souls, Fr Mayer has made a better man even out of one so refractory and rebellious as I.

I am grateful for the opportunity I had for several years to deepen my meditative practice under the watchful eye ('that never sleeps') of Denis Genpo Merzel, of both the Soto and Rinzai Zen traditions, at the Kanzeon Zen Center in Salt Lake City, Utah. His wisdom, humour, and kindness are themselves worthy foci of meditation. A master teacher, he taught me by example and thus not only enhanced my meditative practices but my teaching practices as well.

I have had the rare opportunity of working with Dr Susan Rowland. In her humility, she constantly resists what I cannot help but say after half a century of reading Jung and Jungians—namely, that she is the most innovative and insightful Jungian scholar on the scene today—one who has singlehandedly changed how we read Jung in her analysis of him in literary terms: 'Jung as a writer'. She has changed my understanding of Jung in many salutary ways, a few of which I discuss in this book. These people have been key in my work in one of my two areas of research—depth psychology.

In educational studies, my other focus, the following people have been key in ways that are imprinted in invisible ink on every page of this study. Dr Robert Bullough, one of the premier scholars of the history of the 20th-century U.S. curriculum, showed me how to parse a curriculum as essentially a world-historical text that encodes the whole spectrum of a culture's psychosocial problems and prospects. Dr Stefinee Pinnegar's work in narrative theory, especially her prodigious labours of love with teachers about their sense of calling and the existential roots of their *praxis* has helped transform teacher education in the U.S., and would do so even more if policymakers and university and college administrators had the good sense to listen to her more, and more carefully. Her dazzling mind is matched only by her simple goodness. Dr Robert Carson, author of the *Ourstory* approach to the curriculum, offers in it a vision of the curriculum that is more capacious, daring, and simply more intellectually winning than any other theory of the curriculum I have ever encountered in my 30 years of studying it. Dr Joseph Matthews, veteran principal and noted scholar of the principalship, taught me, both by example and in his work, that in school leadership, as in everything, humour and balance are all. Dr Vance Randall, who was my chairman at Brigham Young University during my two decades there, and an important scholar of private education in the U.S., is the Chairman of chairmen, and everyone who has ever been in a position of academic leadership might well look to him as an example of enlightened and enlightening leadership. My admiration for these five colleagues is rivalled only by my love for them.

My Jewish mother and Italian Catholic father, fleeing their families' wrath because their marriage transgressed faith and ethnic boundaries in New York City in 1950, moved far away, landing finally in the unpopulated scrub-and-saguaro desert of Tucson, Arizona. There, between the Papago Reservation just south of our rough adobe home and the Mexican American barrios just north of it, I grew up, taught by my parents about the beauty of the Native and Latino cultures that bracketed our lives. They gifted me with a peerless education!

Above all, I stand all amazed at God having blessed me with my wife, Evelyn, and my daughter, Elizabeth. It is both a joy and a puzzlement to me that I have them (although it would be more accurate to say that they have me, eternally and totally). For, no man could possibly claim that he merits either one of them, let alone both of them. Each of them highly accomplished in her own right, they love and support me with a purity and consistency that I will spend this life working to be worthy of so that I may be with them forever, after this brief, mortal day has passed and the day that knows no end begins—that Time beyond time, when there is no one who does not consciously live, move, and have their being in the tender, universal embrace of the Divine.

Part I

The archetype and time

Chapter 1

Narrative, archetype, and the individual

Gaining perspective(s): the necessity of narrative

Our narratives are the stories that we are always authoring, adding to, erasing from, and sometimes radically rewriting in our minds for the 'creation of coherence' in our lives (Linde, 1993).[1] Otherwise, we would merely have a log of events, a list of whatever 'happened to happen'. Let that log be as complete as possible in minutest detail. Exhaustive and exhausting, it would also be meaningless. For if all we have is just a log of events, then there is really no story at all. A log's mere events do not just automatically form into patterns to provide a perspective on themselves. They do not interpret themselves.

That is what human beings do. We provide the perspectives. We are the 'meaning-making' agents. We create coherence in our lives—or not. If one is unable to make any deeper connections in events, then one is in danger of being caught up in what Gebser (1985) called 'a-perspectival madness'. Such a person is fragmented, unable to make connections. He is inchoate. This epistemological crisis is a feature of certain neuroses and psychoses, and it may, in the final analysis, be at the root of some of them, perhaps even all of them (Wilber, 2000). In any case, without any life-giving organizing narratives, life is devoid of meaning.

Our narratives are our meanings. Without them, a person may all too easily fall into either a lethargic depression—a 'depressive position'—or into the terror of being fragmented, of shattering, of being persecuted, of 'falling apart'—a 'schizoid position'—as defined early in the history of psychoanalytic theory by Melanie Klein (Klein, 1932/1975). Meaning makes connections between parts to establish a pattern. Thus, meaning, essential to the health of the human being, is narratival patternicity.

Not even the hard sciences using their universal language of maths are immune to the need to create narratives.

Take, for example, the idea of 'goodness of fit' from the field of statistics. This refers to when the formula describing an anticipated pattern of events is compared against the sequence of the events as they actually turned out. If the discrepancy between what was predicted and what was observed is sufficiently low and there is only a very small mathematical remainder that falls below what random variation would have caused in any case, then there is a significant 'goodness of fit', and you can conclude with a certain degree of confidence that the sequence of events is meaningful according to what your formula anticipated. Your formula is meaningful.

Analogously, if the unfolding of sequences of events as we live our lives is close enough to how either our patterns of meaning predicted they would go or, *post hoc*, if we can find a pattern that does explain how they went, then we have a narratival 'goodness of fit' that engenders and reinforces our sense of meaning. I highlight 'sense' to imply that a person's entire grasping of and being grasped by life, a subjective and intuitive inner process, is much more relevant to us as human beings than any objective, mathematical set of formulas could ever be.

Yet even a mathematical procedure like establishing goodness-of-fit has a narratival aspect. And the most subjectively nuanced narrative makes meaning by comparing intuitive impressions and against actual outcomes. Bridging the gap between the subjective and objective domains, our narrativizing in both of our major epistemological modes, subjective and objective, poetic or scientific, evidences our ability, indeed our inner imperative to dwell in various 'realms of meaning' (Phenix, 1964).

Even so, there is no maths to describe the love that flows between a mother and her child as they lie in bed together after a day in the park and then, after eating their favourite ice-cream from the same bowl sharing a spoon, they both, finally, gazing into each other's eyes and stroking each other's hair, drift off at the same moment to sleep. In what matters most to us in our lives, it is our 'subjectivity' that we consult. And rightly so. For meaning is most human when it is most humane, and when it is most humane, it is most ethical. It is the fostering of humane, and therefore, ethical narratives in educational processes that is the purpose of this book.

None of our narratives, however wide-ranging and ethical, accounts for absolutely everything. As for those things that don't quite fit, we reconcile ourselves to the fact that all our meaning-systems come with a mysterious 'surplus'. We are not gods. We are limited human beings who are always adjusting our meaning-systems to be more meaningful under the stern tutelage of experience. Either that, or we fall into a pathology that is opposite to the 'a-perspectival madness' ('Nothing is true …'). We then suffer from (and make others suffer from) what we could call 'dogmatic delusionality' ('Only what I believe is true!').

At any rate, it is our patterning of what happens, in time and over time, that invests life with meaning. And since a pattern of events in one's life is what constitutes a narrative, then the question of whether or not life is meaningful really boils down to the question of whether a life is a workably coherent narrative. No narrative, no meaning. Hamlet's 'to be or not to be' can thus be translated into the question: 'Is there or is there not some narrative that can explain all this wild, wicked and, maddeningly confusing stuff going on in Castle Elsinore?' And of course, that finally translates into the bigger question that is always hovering over us: 'Can I discover or fashion a narrative that makes sense out of all the pain and disappointment, so much apparently random suffering in my life and everyone else's, or can I not?' To be or not to be. To have a narrative or not to have one. That is the question!

Neurosis, seen in this light, is a 'narratival rupture', a temporal discon-nection between point A in time and point B in time and from both of them to similarly disconnected points W and X (Hamlet laments: 'The time is out of joint!'). By this view, recovery in therapy is a 'narratival repair' with the client 'rewriting' an even better narrative than the one before the rup-ture/breakdown. When that happens, then the patient has learned (Mayes, Grandstaff, and Fidyk, 2019, 2017a). This makes of therapy an educational process. Conversely, educational processes have a therapeutic dimension as I hope to show throughout this book, especially when what goes on at school is enriching the student's life-narrative (Mayes, Grandstaff, and Fidyk, 2019).[2]

As for Carl Gustav Jung, he was insistent upon the point that therapy is about crises of meaning. It is not just about happiness. It is not even pri-marily about happiness. For, the stoical Swiss Jung believed that the goal of psychotherapy 'is not to transport the patient to an impossible state of happiness, but to help him acquire steadfastness and philosophic patience in the face of suffering' (1966b, p. 81). Therapy should be about finding meaning and growing in and through difficulty. Neurosis was, in the last analysis, 'the suffering of a soul which has not discovered its meaning' (1984, p. 198). And this meaning need not reveal itself in dramatic breakthroughs or result in great achievements in the eyes of the world. Meaning can be a humble thing, and usually is, Jung believed, discovered in the ordinary give and take of daily life (Jung, 1954, p. 45).

Jung's quiet, stoic tones are reassuring. But Gebser is also right in forcefully characterizing the lack of narrative as 'madness'; for, the root of neurosis and psychosis may well be a fundamental 'derangement' (de-arrangement—i.e., in-cohere-ence) of one's capacity to narrativize. Human beings need this meaning in order 'to go on being' (Winnicott, 1992). At least, they need meaning to go on being in creativity and courage (Frankl, 1967; Tillich, 1952).

Archetypes and meaning in life-narratives

In Jungian psychology, the major way of finding meaning in our life-narratives is through archetypes, which are the central concept in Jungian psychology. The main purpose of this study is to draw these two approaches to meaning together in Part I—namely, the idea of narrative together with the idea of archetypes—as a means in Part II of extending the reach and expanding the scope of my previous work in archetypal pedagogy (2017a, 2017b, 2017d, 2015, 2012, 2005a, 2005b, 2002, 2001, 1998), which heretofore has not incorporated narrative theory in any systematic way.

This synergistic joining of narrative theory with archetypal theory—two fields of study that are intimately involved with the question of meaning—will hopefully result in ever more meaningful ways of shaping, assessing, and improving educational processes so that they are the most deeply and broadly applicable to all the domains of the teacher's and student's lives: emotional, cognitive, cultural, ethical, and spiritual. In general, what we will find in Part I, and will then apply to educational issues in Part II is that the more archetypal the narrative, the more meaningful it is; and the more meaningful the narrative, the more archetypal it tends to be. This is why 'the greatest and best thoughts of man shape themselves upon [the archetypes] as upon a blueprint' (Jung, 1967b, p. 69). It also accounts for the fact that

> whoever speaks in [archetypal terms] speaks with a thousand voices; he enthralls and overpowers, whilst at the same time he lifts the idea he is seeking to express out of the occasional and transitory into the realm of the ever-enduring. He transmutes our personal destiny into the destiny of mankind.
>
> (Jung, 1966a, p. 82)

An overview of archetypes[3]

The first thing to note about archetypes is that they are paradoxical. An archetype is like a coin whose two sides are always each other's opposite. Archetypes contain all that is light in the human experience and all that is dark. They lie at the core of all that is angelic in us and all that is demonic. They are the psychological and ontological source from which 'mankind ever and anon has drawn, and from which it has raised its gods and its demons, all those potent and mighty thoughts without which man ceases to be man' (Jung, 1967b, p. 67). At the same time as they are 'in us' and 'at our core', they are also cosmic realities so distant from anything we can know that they are impenetrable even by our most advanced cognitive faculties and subtlest lines of analysis.

The archetypes are paradoxical as well because they are both so primordial yet also so transcendent that their concentrated energy would simply explode consciousness to smouldering rubble to be in the immediate presence of their overwhelming power, an experience that leads almost inevitably to psychosis (Jung, 1967a). Therefore, they present themselves to us in the secondary, mediated form of archetypal symbols. These symbols, one remove away, as it were, from the core of the archetype, are formations that specially encode the meaning of the archetype as symbols. They are therefore called 'archetypal symbols' that convey a manageable portion of the energy of the overwhelming power of the archetype-in-itself so that we can begin to engage with the otherwise entirely inaccessible. Ordinary ways of communicating ideas will never do in bringing us to the zone of the archetypal, where meaning resides in its most concentrated form—and those forms are always symbols.

Only the special power of the symbolic can bring us into the proximity of the sacred. This is because of the primordial and transcendent nature of the archetypes: Being both pre-rational and transrational, they exist primally before speech and cognition in the realm of sheer instinct while at the same time they exist transcendentally beyond the reach of speech and the possibility of any typical forms of cognition in the realm of sheer spirit. Jung thus said that, on one hand, archetypes are 'organs of the pre-rational psyche' while, on the other hand, they are 'categories of the soul' (Jung, 1978, pp. 67f). Archetypes cover the spectrum of all the major issues and impulses that always have and always will make up the human experience. They are perennial and universal although they dress up in different ceremonial vestments and dance to different rhythms from culture to culture.

In both their light and dark aspects, the archetypes are inherent in every human being. They are therefore 'collective'. They are also beyond the reach of consciousness—so much so that it is not enough to call them merely 'subconscious'—as in Freud's much shallower layer of psyche, the subconscious, where material is personal and therefore recoverable. We must instead call them 'unconscious'—a stronger term than 'subconscious', since we can of necessity never know them directly in their ancient and unreachable depths and heights. Therefore, Jung said that the archetypes reside in the 'collective unconscious'.

Every statement about the collective unconscious and its archetypes is at best a very rough approximation. We can neither primordially remember nor transcendentally intuit the true scope and full impact of the archetype. Archetypes bracket the possibilities of our consciousness from just before that misty prehistoric threshold where the first truly and uniquely human thought arose, and they go to just beyond that indescribable height where the most sublime reaches of mystical communion with the Divine breaks free of the orbit of human thought and language and disappears into the inexpressible rapture of the saint. This is the other reason we can never experience an archetype directly—namely, that it is also the very organ for knowing upon which all knowledge develops within us. Because we see through it, we cannot see it any more than the unaided eye can see itself or than teeth can bite themselves. One cannot see what enables seeing in the first place or know what enables knowing, for they exist by definition before all seeing and knowing.

Archetypes thus precede and transcend cognition. They are unknowable to us in our present epistemological limitations, yet they are simultaneously that upon which all knowledge was originally built at the unconscious level and towards which all knowledge ultimately strives at a supra-conscious level—neither of which is accessible to us in our present limited condition. The one possible exception to this might be the person who has attained very high levels of yogic awareness so that all conscious thought processes reduce to 'zero' and the yogi is left with pure awareness as such. Even then, it is not clear if this pure awareness as such is finally another (although infinitely more refined) state of epistemological self-awareness or if it is actually being in and with the archetypal realm of being-as-such.

Nevertheless, as just noted, we are able to process and interact with the archetype through archetypal symbols. There is no other way for us to even begin to grasp the archetype than by the suggestive, multivalent, intuitive power of symbols. 'The symbol is the primitive exponent of the unconscious' while it simultaneously is 'an idea that corresponds to the highest intuition of the conscious mind' (Jung, 1978, p. 30). Covering the entire spectrum of human experience, archetypal symbols encode major issues and themes in our life-narratives in such a way that those narratives are infused with the indirect power of the archetype but not overwhelmed by it. The same is true of archetypal narrative-structures, which reflect overarching patterns and unfolding processes over the course of our lives.

Together, archetypal symbols and archetypal narrative structures—basically available to us as they inform dreams, creative processes and products, fantasies, and psychological symptomatology—offer potent yet subtle symbolic and narratival means of examining one's present life-narrative to make it more complete and creative, clearer and more powerful. One may then live one's life in ever-widening circles of passion and compassion that include all of life's dualities as one learns through hard-won experience to reconcile them. In this, one becomes wiser and, being more wise, more spiritual. The realm of the merely personal and mundane, the rigidly and simply temporal, is transported to the realm of the universal and salvific. When the present moment is infused with the Presence of that which transcends time, that which is Timeless Time, then, along with Lord Whitehead (1964, p. 14), we discover to our supreme delight that 'the present holds within itself the complete sum of existence, backwards and forwards, that whole amplitude of time, which is eternity'.

It is at this point that many misinterpret Jung as advocating for an escape from the socially normative, ego-oriented time of consensual reality in order to live in a never-never land of complete identification with the archetypes. But Jung never said any such thing. To the contrary, he understood the necessity of living a productive, sane, and reasonably safe life within the boundaries of social realities. Jung's conservatism will be a running theme throughout this study.

What he objected to was when those constraints become so overbearing or unreasonable as to alienate a person from her own soul, which he called the Self, and which one might equate with one's core ethical and perhaps even eternal identity. The great project in Jungian psychology is to establish an 'axis' between one's social identity and one's essential identity so that ego, under the aegis of the Self, is infused with and directed by a higher vision while, at the same time, one's visionary Self learns to manifest itself in ways that are emotionally grounded and socially useful, not run off into irresponsible and possibly even dangerous flights of archetypal fantasy. The establishment and maintenance of an ego-Self axis, fructifying in an ego alive with idealism and coupled with a soul pragmatically dedicated to the betterment of the world —this is the *desideratum* of Jungian therapy and one aspect of what Jung meant by the term 'individuation'.

Jung on archetypes

Jung wrote literally volume upon volume on the nature of the archetype. Let us begin by looking at a few particularly useful depictions of them.

One of the simplest and most poetic of Jung's definitions of the nature of an archetype is that it is 'the inherited possibility of human imagination' (1967b, p. 65). Already, we sense that an archetype goes well beyond merely academic, discursive categories of description and analysis. It has to do with more fundamental poetic capacities to 'imagine' realities that transcend the observable and measurable. And it is open-ended, dynamic, and creative because it is about 'possibilities'. Still, as the archetypes are also 'typical modes of apprehension' (1967b, p. 137) that we were born with, they also have something of the inherent and instinctual about them (1967b, p. 138). Thus, although involved in transcendence, they are rooted in our basic, even primal nature. They are 'typical' of us—even *arche*-typical.

We are then warranted in forming a composite portrait of the archetype as both transcendental and primordial. We might, therefore, speak of archetypes as the spiritual correlates of our instincts—or, as Jung puts it, our 'spiritual instincts'. They are the rarefied 'image of instinct in man' (1968b, p. 179). In a sense, therefore, archetypes are both the source and object of our inclinations towards and intimations of the enormity of Spirit within us.

Although there is, too, as we shall see throughout this study, great individual variation in how archetypes are experienced and enacted from person to person, there is also constancy from person to person, even culture to culture, and epoch to epoch. They are the ways that human beings respond to their situation as creatures *sub specie aeternitatis*.

Thus it should not be surprising that archetypes manifest themselves throughout history as a sort of ethical constant across time and space, being 'the functional disposition [of people] throughout different times, places and cultures, to produce the same, or very similar, ideas' (Jung, 1954, p. 102). Note here that the archetypes are not those historically recurring ideas themselves; for, those we do experience directly. Instead, it is the inborn disposition to produce such recurring ideas. Those we do not experience directly. Indeed, how could we? We only *have* an idea because of the 'functional disposition' to produce that idea. We can no more turn our consciousness upon its source than a telescope can turn its lens upon itself to scrutinize itself.

An example of this is the ancient motif of the God who visits his people since they are in need of saving and he alone is mighty to save. Yet he must undergo a sacrificial death to atone for their sins and restore their land to a place of felicity and fertility. In ancient Egypt, that god was Osiris. For many people today, that god is Christ. The archetype is the same. It is the archetype of the dying and resurrected god who saves his people. But that archetype has been filled by different archetypal characters/symbols/events in the two different sacred narratives. The archetype is similar. The archetypal *images* differ.

It is as if an archetype were an empty container but charged with a certain type and realm of spiritual potential that for some reason gets activated or activates itself, or perhaps a blend of both. When that happens, different things begin to materialize in the box. They all bespeak the archetype, but they do it differently.

Osiris and Christ. They are alike in their archetypal core but different in their cultural and temporal manifestation. Both Osiris and Christ are realizations of the archetype of the Saviour. An archetype, therefore, is a specific type of existential/ethical potential. An archetype-as-such is thus a sort of 'empty potentiality' (Jung, 1978, p. 69) that can generate countless symbolic realizations of that potential without being reducible to any or even all of them.

Hence, archetypes could also be characterized as 'the stock of inherited possibilities of representation that are born anew in every individual' (1968a, p. 156).

It bears repeating that an archetype is a potential, a matrix of possibility, a 'possibility-field' out of which these specific ideational and imagistic crystallizations emerge. Indeed, Jung compares an archetype to the invisible force and abstract principle that governs the formation of a crystal (1968a, p. 80).

Other approaches to the archetype

Frey-Rohn (1974) offers an economical definition of archetypes as 'preconscious categories which [channel] thought and action into definite shapes' (p. 92). Other Jungians have pictured archetypes as 'a kind of mold for the accumulation and discharge of psychic energy' (Odajnyk, 1976, p. 25) and speculated that they might actually *be* patterns of energy at the deepest and most formative levels of the psyche (p. 143). As such, they are 'irreducible and primary', 'the structural nature of the psyche itself' (Palmer, 1995, pp. 8, 114). Samuels has said that archetypes 'constellate experience in accordance with innate schemata and act as an imprimatur of subsequent experience' (1997, p. 27).

I have elsewhere characterized the collective unconscious and its archetypes in the following terms:

The collective unconscious is the dynamic psychic matrix from which all our other psychic functioning—conscious and subconscious—emerges. It is composed of archetypes, which can be pictured as constantly interacting, occasionally overlapping, and subtly morphing 'patterns of energy'—although I use the idea of 'energy' metaphorically since actual physical energy is far from a category that precedes thought, is measurable, and can even under some circumstances be observed; these are the very things that are not true of archetypes.

(Mayes, 2012, p. 63)

Archetypes are thus the unseen 'dominants' (1967b, p. 80) as Jung used to call them,[4] that, on one hand, *engender* ethico-spiritual intuitions, but also, on the hand, are 'discovered' by those intuitions. They are only ever approached in the most indistinct and distant ways, if at all. They simply go beyond any form of human cognition, apperception, or intuition. We do gain a secondary purchase on them, however, as they emerge into existence as archetypal images that will vary depending upon personal, cultural, and historical circumstances and other stimuli.

At any rate, archetypes set the terms and tones of those things that are most important to us. They are everywhere implicit in how we interpret and shape our subjective and objective worlds in a distinctly human manner that has, in the most essential ways, remained fairly constant throughout history and across cultures although the material circumstances have changed and technical knowledge has exploded almost beyond the power to imagine, much less master. This does not touch the archetype. The archetype abides in a cosmic untouchability.

Another example of all of this may be useful. One may watch a series on Netflix set in urban America one evening, a play by Shakespeare the next, a tragedy from the Greek drama on the weekend. Next week, one goes with one's son to the mall to play the latest high-tech sci-fi theme game. All of these different instances of theatre may be equally interesting because, despite the radical differences in the time and place of the dramas, they deal with the same basic trials and tragedies, tensions and resolutions, perils and possibilities, triumphs and catastrophes that have always quintessentially captured the human condition.

It is a beautiful thing to celebrate difference in these times, which may in historical retrospect ultimately come to be called 'the age of multiculturalism', according to the philosopher of the social sciences, Brian Fay (2000). I will invoke multicultural theory throughout this study as I have in previous books, especially in my *Understanding the Whole Student: Holistic Multicultural Education* (2016; see also Thompson and Mayes, 2020).

There is the danger, however, that if that celebration does not also recognize and honour certain timeless, archetypal truths that do not change or go away—no matter the political force exerted on them, and that are indeed essential to the survival of cultures, whether dominant or subdominant ones—then a culture, deriding or simply dismissing those time-honoured verities, puts itself on a fast track to moral dissolution and historical collapse. This is an inconvenient truth for much postmodern theory, which eschews any notion of ethical absolutes. That does not hurt the standing, however, of the fact that all civilizations have either abided by and thrived in these universal truths or perished for the lack of them.

Jung understood this well. Virtually every culture, he observed, has 'a highly developed system of secret teaching, a body of lore concerning the things that lie beyond man's earthly existence, and of wise rules of conduct' (Jung, 1966a, p. 96). One of the 20th century's greatest sociologists, Anthony Giddens, concurs, positing a universal logic and gradation of values that are the infrastructure of most cultures. 'These include prohibiting sexual relations between close relatives, the existence of art, dancing, bodily adornment, games, gift-giving, joking, and rules of hygiene' (Giddens, 1991, p. 46).[5]

Finally, to round off this multi-angled approach to grasping the nature of an archetype, picture yourself standing on the deck of a great liner at night in the middle of the ocean with a full, bright moon illuminating the surface. Winds keep coming up and playing across the water causing different patterns on the morphing surface that glitter in the night. You cannot see the wind that creates various figures in the water but, since you do see the figures, you can imagine something of the dynamics of the wind creating the glittering ephemeral shapes on the ocean. In this trope, the wind is the various *archetypes* that create those visible traces of them on the surface of the water, and those patterns are the *archetypal images*.

Whether there are a certain given number of archetypes, whether they are illimitable in that they are always are coming into being, whether they can be numbered at all because they are constant combinations and recombinations in infinite variety of a universally circulating ontological energy—these are imponderables.

The list of some of the major archetypes includes the hero/heroine, wise elder; anima and animus; prophet and disciple; parents, mate, child; birth and death; heaven and hell, the wilderness of tribulation and the haven of home, and others (1969b, p, 183, 1967b, pp. 171, 190; 1956, p. 391).

The complexity of the idea of the archetype and the range of views about it

There are many ways of approaching the idea of an archetype. Indeed, what an archetype finally 'is' is perhaps the most ardently debated issue in Jungian Studies. As I read it, there are currently eight basic approaches to the question.

First is the position that archetypes actually exist as not only a feature of the Ground of Being but as that Ground itself, and that this carries with it an ethical imperative that one seek out that archetypal infrastructure of one's life and live faithfully to what one finds; all of which implies that an archetype not only exists as such (i.e., has 'ontological status') but also has ethical (i.e., 'axiological') status/implications (Edinger, 1973; Heisig, 1979; Mayes, 2017a; Stein, 2006, 1995, 1990, 1984, 1982).

By the second view, an archetype has a sort of borderline ontological status as an epistemological structure with great clinical (Eisendrath-Young and Hall, 1991) or rich phenomenological (Brooke, 2009) possibilities.

Third is the assertion that the archetype has a dependent but definite ontological status as an evolutionarily adaptive biological structure (Stevens, 2003).

The fourth, also from biology, holds that the archetype has potential ontological status in the form of a fifth-dimensional 'morphic field' out of which the species variously emerged and proceed to evolve (Sheldrake, 1981; see also Conforti, 1999).

The fifth camp, related to the fourth as biology is related to physics, believes that the archetype has ontological status in that the archetypes make up a fifth-dimensional 'implicate order' out of which the physical universe is constantly emerging and operating (Bohm, 1986; see also Cambray, 2009; Peat, 1988, Spiegelman and Mansfeld, 1996).

The sixth position comes from developmental psychology, with claims that archetypes have ontological status because they are a human developmental reality and therefore must, by implication, be reflecting a 'pattern' of some sort in the nature of things (Fordham, 1994; see also Kalsched, 1996; Wickes, 1927/1966).

The seventh position holds that the archetype is just a theoretical construct with no ontological status but limitless mythopoetic possibilities (Hillman, 2004; López-Pedraza, 2012).

And finally from Feminist Studies comes the assertion that the idea of an archetype may or may not (but probably not) have ontological status and that it is in any case a gendered concept, especially in the anima/animus binary, requiring us to deal with a possible ontology of gender as well as its politics (Rowland, 2002; see also Lauter and Rupprecht, 1985).

In this present book, I will, naturally, primarily deploy my own current understanding of this many faceted, highly mobile concept—essentially the first position listed above—as it has developed in my own work over the last 20 years (Mayes, 2017a, 2017b, 2017d, 2015, 2012, 2005a, 2005b, 2002, 2001, 1998).

Grasping the archetype: a joint effort

Most of the sustained attempts at a definition of the archetype in Jungian scholarship have merit, even when they do not agree with each other. The idea of an archetype is so complex, even opaque, that no one theory about it can ever lay claim to being definitive. This is largely due to Jung's own indeterminacy on the subject, which is itself a function of both the intractably difficult nature of the idea, his own shifting views, and his rhetorical (and sometimes frankly politically strategic) objectives from time to time and audience to audience (Mayes, 2017a). This is a question we will take up in greater detail in Chapter 8.

Everyone engaged in theorizing about archetypes stands to learn something from other interpretations. This is true no matter how different those other views are from his, and often especially then, and it is an error to exalt any one view of the archetype. It is arguably the most difficult concept in all of psychology, which is probably why academic psychology mostly just ignores Jung. If it cannot be measured by an institutionally-approved 'tool', it does not exist.

Anyone theorizing about archetypes, indeed about psyche in general, does well to emulate Jung in a letter he wrote to a friend in January, 1929:

> Can't you conceive of a physicist who thinks and speaks of atoms, yet is convinced that those are merely his own abstractions? That would be my case. I haven't the faintest idea what 'psyche' is in itself, yet, when I come to think and speak of it, I must speak of my abstractions, concepts, views, figures, knowing that they are our specific illusions.
>
> (Jung, 1973, p. 11)

Jung called this the principle of 'non-concretization'.

Jung fully understood the puzzlement that readers, even devotees, felt at the idea of an archetype. He shared it. 'I admit at once,' he said, that the archetype is 'a controversial idea and more than a little perplexing. But I have always wondered what sort of ideas my critics would have used to characterize the empirical material in question' (Jung, 1967b, p. 77, fn. 15).

The 'empirical material in question' was and is the persistent fact (never fully explained away by basically geographical theories of transmission through trade, warfare, exploration, intermarriage or the like, which always leaves a mystifying surplus) that 1) groupings of certain archetypal themes, narrative structures, character-types, and culturally variable but semiotically cognate symbols 2) underline how, through art, culture, and religion, humans have since time immemorial tried to come to grips with the human condition.

Whatever one makes of the idea of the archetype in the grand scheme of things (or even if there is no grand scheme of things), the Existential fact for us remains that we are, tragically and happily—the two archetypal masks of the Greek drama—singularly self-conscious beings in finitude.

The human being performs his existence on the stage of mortality against the backdrop of eternity. He lives, moves and has his being *sub specie aeternitatis*—as a sub specie of eternity. And it seems to be the case that most of us wish to do so in a manner that to us, by our individual lights and cultural colourations, is ethically valid. Aware that we and those we love must die, there is the craving in many and, one imagines, most hearts to transcend finite time and attain a higher plane of existence—and to maximize our communion with it in this life too—until we one day dwell constantly where 'sacred time' prevails and finite time ceases (Eliade, 1954; Ricoeur, 1985).

'Ultimacy' and its limitations

An important debate in Jungian studies is, as we have seen, whether archetypes 'have ontological status', as the philosophical phrase goes. Of course, to say that something has ontological status is to express one's belief that a particular word that he is using refers to something that is 'really real'. The opposite position is that that word is just a word. When this person uses the same word, it is not to express her belief that it refers to something that it is 'really real' but rather that it is a tool of philosophical conversation. It is a linguistic instrumentality. It may be important in discourse about all sorts of issues of vital concern to everyone involved in the conversation, but it does not refer to something that exists in some secure ontological zone.

Regarding 'archetypes', one can make a 'strong' statement of belief in their ontological status or one can make a 'strong' statement of disbelief, or one can fall somewhere in the middle. All three of those general positions on the matter are perfectly reasonable. Any decent university library will house compelling works by honest men and women who brilliantly lay out profound arguments why they do believe in ontological absolutes in general, don't believe in them, or take that middle stance. One reads their work with admiration for the quality of their reasoning and the courage of their convictions.

For now, and committed to authorial transparency, I'll state upfront that I take a strong position on archetypes as having ontological status. But not 'strong' in the sense of being certain that I am correct, and certainly not in the sense of trying to muscle the reader into my point of view.

However, since this book rests on the idea of meaning in one's life-story by means of intense involvement with the archetypal realm, the issue of the author's basic beliefs—his 'fiduciary commitments' as it is put in philosophical discourse—is relevant, and the reader not only has the right but the need to know where an author stands in such a study. This is not so that the reader can fall into lockstep with the author's opinions. To the contrary. It is so that the reader, forewarned about the author's biases, can be discriminating and even critical in what he chooses to believe about and from the author. I want to make it clear that when I surface my beliefs and apply them in this book, I am not making ontological truth claims about them but merely indicating my subjective commitment to them. I lay no claim to knowing the absolute truth-value (let's call it 'Truth' with a capital 'T') of my assumptions.

All I know is that my fundamental assumptions, which I will naturally bring to bear upon our discussion in these chapters, are 'true' as best as I can tell at this point (let's call it 'truth' with a lower-case 't'). That is to say, they are for me 'true until further notice', in the words of Sir Anthony Giddens (1990)—'true' until someone makes a case that I find compelling enough, or if I have experiences impressive enough, to cause me to change one or some of my 'truths'.

And at the end of the day, no one knows enough to make strong onto-logical claims about matters as vast as whether 'archetypes' actually exist. There are compelling arguments on both sides of that question. I am simply stating where I have landed regarding that question. For, in the last analysis, after the most voluble arguments swell ... and then taper off into silence, we are, each one of us, left alone with our thoughts and confusions, hopes and apprehensions, our experiences and our imaginings. The heart of any matter under discussion is the heart of the individual discussing it.

Relatively ultimate

Useful in this connection is the idea of what the Existentialist Protestant theo-logian Paul Tillich called one's 'Ultimacy'. The notion of Ultimacy begins with the assumption that one is not only free to state one's basic assumptions as they relate to an issue under analysis, but that one is often required to do so to for the sake of clarity and integrity. At the same time, one must also have the humility and realism to know that one cannot prove those foundational assumptions. This is for the simple reason that one's assumptions, being the foundation of all that one asserts, will inevitably be the point-of-origin of any concepts and methods one might use in that proof. One cannot rely on a debatable precept to prove the truth of that precept.

This unprovable but necessary point of origin—whatever it might be for an individual—is the base of any idea we are espousing, whether we are in a casual conversation or in those formal conversations called 'scholarly dis-course'. This touchstone is one's sense of 'Ultimacy', and it is discursively valid—though, of course, not necessarily ontologically true—according to Tillich, to the degree that one has pursued it rigorously and courageously—in good faith. It does not attempt to control or in any way run conver-sationally roughshod over others, who must be abiding by the same rules if the discourse is to be a legitimate and potentially fruitful one in which everybody comes out of the conversation having learned something from each other.

Whether or not we are aware of it, we all do have a set of ultimate convictions, fiduciary commitments, which consciously or unconsciously guide us in our thinking and acting. Claims to Ultimacy are, of course, espe-cially evident when it comes to religions and their charismatic founding figures, whose originating revelation or teachings believers then scrupulously guard, carefully elaborate in doctrines, and solemnly encode in rituals practiced by the community of believers (Berger, 1967). Still, a foundational belief, even if it's the belief that there is nothing to believe in, is an ultimate judgement call. The rhetorical theorist Kenneth Burke called them our 'terministic screens', for upon them we project the movies of our lives; they are where our projections become 'visible' as the assumption(s) we are 'ultimately' operating off of (1989). They are our 'Ultimacy'.

A firm and final belief that this world is all there is and that when you're done, you're done, is no less a fiduciary commitment than belief in the existence of 'God'. They are both risky commitments, and they both bring with them certain advantages and certain problems. But what of that? Any commitment is a risk. A risk-free life would not be a life. It would be a lie. Our fiduciary commitments precede proofs and are often enough the launching pads from which various 'programmes of proof' then take flight. Our basic commitments are a matter of the intensity of our investment in them. In a sense, our life narratives are one grand concerted attempt to both discover, justify, and account for ourselves in light of our fiduciary commitments. In this sense, our narrativizing is fundamentally an ethical project.

Throughout his writings Jung states that he makes no judgement as to the ontological or metaphysical validity of a person's spiritual experiences and assertions. However, in my *An Introduction to the Collected Works of C. G. Jung: Psyche as Spirit* (2017a, pp. 77–86) I discuss the fact that Jung actually made many statements about the varieties of religious experience and not all of them were neutral. Not only that but his statements were often inconsistent with each other so that it is difficult to get a real fix on where Jung stands on this matter of great importance in any discussion of archetypes. For, the two topics of 'archetypes' and 'spiritual experience' are closely related. Indeed, medieval Catholic theology revolved around the dispute about whether an archetype had ontological status, and it is still a relevant issue in theology.

Therefore, whenever appropriate to do so in the course of this book, I will clarify my assumptions regarding this point or that; however, when I do make one of my fiduciary commitments explicit, I do not do it because I lay claim to the absolute Truth of my assumptions. I do not do it as if I were free of doubts. The person who *never* doubts his 'Ultimacies' is, *no* doubt, prone to fall into polemics and fall out of fruitful discourse. *No* doubt, the person who *never* doubts his positions thinks that is being extremely reasonable. However, as Jung wrote, not only our reasons but indeed our very reason itself is, when all is said and done, 'nothing more than the sum total of all [our] prejudices and myopic views' (1969b, p. 13: emphasis added).

I thus hold firmly to Sir Karl Popper's rule of 'falsifiability'. What is this 'rule'? Simply put: It is entering into a conversation believing what you believe but realizing that all or part of that belief may be wrong. It is being willing to change. It also has the reasonable expectation that the person you are having the discussion with feels the same way and will play by the same rules.

One who engages in polemics, not partnership, in dialogue is also acting unethically, according to the 20th-century Jewish ethicist Martin Buber (1965) in his seminal work *I and Thou*. There Buber defines ethical relationship as one in which you view your conversant as a 'dialogical partner', from whom you are as anxious to learn as she is from you.

Jung and the ontological status of an archetype

Every narrative is subjective in terms of one's ultimate commitments. But that does not mean that a conversation is non-objective, without any need for any proofs of any kind, basically just a free ticket to assert whatever you like. Narratival approaches allow for a great deal of subjectivity—not, however, to such an extent that the game is 'deuces-wild' and any assertion in a conversation is as good as any others. That would lead to a-perspectival madness again, just the thing that we wish to prevent while sufficiently honouring subjectivity and perspective. In this, as in virtually anything, balance is key.

There must be some evidence for one's assertions—a *prima facie* case that must be made before others can be reasonably expected to give them a hearing. I have tried to establish that case throughout my work in archetypal pedagogy over the last 20 years and I will draw on some of that work but also, I hope, go beyond it in this present study.

First, Jung left us clues as well as some passionate statements that point in an ontologically Realist direction. It has always seemed curious to me that so little is made of the fact that probably the most salient term in Jung's 'lexicon of the psyche' (Mayes, 2017a) is 'archetype', which is also the leading idea in Plato.

Jung knew the classics, read Greek well among other ancient languages, had a fine humanities education, and was an assiduous student of ancient literature (Bair, 2003; Shamdasani, 2003). He certainly knew that showcasing the word 'archetype' would inspire all sorts of unflattering associations made by his professional, and especially academic, community between him and Platonism—a big problem for Jung given the Aristotelian Nominalism and dogmatically empiricist assumptions of his peers. It is likely that some very unpleasant talk about his 'Platonism' went on behind Jung's back, and we sense that it hurt him (Jung, 1965)

Did he from about 1919 on, not that far out from the break with Freud, do this to now throw more fuel on the fire, to stir up even more acrimonious resistance to his work? It was not enough that that community in addition to the Viennese psychoanalytic juggernaut viewed him as traitorous or naïve—and in either case, totally 'out in the night'. Now he must exacerbate the problem by associating himself, however gingerly, with Plato and a word that implied a philosophy that the medical and academic community of the time eschewed? (Ellenberger, 1970). This seems unlikely.

Jung relished his role as a physician. His sense of calling as a psychiatrist went to his core (Bair, 2003). He did not cow-tow to the approval of his fellow doctors, but neither did he revel in losing it—its camaraderie and prestige

(Jung, 1965). For, Jung was a conservative man in conservative Swiss culture (Bair, 2003; McLynn, 1997; Shamdasani, 2003).

He was country-born-and-bred and he was a patriot. He took great pleasure in dressing up in his officer's uniform as a reserve military physician in the Swiss Army and marching in parades on festive occasions. He was a man of considerable wealth, too, and out of ideological conviction, no doubt, but also personal interest, he loathed socialism and communism. And equally, he valued his impressive title of Herr Professor Doktor Jung, not only a man of medicine but, even more augustly, a professor at the university. His father was a pastor and his uncles and grandfather had been Protestant theologians of note, and he grew up in a parsonage—not unproblematically, to be sure, but influentially (Jung, 1965). This was not a man who threw caution to the wind.

His use of the scientifically heterodox word 'archetype' suggests some sort of affinity that he felt intellectually and ethically bound to express—if only in a mixed way early on from his first published use of that word in 1919 (Palmer, 1995, p. 115), but one that would crescendo during the later 'religious' stage of Jung's work (Charet, 1993)—such as his famous answer to a BBC reporter's question during an interview if he, now advanced in years, believed in God. 'I do not need to believe; I know'. No less an interpreter of Jung that Jolanda Jacobi (1974) has noted clear similarities between Jung's and Plato's thought.

'Knowing' things as a matter of personal experience, not just theory, was what made Jung a good worker in stone who built a medieval tower in which to study, write, and meditate in solitude. Knowing things in person also made him an observant mystic, as the publication of *The Red Book* (2009) vividly exemplifies with its lustrous illustrations that bespeak personal otherworldly encounter.

Experience was crucial to Jung (1967b, pp. 211 and 213). He did not automatically rule something out of court as impermissible and impossible just because it went beyond the materialist assumptions of his day. Evidence was evidence wherever it came from and a fair mind judges it on that impartial basis, not because its source doesn't happen to suit one's fancy or a 'scientific' bias. Again, we have already come across Jung's assertion that 'reason ... is in point of fact nothing more than the sum total of all [our] prejudices and myopic views' (1969b, p. 13).

So it was with the 'small-t' truth of the religious experience. Jung knew it in his bones during his youth in his dreams and in nature. He knew it from his mother—a gifted mystic. He defended it as a sole dissenting voice in a fashionably atheistic university club. He credited it as an intern, not just conveniently dismissing as pathological every fantastic thing a patient said but keeping a weather-eye out for real visions and actual apparitions as he braced himself on the deck of therapy amidst his patient's psychic tempests. In a practical appreciation (and, I believe, defense) of religious experience as therapeutically indispensable and existentially desirable, Jung wrote: 'A religious truth is essentially an experience, it is not an opinion. Religion is an absolute experience' (1967b, p. 289).

And throughout his career Jung took note in the hushed tones of the consulting room, and stated now as a seasoned psychotherapist, that 'Among all my patients in the second half of life'—that is to say, over 35, and thus entering that midlife crisis that he noted clinically and established theoretically as a developmental reality, 'there has not been one whose problem in the last resort was not that of finding a religious outlook on life' (1966b, p. 202). One could multiply examples of this sort of assertion in *The Collected Works* of the plausibility and even the necessity of spiritual vision in the individual and in her culture for that person and society to survive.

That Jung strove through Analytical Psychology to provide ways and means for his patients to experience hope in discovering, *for* themselves and *within* themselves, organizing spiritual principles to vitalize their life narratives, is evident. He would do this by helping patients frame their issues and processes in universal symbolic forms and narratival structures that now came, uniquely and more or less autonomously to each patient, to invest their lives with meaning.

Jung makes this point throughout *The Collected Works* but nowhere more impassionedly than in a Q-and-A session after an address where, lamenting the loss of the symbolic life—a life lived in the cadences of a more enthused (meaning literally 'en-God-ed') narrative to orient one's biographical narrative—he exclaimed:

> Only the symbolic life can express the soul, the daily need of the soul, mind you! And because people have no such thing, they can never step out of this mill—this awful, grinding, banal life in which they are 'nothing-but' [their social roles].
>
> (Jung, 1954c, pp. 274–275)

These archetypal symbols, whose absence he laments and whose presence he invokes, are not, in Jung's view, just feel-good psychiatric prophylactics against despair. They are curative because they are real.

No account of Jung and his attitude towards the ontological reality and spiritual implications of the idea of the archetype can omit or even easily get around a statement he made in 1952—at the ripe old age of 77 and nine years before his death in 1961, when, 'here, just for once, and as an exception', Jung allowed himself to 'indulge in transcendental speculation' (and we know from the late-revealed *Red Book* that it was for Jung the man more than just speculation) that:

> God has made an inconceivably sublime and mysteriously contradictory image of himself, without the help of man and implanted it in man's unconscious as the archetype … an archetypal light … in order that the unpresumptuous man might glimpse an image, in the stillness of his soul,

that is akin to him and is wrought of his own psychic substance. This image contains everything he will ever imagine concerning his gods or concerning the ground of his psyche. This archetype, whose existence is attested not only by ethnology but by the psychic experience of individuals, satisfies me completely.

(1977, p. 667)

Archetypes and types of time

Biographical time at its minimum (Hamlet, Macbeth, and Us)

Hamlet's 'to be or not to be' echoes down the centuries and is as valid a question in this moment as it was when it was first uttered about 420 years ago. The Existentialist frame-of-mind still sees it as the core human conundrum— the dialectical tension between 'being and nothingness' (Sartre, 1956).

By Jung's view of the operation of the psyche, it is the feeling of meaningless that is the primary cause of psyche's wreck on the rocks of psychic pain. Conversely, it is the discovery of meaning in the individual's life-story that is the 'cure'—the recovery of a creative life in a reenergized psyche. That is the goal of psychotherapy and finally the goal of life (Jung, 1966b, p. 45, 1957). Jung is not alone here. The same focus on a meaningful narrative of one's life as the therapeutic 'cure' characterizes Frankl's Logotherapy (1967), Perls' (1957) Gestalt Therapy, May and Yalom's (1995) Existential therapy, and White and Epson's Narrative Therapy (1990). The difference in Jungian therapy is that the generation of a meaningful narrative is inseparable from those archetypal motifs, symbols, and processes that emerge as meaning also emerges—the two, archetype and meaning, being isomorphic.

Lacking a narrative that draws heaven and earth together—an intercourse of the time of this realm of existence with the Eternal Now that bears fruit in the form of archetypal imagery and energy informing one's life-narrative—we may easily become like Hamlet, caught in a dull maze of error and confusion. He spits out his contempt for his narratively stripped life—a relentlessly mundane 'present' that offers no hope or enchantment, not a salvific 'Present' vouchsafed by Eternity:

> How weary, stale, flat, and unprofitable
> Seem to me all the uses of this world!
> Fie on 't, ah fie! 'Tis an unweeded garden
> That grows to seed. Things rank and gross in nature
> Possess it merely.
> (Act 1, Scene 2, ll. 133–137)

In her classic study of the nature of totalitarianism, the historian Hannah Arendt made the startling conclusion that it was inanity and boredom (primary symptoms of living only in egoic, mechanical time) that best characterized the lives of Hitler's inner circle (Arendt, 1951).

In the case of Hamlet, it was his uncle's lust to vaunt his own biographical narrative that was the originating sin that severed the Danish kingdom from the symbolic narratives of heaven and that set the whole sad story at Elsinore into emotional and moral disarray. Presently, we'll look in some depth at how one's own narrative and the narratives of one's culture are tightly interwoven.

Now everyone in Castle Elsinore, and no doubt everyone in Denmark, is paying the price. But especially Hamlet. He complains of how 'weary, stale, flat, and unprofitable / Seem to me all the uses of this world' because 'the time is out of joint' (Act 3, Scene 1). To be out of joint is to be disconnected from something vital and orienting, something that holds one in place and allows one to function correctly. But where time has gone so awry, so inevitably is narrative, for 'a narration is the symbolic presentation of a sequence of events connected by subject matter and related by time' (Scholes, 1980, p. 209). Narrative and time lie together like lovers begetting the future, which issues in either 1) the emotionally, intellectually, and ethically galvanized evolution of one's life-narrative in archetypally rich energy and imagery as one's narrative tends towards the Timeless, or 2) the stalling of one's life-narrative in its ethical paucity, its only certainty the full-stop of the grave.

Macbeth, too, having, like Hamlet's Uncle Claudius, ruptured Heaven's archetypal narratives about the proper transfer of power in the service of his personal power and biographical aggrandizement, finds himself very low indeed. Wasting and wasted, he despairs of tomorrow, which exists only as a projection of the present, all wrapped up in his now-foul ego, the sound of ticking the only sound he hears, or will ever hear, again so that 'to-morrow, and to-morrow, and to-morrow, / Creeps in this petty pace from day to day, / To the last syllable of recorded *time*' (Macbeth Act 5, Scene 5, ll. 17–19).

I have highlighted 'time' because it is the crux of the question of whether or not a person feels her life has meaning. In a coherent narrative—that is, a story in which the flow of time has a pattern following the templates of the Timeless—the time of our lives coheres as a plausible and productive story. It is our archetypally infused narratives and core fiduciary commitments that alone stand between us and emotional, epistemological, and ethical disarray.

Thus, our narratives may function to guide, sustain, and 'justify' our lives. Inevitably, of course, they do this in most cases in some degree of tension and doubt if they are authentic, not an attempt to sidestep the profound ambiguity and anxious riskiness of being in a world such as ours. We are probably narrativizing right up until that day we lie on our death bed and, in the grieving, receding faces of those surrounding us (they also trying to make a narrative in which the loss they are just now beginning to register in its fullness makes sense) and in the rain irregularly curving its way to the bottom of the pane, we make one concluding pass at piecing together a life-narrative of all that transpired in the life we are passing out of. This is the ultimate 'exit interview', but of oneself with oneself, and with perhaps the hope of a new type of narrative in a transfigured, transfiguring time that may just possibly await us.

And not only in this moment but over the span of a lifetime, 'man's search for meaning' (Frankl, 1967) is just that—a search, a rugged ride on a rough rollercoaster; the 'dialectic between time and eternity', which the philosopher and narrative theorist Paul Ricoeur (1985) identified as our central existential tension. We live to tell stories; we tell stories to live; and moral courage requires that we do it as honestly as we practicably can—under the Sign of the Question Mark. The syntax of our existence is fundamentally interrogative, not declarative.

We are such thoroughly narratival creatures that after a day of narrativizing even in the heat of the quotidian hustle-and-bustle (indeed in order to survive that spiritually dull maelstrom of the mundane) we go home to sleep, only to narrativize even more, and more fantastically too, in the shape of dream narratives, richly symbolled—each one potentially containing up to 11 planes of meaning that are extensions of similar themes and symbols in dreams the nights before, sometime stretching back years, even decades (Vedfelt, 2001). Our capacity to tell stories to make sense of our lives is both mindboggling and mind-enabling. It is perhaps the principal thing that distinguishes us from other animals (Burke, 1989, p. 55).

Egoic time v. Eternal Time

According to many narrative theorists, the gist of most of our waking narratives, no matter how self-effacing we may make them at a surface level, is:

> I am a good person. I have tried to do the right thing. Where I have not, circumstances have been against me. Where I have done right, that is truly who I am. And even though I have done wrong, I am more sinned against than sinning.

Asks White, 'Could we ever narrativize without moralizing?' (1980, p. 27).

The land of the egoic is also the dominion of the mechanical time that the clock reigns over, in the socially confirming, socially conforming spaces of our consensual realities. In psychoanalytic parlance, the term 'egoic' is not to be confused with 'egotism' and rank selfishness. It simply refers to the ego structure that we must all develop as members of functioning collectives in which we are a distinct unit—one who to a certain degree has a distinct identity but mostly one who knows the rules of social order and more or less plays by them. We must all to some extent live in that realm: Its rules and roles, tasks and irritations, strategies paying off or gambits gone wrong, over-blown triumphs and covered-over failures. And we must present a face to the world that assures our fellows that all is basically well and that a certain homeostatic normalcy is being maintained.[6]

Goffman called this 'Facework', and as he points out, it is not necessarily a bad thing (1997). Jung makes the same point about his famous idea of the persona (1967b, p. 174). We can't go about simply saying what we think about everyone and every situation we come across in the course of the day. We'd all come home with bloody knuckles and black eyes at the end of the day—that is, for as long as we still had a home. For, social order would rapidly collapse. Facework and personas are a necessary part of social cohesion, the generally equable flow of that social narrative that allows us to live together.

The problem arises when our Facework so consumes us that we fall out of touch with those deeper parts of ourselves that we should rather be constantly accessing in order to live an existentially authentic life. When our existence is so governed by regimented social time, sprawled before its Imperial Master, King Clock, then that is the agony, and that the neurosis, of what I am calling biographical time at its psychospiritual minimum, and its lock-step march to the dull drum of that mechanical device that ticks us together in our tasks. It is unrelieved by higher vision and infusions of the Eternal Now into the otherwise unredeemed day, which often becomes a landscape of emotional evisceration, phenomenological vacancy and ethical vagrancy, stemming, I will propose throughout the rest of this study, from an individual and her culture feeling cut off from an ontological source of time—Ricoeur's 'Eternal Time'. This contrasts with the experience of time in its most spiritually denuded aspect, stripped down to nothing but itself. It is biographical-time at its minimum.

Thoreau (1966) said that time was the stream that he fished in. But we have it on even greater authority that we are the fish who need to be snatched out of the river of time,[7] liberated from the mere hydrodynamics of ordinary time-as-such, 'time' with a lower-case 't'. But in Ricoeur's dichotomy, 'Eternal Time'—'Time' with an upper-case 'T' indicates a higher, restorative order of Time—where 'passage' is not passage as we know it but a balletic stillness-in-movement and movement-in-stillness perpetually emerging in and as a transcendent but also immanent Now (Suzuki, 1964; Tillich, 1963).

Macbeth's 'tomorrow and tomorrow and to-morrow' is the utter collapse of biographical time. The eternal Now, as the source and the goal of biographical time, is the human being's release and realization. Hence arises the awareness (and the burden of both Hamlet and Macbeth) that our biographical narrative is following the wrong ethical tempo. That correct 'measure' is the ontological and ethical cadence of eternal Time, the fountain of time, as it is pictured in Vedic metaphysics, overflowing with the archetypal treasures of history's most sacred narratives, carrying the boat of one's own biographical narrative along on it as well in an easy flowing together of the individual consciousness and the collective unconscious. This is the time sensed in the sea, that oceanic metronome that suggests infinity by beggaring the smallness of our watches and clocks.

Our stories in time/Our stories as time

By this view of things, time is not an objective, stainless-steel container in which we place the story of our life for impartial analysis; it *is* the story of our lives—different with each person and therefore resistant to categorical analysis—as either 1) Time as the meaningful patterning of our lives as a *pas de deux* of biographical time and eternal Time, rich in archetypal imagery and energy or 2) time as the breakdown of biographical time in its self-alienation from eternal Time, with personal narratives that are empty of that energy and imagery, being instead simplistic, repetitive, and prosaic. The question is either the marriage of 'time' and 'Time' or their divorce.

In the Eastern spiritual tradition, release from merely mundane time is 'liberation'—the sempiternal fruit of 'right practice' and divestiture of ego. In the Western tradition it is called 'salvation' and it is a Grace bestowed in the transaction between a Divine Mercy and a faith that has been 'refined ... in the furnace of affliction' (Isaiah 48: 10). In Eternal Time, ordinary, mathematical time stops and incalculable Time begins. Or rather, sacred Time does not so much 'begin' (for it has no beginning and suffers no end) as much as it discloses itself to a human consciousness that is now no longer occluded from itself by itself.

Eternal Time is what it has always been, presently is, and always will be (and yet is in constant transformation, too). It is the 'Ever-Present Origin' (Gebser, 1985). It is as present in this very now in which you read these words as it has ever been in any past-now or future-now. This 'now' is the same 'now' you and I have always been in. This is the very now as that instant in which you realized that no one was holding on to the bike and you are steering it alone! It is also the now in which you signed the divorce papers. The 'now' in which we die is the same 'now' in which we were born. All our 'nows', individually, collectively, and as a specie, are this same 'Now' that was before all our beginnings and is after all our ends.

Eternal Time also 'moves', but not through any space we could identify, occupy, or travel to in any physical way because it goes 'beyond' our dimensions. Although Eternal time 'moves', it does so both in and beyond itself, both absolutely 'other' than any space we could possibly inhabit as things presently stand, yet also at the centre of our world, whose dimensions emerged out of its archetypally maternal womb in its capacity as the archetype of the Cosmic Great Mother (Graves, 1959; Jung, 1971, p. 187).

As with temporality, the Eternal 'moves' but not towards any destination that we can conceive of or plot on any Cartesian graph, but in its own metaphysical rhythms and richness, its own transcendental paces and passages, towards its own purposes, and perhaps transcending even Itself in Its own 'evolution'[8] that we are not poised (enough) to see from the shaky interrogative ground onto which we have been thrown. For, here we are—without our consent, with no travel plan, and as aware that we must move forward as we are unaware of where True North lies—the human condition, according to Heidegger, who devised a compound German neologism to describe it: *Geworfenheit* ('Thrown-ness').

In what follows, I will address these temporal dilemmas from an archetypal perspective. In Part II we will take what we have discovered and apply it to educational topics and practices. There we will find that the key to the resolution of these dilemmas lies in the idea of the symbol, especially the archetypal symbol.

Narrative and time in relation to the archetypes and the collective unconscious

Throughout this chapter, I will continue to examine the question of time but increasingly in relationship to the nature of an archetype and continuing to consider the complexity of views in the current Jungian world that swirl around the question of what an archetype 'is'.

These range from 1) those that portray the archetype as simply a cognitive construct or phenomenological possibility that channels thought, thereby granting the archetype enormous epistemological, therapeutic, and even literary power and potential but little or no ontological status, to 2) those that see an archetype and the ever-shifting web of connections among it and other archetypes in the Collective Unconscious—that matrix within which the archetypes have arisen, presently operate, and perpetually transform—as an integral aspect of the Ground of Being and even possibly as that Ground of Being Itself.

The latter position makes of the archetype something that is not only psychologically foundational but also ontologically foundational so that *psyche in its most matured and integrated forms, which Jung called 'individuation,' corresponds to, or at least is organically woven in some substantial way, into the Ground of Being Itself. By this view, psychology and psychotherapy are not a psychodynamic inquiry and medical techne but a psychospiritual devotion and ethical project.* We will take up the topic of psyche and ontology and its educational implications in Chapter 8.

As for Jung himself, he's all over the map on what an archetype is, although, as he aged, he grew ever closer to the latter, more spiritual view (Charet, 1993), especially in his alchemical studies, the crowning volumes of his life's work (Edinger, 1985; Jung, 1970c, 1969a,b, c).

One hears in this debate an echo of an issue that has defined the divide in Western philosophy since its Greek origins.

Plato and Aristotle: the double concerto of Western philosophy

To illustrate this division that runs like a fault-line throughout the history of Western philosophy, let's look at two very different answers Jung provided regarding the question of whether or not an archetype has 'ontological status'. This is the question about whether or not the archetypes are really real or whether the word 'archetype' is simply a linguistic tool that we deploy to discover and discuss various matters that bear upon our lives in many substantial ways but that does not indicate the existence of something that really exists in another realm of being. Depending on what one is reading in *The Collected Works*, Jung affirms each of the poles and just about every cline in between. Since this issue is important in what follows, I will pursue it in a bit of depth here. Moreover, this has been an issue in general, and particularly regarding the idea of the archetype, since the beginning of Western philosophy until this day.

On one hand, Aristotle took the view that categorical statements and universal propositions are essentially just linguistic gestures, categories based on our observations of things in the world, but not indicators of abstract ontological or metaphysical 'entities' that actually 'exist' in-and-of-themselves (the *esse-en-se*: Kant's [1781/1997] Ding-an-Sich, Sartre's [1956] Etre-en-Soi) in a higher realm of being (Aristotle, 2000). They are words. This is why this view is called '*Nom*-inalist'. These words are preconditions of thought and tools of analysis that have quite crucial analytical/pragmatic and poetically unlimited uses, but they do not have ontological status.

On the other hand, the 'Realist' position, formulated by Plato, understood linguistic universals as reflections and expressions of a higher order of reality whose general categories do point to transcendent entities called 'archetypes', which, transcending our realm of reality, do have not only ontological but also metaphysical standing—that is, are not just linguistic operators but are really real in higher realms (the '*Real*-ist' position) and are to some considerable degree discoverable by inquiry, especially in the dialogical mode (1968).[9]

Between these two poles is probably where most Jungians land. In Jungian terms, that would be between: 1) the Nominalist, post-Jungian pole with its insistence upon the linguistic deconstruction of all archetypal reality-claims and value-statements, on one hand, and 2) the Realist, classically Jungian view, which insists upon the ontological status of the archetype as both pre- and trans-linguistic, a primordial and transcendental 'fact' and thus having an 'ethical dimension'. I take a classical view but one that has been influenced by postmodern theory (Foucault, 1980, 1972) as well as multicultural theory (Banks and Banks, 2001; Nieto, 2000).

'The dialectic between time and eternity'

We are narratival beings. It is in the narratives of our lives that we live, move, and have our being. I thus move on to an elaboration of our existential condition as a narratival tension between two temporal domains. Paul Ricoeur characterized this as 'the dialectic between time and eternity' (1984).

Thus, if one believes that a 'higher' realm, even if it did exist, does not touch the human being in any redemptive ways, one is nevertheless still carrying on in the context of that powerful absence, vociferous in its cosmic silence—and therefore one is still moving through one's life with reference to it.

In many discussions, what is not said is as important as what is said ... and sometimes even more so. In a curriculum, what is not is studied or allowed to be discussed is as important as what is. Negative space is just as important as positive space in a painting. The absence of the Divine in an existential narrative is as impactful as is its presence, and sometimes more poignant. And whereas statements of faith may ring out in chorus, the silence of God is deafening.

In terms of genre literary criticism (Frye, 1957), this renders our narratives either 1) ultimately 'tragic' if it is felt that that the Divine, if it even exists, is not guiding the individual's biographical narrative towards transcendence of merely secular time which always empties out into the grave, or 2) 'comedic' if Eternal Time is rippling through the individual's biographical narrative and folding Its time into her time so that she is moving towards transcendence of merely secular time. This theme of universal salvation has had great visionary spokespersons such as the heterodox 3rd-century Origen, where the devil himself is redeemed at the end of time—indeed, the devil's redemption is precisely what makes time end; and the 14th-century mystic Juliana of Norwich, whose visions of cosmic felicity, where earthly time is gathered up into the Eternal Time of the ever-present Now, were summarized by her incantation that 'All shall be well. And all manner of things shall be well.'

Hence, there are the two archetypal masks in the Greek theatre—one tragic, one comic; one aflame in the human time of agony and sheer endurance, the other transfigured in the eternal Time of release and endless presence in the Eternal Presence. Our life-narratives are already archetypal in that they are essentially one or the other of these two genres or fall somewhere in between.

Anciently, these narratives took the form of religious stories in both the Buddhist/Hindu and Judeo-Christian traditions (Eliade, 1959, 1954). These stories were used as exempla of 'right living'. They told of what the gods did at the formation of the universe, how the gods went about living their lives in it and beyond it, and what together they and certain mortal culture heroes did to found this specific culture. This all happened long ago, in *illud tempus*, so long ago, in fact, that it was emphatically (in dreams, words or images are often doubled to suggest their transtemporal nature) 'long, *long* ago', where mortal time effaces, dies out, is transformed, and then feeds into a different stream of time—into Eternal Time. It happened so long ago that it happened 'once' 'upon' a time, for it is an order of time that is above time, 'upon' it, and it is always happening in an eternal now and thus is always happening 'once'.

These accounts evolved into devotional practices and liturgies that one applied to one's life so as to orient and make sense out of one's personal narrative by comparing it to, even placing it under the sponsorship of, a sacred narrative.

For, a 'sacred narrative' is what a liturgy is or commemorates. It is a recounting or text that has been given to the culture and is guarded by the elders, they whom mortal fires have 'holocausted' into purity through affliction and a physical diminishment that allows Spirit to emerge and possess them. The sacred narrative issues directly from heaven, it is claimed, and it evidences its *bona fides* by its own sheer power; it legitimates itself by how irresistibly compelling it is in its profusion of archetypally rich symbols, themes, and narrative patterns.

The sacred narrative calibrates a biographical narrative towards a more deeply significant and satisfying goal than merely a stand-alone biographical narrative could do; for, the Sacred narrative radiates the Time of Heaven and infuses the present with its metaphysical electricity—a present that would otherwise be empty, purposeless, randomly driven, and perpetually adrift in a vacant cosmos. But an individual may be saved by participation in the sacred narrative as it moves through her life, and moves her through this life, onto a higher plane of existence, wedding merely mortal time to Immortal Time, which could, to be sure, also be experienced in mortality but never in its fullness (Eliade, 1959).

The human being sub specie aeternitatis

This situation is captured in the idea that the human being is uniquely that creature who lives *sub specie aeternitatis*. Drawn from Spinoza, the phrase *sub specie aeternitatis* has had a colourful career in its wide variety of interpretations. In any case, the idea caught on and has been variously interpreted and deployed. Jung (1965, p. 3) speaks of symbolism and myth as our only way of *realizing* (in both the sense of knowing and bringing to completion) what we feel ourselves to be at our spiritual maximum: beings who exist 'under the aspect of eternity'—*sub specie aeternitatis*.

I will use the phrase at several points throughout this study. By it, I will mean: A human is that unique creature who is aware of being fatally bound by finite time but who longs to finally bound beyond finite time into a Time-beyond-time, a timeless Time, a cosmic Time, a sacred Time by which he feels himself to be surrounded in this realm of existence but from which he also finds himself to be separate. For although 'the phenomenology of temporal impermanence' pervades all our personal narratives in finite biographical time, the human being can in finite time only intuit the possible existence of that higher realm and desire to communicate with and gain entrée to it in this realm of being (Sovatsky, 1998, p. 16).

By my reading[10] of the phrase *sub specie aeternitatis*, it is to compassionately regard the human being as that creature who is aware of herself as existing between two temporal planes. On one side, there is the 'ordinary time' of mere cause-and-effect, bracketed by the absolute endpoints of birth and death. On the other side lies the Presence of or Hope in the Eternal, or the possibility of liberation from ordinary time into a realm of Being where experience is now not only unfettered by ordinary time but triumphs over it. With Paul, one, from whatever faith perspective, then revels in the rhetorical questions: 'Where, O Death, is your victory? Where, Death, is your sting?' (1 Corinthians 15: 55).

And it is the ship of narrative, powered by the invisible winds of the archetypal that billows and fills its sails, that carries the individual over the violent waves of experience (often bitter to the point of inconsolability) in the punishing weather of the dialectic between time and eternity on an oceanic journey. It is the only journey there is, the one that stretches from a mortal land to a now-plausible, immortal shore.

Archetype, time, and meaning

This, then, is the fundamental dichotomy in our lives and it is narratival. It presents itself as two narratival questions, and upon their answers hangs the issue of whether our life-narrative is fundamentally in the 'tragic' or 'comedic' mode. Which of those two genres do we finally exemplify? If our life is narratival, then the meaning of that life, or its lack of meaning, is finally the nature of our narrative (Frye, 1957): What genre are we? That is the question! Or rather, it is two questions.

Question One: Is the narrative of our lives merely egoic, socially constructed and linguistically deconstructible; just empirical, ontologically limited to the rational, ultimately only mortal, and pointed, finally and insuperably, to the mute victory of the mossy grave and the decaying bones within it? In other words: When all is said and done, is the story of the individual life a mere biographical narrative lived out day by day—'tomorrow and tomorrow and tomorrow', event after event—until one day we run out of tomorrows, have used up our mortal duffle-bag of 'events' and that is that? Does the egoic-narrative of Newtonian time and the *ennui* of the empirical have the last say—which ultimately leaves us with no say at all about our final disposition or destiny? Or,

Question Two: Is our biographical narrative lived under the sponsorship of the Divine? However distant, detached, or even as absurd as that Divine may sometimes seem in Its presently occluded Form-Beyond-Form (as in both the Diamond Sutra in the Eastern tradition and St John of The Cross' Dark

Night of the Soul in the Western tradition). Yet, for all that, is the Sacred now (in this very moment of sheer-facticity and mere-time that hides Itself from our timed-out eyes) folding our biographical narratives with all their otherwise senseless details into Itself?

And what is more: To the extent we can each receive It, is It, the Ever-Expanding God, folding the details of Its evolving Self into us, too? Is the Transcendent investing our narratives with a redemptive significance in which our agonies and indignities, our history of inflicting and suffering wrongs, and the simple boredom that we must often just slog through in this life—is all of this not only *that* (although in Existential courage we must confess that it *is* that) but inescapably part of a pilgrimage through mortality to a final Jerusalem-of-the-Heart, where we find our dynamic rest, ceaseless creativity, and indivisible community with other similarly shaped beings, which is to say: Every human being?

The evolving God in the archetypal life

Ricoeur called the tension between Question One and Question Two 'the dialectic of time and eternity' in our narratives and makes of this tension the existential engine that powers our life-narratives (1984, p. 28). Hamlet's 'To be or not to be' is still the simple question, and that simple question is our complex condition.

In sum, are 'the sacred and the profane' united, or do they cancel each other out (Eliade, 1959)? Are time and space simply that and forever out of communication with the Divine, if there even is a Divine? Or can we, in our individual narratives, make of those specific stories individual instances of a universal process in which we redeem our naked biographical time by enfolding it in eternal garments?

This sacred time, which I, combining Ricoeur (1985) and Sovatsky (1998), will call the cosmic time of spiritual narrative, refers to another type of time ontologically—or, at a bare minimum, a different 'knowing' of time phenomenologically—but, in either case, with an experiential immediacy and an ultimate hope that is healing, even salvific, for the individual. This cannot be far off what Jung meant when he famously asserted that he never saw a 'cure' in therapy that did not involve the growth of a 'religious attitude' in the patient—not necessarily linked with any particular *ecclesia* or dogma (Main, 2004, pp. 297ff).

To live one's life in psychological health and spiritual purpose—that alone, according to Jung, constitutes a cure. An alternative to time has thereby arisen and been offered (or better: an alternative is internally generated as one is grasped by Spirit). It does not negate merely mechanical, linear, and mathematically manipulable time—finite, quotidian time, in which we are, without the saving grace of Sacred Time, inescapably bound. It does, however, go beyond it, for it is, rather, a transcendent experience, not an abstract imposition as mechanical time so often is upon all of us in the course of a day, as we watch the watch as if it were our drill-sergeant.

On the other hand, Eliot in *Four Quartets* vouchsafes us a vision, a glimpse of sacred time. A place both in time and out of time, localizable in every point in time-space but utterly and simultaneously transcending our time-space in a radical bifurcation of our world and the environs of the Divine. This heavenly terriority is suffused by a white light, both mobile and quiescent, this paradox implying the limits of our understanding and the necessity of approaching the Divine (if we may approach it at all) in terms of paradox. Jung captures the necessity of the apprehending the Ultimate in such terms, for, as he wrote, 'Wholeness is perforce paradoxical in its manifestations' (Jung, 1969c, p. 145).

This is the Eternal 'Now' (Tillich, 1963). In eschatological terms, the present is already folded into eternal time. The present simply does not know it yet although the Eternal always has. In Christian theology, this is called 'realized eschatology', which is to say: 'You are already saved'. Or: 'You are already liberated' in Buddhist terms. It is a moment both in time and out of time when you realize that you are an immortal being experiencing mortality but that mortality is not your home and it is certainly not your end; then that knowledge is already salvific. You are 'awake' to find you already are eternal: You are the Buddha. You are the Christ in a smaller figure but of similar substance. And not only you but everyone will see this about themselves (so Tertullian's doctrine of universal salvation had it) in the moment of their own great awakening. They simply do not know it now as you did not know it then. But all will know it, in each other and in ourselves, according to the promise of 'the perennial wisdom' (Huxley, 1945). And we know it—or rather we intuit it—when we grasp the medieval mystic Juliana of Norwich's ever-ancient, ever-new words to us six centuries ago: 'All shall be well, and all shall be well, and all manner of thing shall be well.'

Transtemporal, salvific time stands in stark contrast to the rectilinear, algebraic, mechanical time of our present life, which, at the pragmatic level, is filled with the daily round of mostly indifferent things, situations, business affairs, biological functions; and at the theoretical level, it is abstractly contained in the universal black-box of the Newtonian cosmos. It is clock-time. It is alternately drab or bedevilled in our biographical time, with some moments of release, but even those moments in and out of time are pestered by our awareness, at the same time, of their impermanence. Recent psychoanalytic theory captures the problem in calling it 'our ordinary, everyday unhappiness'.

Ordinary time, mechanical and mathematical time, clock time—prepackaged passages of precise impersonality—are perfectly suited to the logistics of empirical tasks in the quotidian world. And that time has a history (Mayes, 2005c). The advent of the clock in the 14th century and the discovery of the calculus in the 17th century allowed linear time to be harnessed and used with admirable efficiency in the production and delivery of goods and services, especially its military and industrial uses in organizing people and materiel in concerted campaigns of cash and conquest (Nowotny, 1989). This is why maximizing the 'yield' of such time is of the highest importance in the design and execution of policy, and wherever 'time is money'.

Mechanical time has its uses of course, crucial in the ordinary run of life. No one doubts that. We all live *in* and *with* that. The problem is when we find ourselves living *under* that. Problems arise in the hegemony of mechanical time—when it attempts to 'corner the market' and become the sole criterion of what may be called a 'valid' experience, summarily declaring any other experience of time irrelevant, untrue, or even pathological because it is 'merely subjective'.

In fact, it is a timely attempt of the galvanized soul to break loose of the fetters of this minimalist time and shake off its hegemony—the killing cruelty of sheer objective temporality and mere facticity—in which psyche is presently too straightly bound. Both in and as an alienated, dispirited egoic-eye/I, the individual comes to find he has nothing to measure experiential passage as ego surveys its empty empire other than Newton's clock with its tiny second-hand sweeping around the dull idiot circle of the clock's face, the little penny-piece of tin engraved with differential equations, sweeping round and round, purposelessly, a historical dog chasing its own tail/tale. In what will soon follow in Chapter 2, we will explore ways to break the stranglehold of merely mechanical time on educative processes through inquiring deeply into some of the possibilities of archetypal pedagogy.

It is crucial that we do so. When mechanical time is set up as the one true system and the *only* ontology of time—and in the balance negating other psychologically and culturally differential experiences of time—then ordinary time is not just non-subjective. It is anti-subjective. Obsessively objective, it is unforgiving of any personal variation in felt-experience, attitude, enactment, or presence. Thus established, clock time commands heart, mind, and soul to shrink, conforming themselves to a double-entry bookkeeping accountancy of what it means to be a human being. And it 'disciplines and punishes' heart, mind, and soul through the instrumentalities of weaponized educational, psychiatric, and social-services systems (Foucault, 1980, 1979, 1975, 1972).

Sacred time is of a different and higher order than we typically comprehend because we are limited to experiencing things in Newtonian space and time as Kant (1781/1997) demonstrated in his presentation of the 'mathetic function' in the *Critique of Pure Reason*. However, sacred time is apprehensible through the other epistemological faculty he posited, the 'poetic function', which is capable of not only linear ratiocination but also nonlinear intuition. For, while secular time serves its purposes, Eternal Time *is* the Purpose.

What this means for education, which in *itself* must be counted as one of the most central archetypes in our psychospiritual economy, is the topic of Chapter 2: Narrative, archetype, and culture.

Notes

1 See for example: Booth, 1961; Gardner, 1978; Linde, 1993; Ricoeur, 1985; Schafer, 1980; Scholes, 1980; Sovatsky, 1998; Watson and Watson-Franke, 1985; White and Epson, 1990; Zoja, 1998.

2 On the topic of the therapeutic dimensions of education, see, for example, Barford, 2002; Britzman, 2003; Ekstein and Motto, 1968; Field, Cohler, and Wool, 1989; Mayes, 2017a, 2009; Salzberger-Wittenberg, 1989.

3 Hopefully, the reader already has a basic understanding of what an archetype is. However, for the reader who has no or little knowledge of Jung's use of this term, I have endeavoured in this book to present the idea of an archetype in such a way that the reader may pick it up as he or she goes along. There are also good, accessible introductions to the idea of the archetype in Jungian psychology. See, for example, Conforti, 1999 and Stevens, 2006 (from a biological perspective); Samuels, 1997 (from a postmodern perspective); Gray, 1996 from a sociological perspective; Eisendrath-Young and Hall, 1991 (from a cognitive/neuroscience perspective); and Edinger, 1973; Jacobi, 1974; Matoon, 1981; Mayes, 2017a (from a classical Jungian perspective).

4 Or 'a system of structural dominants shaping consciousness', as Frey-Rohn characterized them (1974, p. 117).

5 For the notion that moral issues are central in Jung's work, see the following: Hollis, 2000, p. 111; Meier, 1986, p. 92; Nagy, 1991, p. 22; Neuman, 1973, p. 23; Odajnyk, 1976, p. 186; Pauson, 1988, p. 53; White, 1982, pp. 153, 171.

6 According to some narrative theorists, the gist of many of our narratives, no matter how self-effacing they may seem, is: 'I am a good person. I have tried to do the right thing. And if this is not true in specific instances, and even if it is not true in general of my life, it is because of things that have happened to me. I hurt myself. But I alone bear those scars. And even if I hurt others, others have hurt me too, and maybe even more. And at my core, I am good and where I am not it is because I have been dealt a rotten hand.' See especially Linde, 1993; see also: Clandinin and Connelly, 2000; Schafer, 1980; Watson and Watson-Franke, 1985; White and Epston, 1990.

7 'And [Jesus] said to them, "Come. Follow me, and I will make you fishers of men"' (*Matthew* 4: 19).

8 For the teleological notion that the Divine is Itself in eternal evolution, see: Bergson, 1902; Chardin, 1975; Fox, 1988; Hartshorne, 1984; Rohr, 2016; Whitehead, 1929; Wilber, 2001.

9 *The Stanford Encyclopedia of Philosophy*, 'Nominalism in Metaphysics', https://plato.stanford.edu/entries/nominalism-metaphysics/ (accessed 2/18/19); The Stanford Encyclopedia of Philosophy, 'Realism', https://plato.stanford.edu/entries/realism/ (accessed 2/28/19).

10 I had the good fortune of studying modern American fiction in 1978 in a doctoral seminar on 'The 20th Century Existentialist Novel' at the University of Oregon with the great Formalist literary critic, the late W. J. Handy, of blessed memory, from whom I learned this phrase and this interpretation of it during a stroll one late Autumn day (Mayes, 2004, p. 1).

Chapter 2

Narrative, archetype, and culture

The three layers of time

As Julius Cesar divided Gaul into three parts, so the French philosopher Paul Ricoeur (1985) divided time into three layers of ascending importance: biographical, world-historical, and eternal. Doing so reveals three general types of human experience in time, which, of course, is tantamount to three different general narratives: personal (the biographical narrative), collective (the cultural world-historical narrative), and Sacred (the Transcendental narrative). When the three strata of this hierarchy of 'time' are 'out of joint', as Hamlet puts it—that is, 'not in right relationship', 'disordered', 'unhinged', and in its literal sense 'out of contact with each other'—then things go terribly wrong.

I will rely on Ricoeur's tripartite model of time in all that follows.

So far, we have looked at the first and last of Ricoeur's three dimensions of time, the personal and the Transcendent, and the problems that ensue when they are alienated from each other.

Now we turn our focus to Ricoeur's second and mediating dimension of time between the personal and the Transcendent. It is cultural/world-historical time.

In *The Wasteland*, T.S. Eliot rendered in wasted-earth tones the 20th century's singular brand of the individual and cultural despair that prevailed because Western culture, in its excessive fascination with and commitment to secularism and rationalism, had, especially since the Enlightenment, increasingly cut itself from the Divine. Of course, Jung's analysis of the plight of 'modern man in search of a soul' (1957) was very similar and his work is in large measure an attempt to offer a solution to this spiritually cataclysmic turn of history. It was not the first time it had happened. However, now that humanity possessed weapons easily capable of decimating the entire planet, Jung feared it might be the last. He wrote under this shadow.

In vision, Ezekiel spoke of a landscape filled with bare bones in the 'Valley of Dead Bones' to portray a similar cultural decay after his people have distanced themselves from their transcendent source. Ezekiel reported: '[God] said to me, "Son of man, these bones are the whole house of Israel." Behold, they say, "Our bones are dried up, and our hope is lost; we are indeed cut off"' (Ezekiel 37: 11).

Almost a century ago, Eliot, referring to Ezekiel, wrote of our own world-historical epoch of despair and anxiety. Eliot speaks, in Ezekiel-like strains, of a wholly desolate place, strewn only with stones and trash. The reader, addressed in Old Testament terms as 'son of man' is challenged to find any meaning in this arid, empty zone, but he is already doomed to fail this challenge since his world is now only 'a heap of broken images' (Eliot, 1971, p. 38).

'A heap of broken images' is an apt description of a culture whose sacred symbols, once harmonized as a saving narrative that sustained the individual in the culture and the culture in the individual, are now broken and in disarray. The decomposition of a culture's religious symbology, the levelling of its once-storied history, is a sure preface to its decline and collapse. This reading of the state of Western culture exemplifies what Ricoeur (1991) has called 'the hermeneutics of suspicion'—the analysis of a person, text, or situation in order to ferret out what is wrong with it, even corrupt, and sometimes beyond repair. There is obviously a great deal in our cultural condition that merits such suspicion.

On the other hand, we may invoke Homan's (1995) 'hermeneutics of hope', which Homans coined precisely in order to describe Jung's approach to things and how it differed from what Rieff (1961) also called Freud's 'hermeneutics of suspicion' and look for that which is promising in a present situation, what is not only salvageable but what might be evidence of a natural progression towards higher levels of organization and health.

Instead of a valley of bones, we might picture a cultural bridge between the biographic and the Timeless made up of archetypal symbols—some ancient and restored, others newly minted from the imagination—that suggest not a civilization simply in distress (although it is undeniably that), but potentially, and more hopefully, a 'civilization in transition', as one of the volumes of Jung's *Collected Works* is titled (1970).

This is still a possibility available to the moral imagination, according to Jung, and our primary chance at cultural redemption and renewal. Admittedly, it was getting late in the day historically, Jung felt, and if such a transformation in culture were to happen, it would have to be soon and it would have to be very deep. But Homans is right. The hermeneutics of hope beat strong in Jung's breast and he made it his life's work to do his part to help save Western culture from the desymbolized godlessness into which it had thrown itself with a culpable abandon and from which it was on point of perishing.

Invoking the dominical injunction that that 'new wine should not be put into old bottles' (Matthew 9: 16), Jung said that the Spirit's universal messages must not be constrained by old myths. This did not mean jettisoning the old myths, however. That would simply result in individual despair and collective disorientation at the jolting disappearance of these culturally anchoring stories. What was needed was that the myths not only be *retained* but *reinterpreted* from epoch to epoch so that they would remain vital in the person's life, not just curiosity pieces in a museum of the moribund (Jung, 1969c, p. 181).

The quintessential conservative, Jung understood the need for sacred symbols to orient a culture toward the Timeless so that the individual might thereby find his own spiritual orientation, for the human being is inescapably a cultural being who knows himself in the terms his culture provides. His identity is quite inseparable from the social context(s) in which he has been shaped at every level and in every dimension of his existence.

Jung is often accused of being apolitical. That is not true. He was quite political and a singularly astute cultural critic. Only, his conclusions were of a distinctly conservative bent, and this is what his critics, particularly his post-modern ones, cannot abide. But there is finally no sidestepping the fact that, for Jung, cultural renewal is fundamentally a project of cultural retrieval—a restoration of ancient symbols that had, until fairly recently historically— over the last two to three centuries particularly—anchored the common man, provided him with cultural harborage in an otherwise terrifyingly uncertain and peril-infested universe.

On the other hand, Jung was no reactionary. He was not so fond as to believe that religion in its old forms could simply be brought back and imposed upon people. Jung understood that 'modern man in search of a soul' (1957) was much too sophisticated for that. The symbols had to be reworked so that they remained relevant to the modern individual. How exactly this was to be accomplished is never made very clear in Jung except his notion that it cannot happen programmatically but must happen person by person.

One sometimes feels in reading Jung that his solution to our cultural mal-aise was for everyone to undergo Jungian therapy. His justification for this, or something like it, was that 'the task of individuation [is] imposed on us by nature, and the recognition of our wholeness and completeness [is] a binding personal commitment' (Jung, 1969c, p. 70). In the second part of this book, I will suggest some ways that this goal of the re-sacralization of culture might be accomplished, or at least approached, through educational means.

In calling for a complete revamping of our cultural heritage, Jung was a revolutionary. But just as Disraeli had fashioned himself, so it could be said of Jung that he was a 'radical conservative' (Bradford, 1982). For instance, in his Second Preface to *Two Essays on Analytical Psychology*, Jung in 1918, the year the First World War ended, called for a revolution, as many radicals were doing then. But Jung's was not the kind of revolution Europe had become used to in the preceding 150 years with one political firebrand after another littering the streets of her capitals with their garrulous calls-to-arms in their pamphlets. In more muted but no less insistent tones, Jung declared: What was needed was an inner revolution that could come about only through deep exploration and radical reformation of oneself. This, in turn, would lead to greater tolerance of one's neighbour since one would not be nearly so prone now to project one's own darkness onto him (Jung, 1967b, p. 5).

Citing the dominical statement that 'the Kingdom of heaven is within you', Jung went on to gloss it: 'The idea at the bottom of this ideal is that right action comes from right thinking, and that there is no cure, no improving of the world that does not begin with the individual himself' (1967b, p. 226). But then again, Jung's emphasis was ever on the dignity and the responsibilities that being a moral agent bestowed and demanded, for 'morality ... rests entirely on the moral sense of the individual and the freedom necessary for this' (1967b, p. 153). After all, Jung rhetorically but emphatically queried to rest his case in just this one volume, *Two Essays on Analytical Psychology*, not to mention the other volumes in the *Collected Works*, where he argues the point no less vigorously: 'Does not all culture begin with the individual?' (1967b, p. 205).

What this would require of most people would be the recognition that, although archetypal symbols present themselves to the individual in culturally variable forms from culture to culture, this did not mean that a culture's sacred symbols are 'just relative' and of no real ontological or ethical moment. Just the opposite. For, the unknowability of the archetype as such, housed in the equally inscrutable collective unconscious, is the same across cultures—and that Unknowability points to the Eternal in each set of sacred symbols known as a religion—at least in the major ones that had proven their depth and durability over centuries, even in some cases millennia, of trial, reformation, and persistence (Jung, 1969a, p. 68).

It was now, however, high time that each religion finally came to understand itself as a legitimate approach to the Divine (which endears him to liberal schools of theology) but not the only such approach (which makes him a hiss and a byword to conservative ones). This would both validate faith but also school each faith into a humble recognition of the legitimacy of other faiths as well. The only alternatives would be warring fundamentalisms or a withering atheism, both of which had proven themselves to be world-historical nightmares.

If sacred symbols were our final hope, it would require a major shift in consciousness for people in general to understand, accept, work with, and finally appropriate their own culture's sacred symbols in this new way and on this basis: Not as in the old form of spirituality as a matter of institutional obligation that aggressively excluded, even went to war on the basis of, other faiths' different experiences and interpretations of the Holy. That was no longer possible for 'modern man in search of a soul' (Jung, 1957). Neither could sacred symbols and religion in general be seen as just psychological phenomena, for then they would have no spiritual force or binding social power.

Rather, there needed to dawn a new age of psychospiritual religiosity, nothing less than millennial in scope, in which the individual made the ancient symbols his own in his own way, along with whatever private symbols might emerge from his dreams, meditations, artistic production, active imagination, and so on. This would require a revolution indeed. But there was nothing else for it if that intermingling of the cultural and the Eternal—so crucially and indispensably a part of the individual's narrative—were to hold. For, when a cultural narrative shipwrecks, it takes its passengers down with it, and all perish in the unforgiving waves of godlessness. To find ways, in no small measure through the instrumentality of psychology and therapy, to empower the individual to not only cope with but thrive in a modernity that had divested itself of any sacred garments, and to 're-dress' that problem by robing culture with a new access to the Divine—this in many respects is what Jung set out to do in his writing—and in his clinical practice too, no doubt. To call it an ambitious programme would be to greatly understate it. It was a massive project. But so was the problem. Two things need to be considered.

First, a culture's symbol systems—beginning with the very language through whose semantic categories and spatiotemporal indicators any individual comes to know herself and others as meaning-making creatures in time and space—are largely provided by that individual's culture (Blumer, 1969; Burke, 1989; Hewitt, 1984; Vygotsky, 1986). A reconstitution of a sense of the sacred in the individual could not happen often or profoundly enough—there could be no critical mass reached—in a society that remained entrenched in rational materialism. There needed to be a cultural commitment to moving beyond this present age that had put its money on technical rationality and come up empty-handed at the roulette table of history.

The second consideration is theoretical but also pivotal from a practical standpoint. From a classical Jungian perspective, the archetypal realm is inevitably being mediated by something, or else the archetypes could never be known. But what? That they are known, and are known to exist in such cultural diversity, strongly suggests the existence of some sort of 'multicultural mediator' that is in communication with both the ontological realm of the archetype and the cultural realm of specific rules, roles, and enactments. Indeed, it would serve as a conduit between both realms.

The existence of such a 'mechanism' could account for the diversity of forms that those foundational myths take, and the rites and rituals they are played out through from culture to culture, despite the universality of their core themes across time and place—or rather: precisely because of that universality. However, imagining what, specifically, such a 'multicultural mediator' might be, what its structure and dynamics might 'look like', is something that Jung never really did.

Henderson's 'cultural unconscious' (and the founding of world-historical time)

The massive effect of culture on cognition is by now recognized in fields ranging from medicine to theology. It has been especially clear for at least the last century (Vygotsky, 1986) and, depending upon how one reads Marx, arguably for going on two centuries.

Jungian psychology was, with a few exceptions (Henderson, 1990; Odajnyk, 1976; Progoff, 1959), slow to adequately respond to this for reasons that would take us too far astray from the present discussion to explore. However, it is now happily the case that this has led some post-Jungians in the last two decades to begin to correct this error (Adams, 1995; Gray, 1996; Samuels, 1997, Singer, 1988). They have done so by elaborating on a dynamic that Henderson in his groundbreaking work called 'the cultural unconscious' (1990, pp. 103–117).

So far, I have been maintaining that one's biographical narrative/consensual-reality time may find its maximum voltage of meaning and psychospiritual electricity if it is drawing its 'juice' from the idea of the Eternal. What I would like to do now is to blend in a notion that will prove key in this study. It is that *the redemptive action of the eternal, archetypal realm on the biographical realm occurs largely through the mediation of that process by Henderson's cultural unconscious.*

The cultural unconscious, a highly theoretical construct, can be pictured topographically as lying between the personal subconscious and the collective unconscious (Henderson, 1990, p. 117; see also Adams, 1995, p. 40). Whether it has the same type or degree of ontological status as the collective unconscious does, is not clear. However, its potency is clear in that it acts as a translator in service of the collective unconscious and its pure archetypes (which we cannot encounter directly), but is at the same time superordinate to merely egoic/subconscious functioning because it produces the culturally variable archetypal images, on which we can and do rely to encounter the pure archetype. This we do primarily in culturally foundational images, but also in dreams, art products, and in neuroses and psychoses too, these also having cultural determinants. One might picture it as a dynamic, not a structure (Jung, 1969b, pp. 179, 212). Still, it is likely that a hypothetical dynamic that explains so much, as the notion of the cultural unconscious does, bids fair to be something more than just a hypothetical at some point—hopefully sooner rather than later given the crisis into which some postmodern theory and its panic at anything like an ontological absolute has thrown a good deal of Jungian Studies.

As Henderson, whose groundbreaking work posited this mechanism, pictured it:

> The cultural unconscious is an area of historical memory that lies between the collective unconscious and the manifest pattern of the culture. It may include both these modalities—conscious and unconscious—but it has some kind of identity arising from the archetypes of the collective unconscious—which assists in the formation of myth and ritual and also promotes the process of individuation in individuals.
>
> (1990, p. 103)

Doing its work as a mediator between the collective unconscious and the personal subconscious, the cultural unconscious is a powerful psychospiritual reality in being the conduit between the forever-unknowable operation of the archetypes at the ontological level and the individual's conscious/subconscious mind at the biographical, phenomenological level. It is a psychospiritual-dynamic, a sort of 'universal translator', that serves as a relay station between the Timeless and time. And it does this differentially for each culture in the terms that make sense to that culture's members.

In other words, the cultural unconscious' primary function is to produce the culturally variable archetypal symbols and stories that commemorate and embody those moments anciently—in a time beyond time, *in illud tempus*, 'once upon a time'—when the Timeless touched a group of people who, seized by that moment or moments, were founders of that culture. Or perhaps such an originary moment is only 'imagined' by a group of later exegetes in the culture, glossing the very stories they created in order to set the standard for a culture ethically. Little matter, for that is itself an archetypal event.

Archetypal symbology as expressed in art, dreams, and so on, in turn relies upon these culturally specific archetypal images that exist in their most immediate form in culturally foundational narratives. These are now to be newly appropriated in a mass and massive project of both cultural reclamation and cultural reformation. It is through the mediation of the archetypally super-abundant cultural unconscious, in other words, that the Eternal becomes conceivable to the human being, tangible to him or her, and it does so in culturally specific terms, which the members of the culture, both individually and collectively, are called upon at this world-historical moment to reimagine. That is the daunting task that Jung sets us.

In the remainder of this chapter, let us carry these points forward, teasing out some of their antecedents, assumptions, implications, and applications, which will then be applied to a wide range of educational issues in Part II.

In illud tempus, *'once upon a time ...'*

In an intersection of the Timeless with time (so many culture's most foundational stories begin), the founder(s) of the culture collectively witnessed and took part in the breaking-through of the Sacred into the world-historical realm—indeed, in most cases this event was the establishing of the world-historical realm. This was also the moment or epoch of the founding of that culture. The Timeless now lives on in this particular form in this particular culture because of this culture's particular experience and expression of the Timeless as captured and recounted in its sacred lore. Its cast of characters is typically comprised of its archetypal culture-heroes as they interacted with those very embodiments of archetypes known, venerated, and sometimes still worshipped as a culture's Divinity or Divinities. To grasp and be grasped by one's culture's foundational narratives is perforce to exist in the archetypal mode and milieu.[1]

To adapt them to one's personal and cultural situation, to appreciate both their ontological validity and historical contingency, and to coexist with other cultures involved in a similar task, this is what lies before us, according to Jung. That the task requires an evolutionary leap forward of the first order is clear and Jung realized this. He also realized, however, that there was nothing else that would do if we were not to blow ourselves to smithereens or be forced to live in a relentlessly apocalyptic, Mad-Max world of a primitive tribalism armed with high-tech weapons that promised a future of wave upon wave of physical mutilations and biological horrors. Moreover, the project, being a culturally infrastructural one, would necessarily be a religious one, for as the Existentialist theologian Paul Tillich declared: 'Religion is the substance of culture, and culture is the form of religion' (1956, p. 103).

If the task is doable, it will only be because there is nothing that is so thick with archetypal imagery and energy at our disposal as foundational narratives. The material is there to be worked with. Jung spent his life demonstrating that much. The question—and for Jung, the fate of civilization itself hung in the balance—was and remains whether humanity could muster the will to do this individual and collective work.

Eliade's 'the sacred and the profane': on the diastole and systole of time

Traditionally, our ancient foundational narratives occurred in settings that were understood to be at once mythical and historic, *in illud tempus*, 'long, long ago'. They were so long ago, in fact, that although it was in a 'time' they happened, it was not any type of ordinary time. It was a time *upon* a time and thus not just in it, but resting upon it, even brooding over it— and thus melding the eternal and the secular and in a necessarily sym- bolic because sacral relationship. And it was *once* upon a time in the Now that is always present and therefore always holy—once and always. *Saecula saeculorum.*

These narratives took the form of theatre in both the Buddhist/Vedic (Nielsen, 2002) and Judeo-Christian (Sourvinou-Inwood, 2003) traditions. Moral exempla, they became shared liturgies and personal practices com- memorating the sanctifying sortie of the Eternal into the backward, bunkered-zones of the temporal. It was applying the mystical template of these stories—in effect, the archetypes of the story, for an archetype is a template—to one's own life that was the purpose of the theatre and the litur- gies. This alone made sense out of one's biographical narrative, to be sketched unto fullness under the template of sacred narrative (Durkheim, 1912/1995; Eliade, 1959; Levi-Strauss, 1987).

Sleeping or waking, walking or dancing, working or recreating; even being born or dying—it is not enough in some indigenous cultures that one is engaged in this-or-that act, however intensely felt, if it is only in the here-and-now. That is simply to be doing something, merely carrying on in 'profane' time, as Eliade (1959), elaborating on Durkheim (1912/1995) a half century earlier, put it in *The Sacred and the Profane*.

Profane time, time just in-and-of-itself, pregnant with no transcendent purpose, engenders only the routine. Nothing to show for itself except the minimalism of itself, profane time has no basis upon which to lay claim to anything greater than itself, no standing to petition for any degree of proximate liberation or ultimate salvation.

The basic problem with profane time is not that it is profane. Eliade makes it clear that good, or at least socially necessary, things happen in profane time and evil things may happen in transcendent realms of time. 'Sacred' and 'profane' are descriptors, not ethical evaluations, in the structural anthropology of the 1950s and 1960s—its heyday and Jung's. The 'sacred' meant merely 'that which is set apart from ordinary reality and practices'. ('Sacred' is etymologically related to 'segregated'.)

Ordinary acts can be virtuous and supernatural acts can be dark. The Gnostic Jung never tired of driving that point home (Hoeller, 1982; Pagels, 1992). He insisted upon it in his theologically renegade *Credo* that God, who created the darkness as well as the light, must contain both in Its nature. Jung scolds God for this in *Answer to Job* (1970b), which can be read as Jung's Gnostic gloss of Paul's notice in *Ephesians* 6: 12 that there are 'spiritual forces of wickedness in the heavenly places'.

Furthermore, we survive as a specie because we live together in societies that protect us from nature 'red in tooth and claw', in Lord Tennyson's colourful phrase. Any large social structure relies on the quotidian rhythms and consensual realities of ordinary, 'profane' time and people's corresponding responsibilities. In the last analysis, said Jung, one does not attain to any measure of individuation if she has not first met those responsibilities (1967b, p. 224). The stalwart Swiss Jung cautioned that the individuation process is not ethical lassitude. Individual ethical insight that the individual has gained from her own hard-won experience married to the Buddha's universal call to 'Right Action' will define the code for her to live by, according to Jung's ethic, which is both rigorous in its demand that one live true to oneself but liberal for the very same reason. The individual celebrates her personally defined ethic, carefully yet courageously crafted, as the moveable feast of circumstances warrants.

What is more, an authentic morality—not just obedience to an ecclesiastical checklist of dos-and-don'ts—is integral to the individuation process since morality is itself an archetype. Thus, for Jung, the primacy of the individual was an ethical axiom (1967b, p, 153). It is the individual's existential right and burden to be that being who is always being called out of nature to be true to her nature by making ethical choices in all their complexity and cost. Still, there are ethical imperatives that stand as axiological facts, for without them we could not live together, and this is intolerable in most cases to a creature as social as the human one. Jung insisted that 'morality is a function of the human soul, as old as humanity itself'. We err, therefore, if we conclude that morality has been forced upon us by social convention and compulsion, for the fact of the matter is that 'we have it in ourselves from the start' (1967b, p. 27).

Edgar in King Lear proclaims that 'ripeness is all' (Act 5, Scene 2, l. 11). In order that an individual rise to her full stature as a mature human being and thus an 'individuated' one, she needed to feel her way, not breezing through theory or speculation, but organically, even messily, through intuition and experience, to the realization of her singular role and responsibility as a free agent.

The problem with the profane is when it overreaches itself, which it too facilely does. It then dismisses and often-enough derides that which does not fit in. It may even legally exclude difference or subtly 'define it out' (Devine 1995) in official pronouncements and other social texts whose cruel message is that difference is illness, to be 'cured' in clinics, which were often theatres of physical and emotional sadism in earlier centuries (Foucault, 1975). What is more, that which is being muscled to the margins, even defined into darkness may, in fact, be something altogether lovely and rare. To pathologize it is nothing less than an assault on the Eternal. Emily Dickinson captures both the absurdity and the violence of this in her proclamation that

> Much Madness is divinest Sense—
> To a discerning Eye—
> Much Sense – the starkest Madness—
> 'Tis the Majority
> In this, as all, prevail—
> Assent – and you are sane—
> Demur—you're straightway dangerous—
> And handled with a Chain.
>
> (Poem # 620)

He whose extraordinary vision cannot be comprehended by norm-referenced, consensual reality is often seen as 'dangerous' by his society. Jesus, preaching in the synagogue in his own hometown, is rejected and reviled. This does not surprise him, according to John, 'for Jesus himself had pointed out that a prophet has no honor in his own country' (4: 44).

It is in transpersonal experience or vision and thus extraordinary time that a certain person or group of people, receptive to the action of the Eternal, first experienced it, credited the account of someone who had had that experience, or simply devised a sacred fiction about it. That 'theodicy' gets commemorated in sacred stories that become the culture's foundational narratives, its mythico-historical infrastructure.

By attacking incursions of sacred time into cultural time, the policeman of profane time is undermining what he purports to be defending, for he is attacking the idea of sacred time in general, but it is precisely upon this that his culture rests. For, where sacred time is not only not honoured but ridiculed, a culture's own founding stories will soon also be at risk of being either trivialized or satirized and finally excised from collective memory. It becomes open season on 'the idea of the holy' (Otto, 1960). Cultures shudder and fall—subdominant ones just as surely as dominant ones.

From the other end of the political spectrum, a good deal of postmodern cultural analysis, putatively crusading against the policing function of hegemonic institutions, emerges as yet another mode of aiding and abetting one of the Total State's most culturally destructive practices—the dismissal of the Holy. The profane-time policeman and deconstructive word-warrior are closer than they think. They equally block the road to a culture attempting to recover the Sacred in the past for the sake of the future. They both alienate a culture from its storied past and block it from finding a way to a culturally renewing story in the future. Each one phenomenologically 'freezes' time in the sterility of a meaningless present. This renders null and void the project of reclaiming a nation's sacred narratives, revisioning them in the present and using them as a springboard into a hopeful future.

There is no greater threat to the State than he who, in the name of the State, would establish 'state-time' as the only time, divorcing it from Sacred time and therefore alienating the State from its redemptive narratives of the past. Nor, on the other hand, is there a greater impediment to a culture's future than he who would deconstruct its past as being but a timeline of lies; for if a culture is presently only the product of lies, then that culture is false to the core and the only ethically defensible act would be to eradicate it, not project that corruption onto any future it would necessarily besmirch, having no basis on which to produce any other kind of result.

As we will see later in this study, an official state curriculum can easily fall prey to this dual danger of either 1) glorifying the present arrangement of things (an extreme conservative move that forecloses the possibility of vision from the eternal realm, which it may not only reject but pathologize) or 2) unduly critiquing the sponsoring state (an extreme radical move that sets out to invalidate the state at its core); leaving no world-historical or cultural means for students to access the realm of timeless Time, children do not learn to come into contact with the Divine.

On the other hand, in various First Nation cultures, their foundational narratives still have a socially and spiritually cohering effect because they are still felt to emanate from the realm of the Timeless. In Part II, we will discuss this defence of multicultural education on ontological grounds, not merely political ones. For, it is often the case that the politically subdominant culture is richer spiritually than the dominant one, which, awash in material goods, is destitute of sacred narratives and the abundant archetypal imagery that they yield culturally (Mayes et al., 2016).

A militantly secular society offers no passageway from the here-and-now to time-beyond-time or place-beyond-place. Even more tragically, the individual in his state-seduced/state-reduced narration has prepared no place, issued no invitation, for the higher-vision to come act on him, to take up residence in him—although without its action in him, there is finally no rest for him. Multicultural education, properly conceived as a sharing of world views under the Sign of the Sacred, emerges as not just a form of education in the 21st century but as itself an archetypal process that both encodes and brings into being the world-historical shift and cultural reorientation towards the Sacred that may be the last hope for our 'runaway world' (Giddens, 2002).

Two princes and the three layers of time

There is another narrative that predates Hamlet's—which we have already touched upon—by roughly 1,600 years. It is useful to look at both pieces of literature, Shakespeare's play and the Four Gospels, because both concern themselves with the three layers of time 'out of joint': 'time unhinged'. Juxtaposing these two documents will prove useful in understanding the three layers of time, the connections among them, and what makes the Hamlet narrative 'tragic' when the layers of time stay out of sync and the Four Gospels 'comedic' when the three layers of time are put right.

In both stories, individual narratives are unhinged, some even ending in suicide as in the case of Ophelia and Judas. Even the larger narratives that had shaped each nation for its own kind of historical greatness are now unhinged and twisted, betrayed by the present occupants of the seats of power in the two lands where the stories are set. And crimes against heaven are regularly committed by the rulers of both lands. This is how the two princes find conditions upon their appearance. The State, which should be the political and cultural encoding of sacred Time where the individual largely finds identity and shelter, has lost its spirit and grown cancerous.

Hamlet: the narration of a tragedy or the tragedy of narration?

Macellus' complaint to Hamlet no doubt echoes his prince's own jagged thoughts on Elsinore's walls in the depths of night after the ghostly apparition of Hamlet's departed father: 'Something is rotten in the state of Denmark' (Act 1, Scene 4, l. 90). Jesus also laments his city's moral decline as he sits alone on a hill just outside (emblematic of his utter rejection) the walls of Israel's principal city and cries: 'O Jerusalem, Jerusalem, the city that kills the prophets and stones those who are sent to it! How often would I have gathered your children together as a hen gathers her brood under her wings, and you would not!' (Matthew 23: 37).

Something wicked this way comes and both marginalized princes know it. They know that it always does whenever time is out of joint and narratives go akimbo, grow disfigured. In Denmark wickedness has already arrived and murderously installed itself as mock-majesty on a sham-throne—the sexually and politically appetitive king. Claudius (uncle-cum-father, brother-cum husband; this family's narrative is weird and redolent of the perverse) has a wretched hold upon its queen, whose own appetites regarding her son are already dubious enough.

Denmark is in the throes of what Habermas called a 'legitimation crisis'— which is when an *official* government is not a *valid* one (1975). Jung would diagnose the cause of this as psychodynamic and archetypal more than merely political. For where the State has run so foul of family—even more, when the State is ruled by such a foul family—no good can issue from it. The family is a link, and traditionally the most important one, between personal and national narratives. It is the shaping force between who one came into the world naturally *as*, and what one's family will train one *into* as a citizen. This is why the archetypes of father, mother, child, husband, and wife figure so prominently in the political and especially the religious life of a culture (Jung, 1969a, p. 156).

Denmark's ruling family, doubly distorted in this borderline-incestuous state-of-'affairs', no longer has the moral credibility or emotional balance to craft, much less model, a compelling-enough narrative to make the centre hold or the State whole. Things are on point of 'falling apart' and the prospect of 'mere anarchy being loosed upon the world'[2] seems all too real, as Yeats also had cause to fear in his day. In such liminal times, there is a special need for cohesive narratives to hold things together. But it is precisely that which Hamlet cannot find within himself and therefore cannot offer to his people.

It is thus not finally a question of *who* will rule in Denmark but of *what* will rule. Or rather, whether there will be any perdurable and ordering narratives at all anymore in Elsinore. The issue is whether Elsinore can hold onto itself as a space in which cohesive narratives are now even possible, for where the State no longer operates as the historical ligament joining the individual to the Divine, all narratives get out of whack … and the time goes out of joint.

Thus, the narratival crisis at Elsinore is not finally about what happens when a single individual's narrative falls a-*part*—even if it is a prince's. It is about what happens when everyone's narratives fall a-*part*: That is, when the narrative of oneself as a biographical being is a-part, decoupled from one's most intimate circles of others; a-part, de-coupled from one's sense of oneself as a vibrant world-historical being; a-part, as when oneself and one's culture are decoupled from a Sacred Narrative that ideally joins everyone's biographical and world-historical narratives to Itself, including all in a Universal Embrace, in a concordance of all narratives with and for each other under the Sign of the Divine.

To de-couple self and society from the Eternal is an ethical mistake. But it is just as much a mistake in narrativizing, as various narrative theorists point out. They argue that the most viable narratives have not only a social but also a religious function; they answer the longing for the Timeless in our experience of time, whose degrees of intensity must reach toward the Infinite or fall into despair and then disrepair (Ricoeur, 1985, pp. 26, 28). The socio-religious function of the national narrative has been short-circuited in Denmark. All pay the price in their confused and reduced personal narratives.

For, again, the narratival crisis at Elsinore is not primarily about the addled narrative of a prince. It is not even about the adrift narrative of a nation. It is not just Denmark's political problem with particular persons that lies at the heart of this drama. That would be a matter of state. Even less is it a personal problem with particular people. That would be a soap opera. It is about national narrativity as a crisis when it is not keyed to the Transcendent. It is not the narrative of a crisis. It is a crisis of narrativity.

Hamlet is not, in other words, primarily the narration of a tragedy. It is about the tragedy of a nation's narration—and the general desolation that obtains when citizens grow dispirited because the Spirit has left the State—or rather, the State has abandoned the Spirit and thus denuded itself of the Divine. The State is then no longer a relay station between the individual and the divine, but a narratival dead-end where the Sacred stalls because the State has run out of gas and the people now have no transport to transcendence.

Hence, the most hopeful, and therefore the most spiritual, narratives are those that 'break the spell of death over life' and are thus 'comedies' as in Dante's Divine Comedy (Dunne, 1973, p. 23).[3] The crisis at Elsinore is the crisis of the world, separation from the Transcendent, and it is a crisis of narrativity. It is not only most of the principal characters in the play who lie dead on the stage at its end. It is narrative itself. Shakespeare's narrative is not so much about Hamlet, Ophelia, Gertrude, Claudius, or Polonius. Shakespeare's narrative is about narratives and how they die when they are 'out of joint'.

In Part II, we will look at the spiritual violence done to the teacher and student when a State that has succumbed to corporate interests—indeed, a State that now has forfeited its role as a cultural conduit to the Divine and become a largely ideological cover for corporate interests in a quasi-democracy (Scott, 2007)—makes and enforces school policies that negate what Dewey envisioned schools as being: The principal sites where the sacred world-historical mission of democracy was advanced.

The Four Gospels: resurrection as narrative/narrative as resurrection

The state of his State will destroy Jesus, too, another rightful claimant to a throne. However, in an Aristotelian peripety of singular dimensions in the world's religious literature, we learn that Jesus somehow bears, and bears away, in his own flesh, the sins of not only his State but those of every State in the world. And as if that were not enough, we learn that this metaphysical *Pax Iesuiana* extends ultimately to every single human being. So the four-part Gospel's combined narrative is encouraging us, by the sheer force *of* its narrative, to *believe*—and, in believing, to experience a restoration of our own personal narrative in renewed communion with the Eternal, which appears as the Archetypal Man, who is the protagonist of this story.

Hamlet, confronted with a clear, ethical transgression that it is both his right as the rightful prince and his duty for his father's sake to remedy, forfeits that right and evades that duty by circling around it in every possible specie of narratival eccentricity. His sanity is questioned throughout the play. He draws everyone around him into his wake, until virtually everyone of note lies dead on the stage. Hamlet avoids the majesty of his calling by getting more and more self-absorbed in interior narratives that paralyse him. Baleful biographical narratives ignore a deeper teleology beyond themselves. It is the folly of youth, and Hamlet is young.

Oppositely, Jesus, as simultaneously God and man under the characterological assumption of the Christ-narrative, needs no 'right' and requires no 'duty' (he is himself the author of the law) to do what he does out of sheer grace, without which, death would, as in Hamlet, be our last 'stage', with no surplus of hope for anything after it.

Hamlet's fatal indecisions stem from his not being able to reconcile his personal narrative with a world-historical one by drawing upon the power of the Sacred narrative to bring it all to pass. Hamlet is caught in the Jungian Puer-Complex—the eternal boy who will not grow up and make the hard choices. Hamlet's inner divorces from himself snuff out the potential unity of his narratives of which he was capable, which history required of him, and God wished for him. This is existential defeat in narratival implosion.

Contrastingly, Jesus' constant interweaving of the three narratives into an all-season garment of an integral and efficacious life that is the clothing of the wise, stands out as exemplary, even in the ethically demanding context of the world's great religious literature.

At the biographical level of Jesus' life-narrative, he evidences the tenderest of personal care, as with the Samaritan woman at the well (John 4). Yet this he does with a firmness that keeps empathy from sliding over into mere permissiveness, which would simply be wrong and ultimately do the individual no good. He fully grasps and patiently works with a person's foibles, flaws, and even serious transgressions. To the woman taken in adultery by mean-spirited Pharisees (who, by the way, let the man involved go scot-free) and whose otherwise-inevitable death by stoning he adroitly adverts, his judgement is abundant in care: 'Then neither do I condemn you', he graciously says as she, no doubt relieved beyond words, turns to leave. But as she does, he, in the next breath, gravely instructs her to 'go and sin no more' (John 8:11). Forgiving, he is also demanding with that perfect balance of 'care' (in the domain of the archetypal Great Mother) and 'demand' (in the domain of the archetypal Great Father) that characterizes the best teaching and parenting—an idea we will explore in Part II: Not 'permissiveness' (excessive care) or 'authoritarianism' (excessive demand) but 'authoritativeness', the synthesis of both in just the right blend of both (Conger and Galambos, 1997; Crain, 2010).

In family life (our family narratives and our biographical ones being isomorphic to each other), our hero is generous in imparting his gifts and doing his duty as a son. He turns water into wine at his mother's behest although it does not suit his purposes at that moment (John 2: 3–4). Yet, he never lets 'the good' sentimentally divert him from 'the best': His relationship with the Divine.

> Someone told him, 'Your mother and brothers are standing outside, wanting to speak to you. He replied to him,' Who is my mother, and who are my brothers?' Pointing to his disciples, he said, 'Here are my mother and my brothers. For whoever does the will of my Father in heaven is my brother and sister and mother.'
>
> (Matthew 12: 47–50)

At the world-historical level of what the evangelists claim is his world-historically culminating life, Jesus tenderly weeps at the beauty of his nation's calling and his all-consuming wish to serve it like a hen brooding over her chicks (Matthew 23: 37). However, no mere 'Nationalist' with the ethically insupportable motto: 'My country, right or wrong!' always on his lips as the answer to every critique of his nation, Jesus severely reproves his nation for what he clearly believes is its misalignment with the political Mind of the Divine, for they stone and kill God's corrective messengers, the prophets: a world-historical error that problematizes its special status as elected to lead the march of history back to history's source and goal: the Kingdom of God.

As for the transcendent meta-level of this singular narrative, there is no passage of it to single out as uniquely representative, for a totally focused awareness of the Sacred is present in every word uttered by the protagonist. But given the prominence of eating-imagery in the Gospels, if one had to choose a passage where Jesus' complete personal identification with the Divine is best conveyed, the following would work well:

> His disciples urged him, 'Rabbi, eat something'. But he said to them, 'I have food to eat that you know nothing about'. Then his disciples said to each other, 'Could someone have brought him food?' 'My food,' said Jesus, 'is to do the will of him who sent me and to finish his work.'
>
> (John 4: 31–35)

Unlike Hamlet, whose physical and linguistic gestures are filled with confusion, ambiguity, bivalence, and strategizing, every gesture Jesus makes reflects a narratival unity of the personal, historical, and Divine in impeccable balance and just proportions. Each of this protagonist's gestures, either physical as in his healing of lepers; discursive as in his announcement of his messiahship in the synagogue in Nazareth; and performative in the bestowal of Divine forgiveness from the Cross radiates with the Presence and the Purpose of the religious tradition that the Gospel authors claim he both fulfils and transcends. It is the tradition of 'the One'.

For, if Hamlet's narratival time is 'out of joint', shattered into Humpty Dumpty parts, Jesus' narrative is a unity at every point, mirroring the basic assumption and proclamation of his religious tradition, in which the Name of the Divinity at its centre is so holy that it may only be referred to indirectly, adjectivally as 'One'. It may not be uttered by a merely mortal voice in the illusory echo-chambers of personal and historical time, where it would inevitably wind up distorted. It may only be referred to indirectly, adjectivally as *echad*: 'One'. '*Adonai echad!*' 'The Lord is One.'

Structure mirrors meaning in this piece of literature and the structural unity of Jesus' narrative reflects Judaism's first and last proclamation to the world: 'God is One.' If we interpret 'one' archetypally, not mathematically, which Jung suggests we should, it being the case according to him that numbers are primarily 'an archetype of order which has become conscious' before they are tools for counting, then we see that the ultimate unity of narratival temporalities reflects an Ultimate Unity cosmologically (as cited in von Franz, 1991, p. 268; see also von Franz, 1974).

According to Jung, one of the meanings of 'One' is the Anthropos: the mythical Archetypal Man. This Anthropos is comprised of two 'capacities': 1) his 'manifestations', which is to say, his many identities as they reveal themselves in action in various venues and 2) his 'psychic functions', in which those actions originated and by which they are presently assessed (Jung, 1968b, p. 176). But to reflect upon one's actions assessed in various contexts over one's life is none other than narrativizing. Archetypally, then, the Four Gospels are the narrative of Anthropos in biographical and historical time. Not only does the Word become flesh in these narratives; the Myth of Anthropos became flesh, too—thereby uniquely interweaving the three layers of time into one narratival tapestry. What does this mean?

It means that Jesus as the Anthropos, the Archetypal Man in the Four Gospels, comes to specifically biographical men and women. The Archetype became flesh, not making theological arguments or laying out lists of dos and don't's. He, the Myth of Myths, comes in a narrative, *his* narrative, which thus sanctifies the very idea of individual narrative, and this in turn sanctifies the fact that each of us in our individual narratives is potentially divine.

The Gospels are remarkable not only in that they purport to be presenting the Messiah. They are equally remarkable in the fact that the Messiah presents himself as a narrative. Given the Evangelists' assumptions about who and what he is—the Divine Himself deigning to take on a specific temporal identity—Jesus, by the very act of living in and living out a life-in-narrative, thereby sanctifies narrativity and sanctifies us since we are our narrations. The Messiah come in a narrative, true. But this now means narrative itself has become messianic.

But first he must suffer death in his biographical narrative, its crucifixion in mechanical time and space. Indeed, some medieval interpreters saw the cross beams as emblematic of time (the horizontal beam) and space (the vertical beam) on which the mortal man, Adam, condemned to die for his transgression, was released by the perfect Atonement of the perfect new Adam.

This makes our narratival hero in the Four Gospels 'heroic' not only in terms of his specific narratival situation and its resolution in time and space: Jesus ben Joseph in Jerusalem, c. 30 ce, carpenter and itinerant preacher. Rather, he emerges finally and more generally as the cosmic conqueror of the limitations of biographical time. Never losing his personal identity and its consummate moral beauty, he now takes on his larger cosmic identity as the embodiment of Universal Process: He exists as the divinization of the mortal human being, through time, beyond time, into Sacred time, from mortal human to Immortal Human, from the fleeting 'now' that never really 'was' to the Eternal Now that finally always is.

Henderson's 'cultural unconscious': ferryman between the collective unconscious and the biographical individual as a world-historical and transcendent being

I will conclude this chapter by developing the notion that the bridge between the biographic and the eternal cannot be created without the archetypal symbols to do so. For where regular language breaks down at the ports-of-entry to the Limitless, that is precisely where the words of poetry come together. Symbols bump us over into the fringes of the Divine. And those symbols are largely what a person's culture-of-origin provides by means of the cultural unconscious.

Whatever agonies are his in this life, whatever abasements, however much sinned against and sinning, a human being's biographical narrative is nevertheless assured and, after a modest fashion, enshrined if enfolded in larger narratives. And why is this? It is precisely because those things happened, yes, but they did not happen in a vacuum. They took place in the Light of the Timeless as that Light presented Itself to that person through the prism of his culture and on the ground where he stood—an individual, yes, but also a member of a world-historical cohort.

And it is his culture in its final stewardship (good or bad as that stewardship may have been; good or bad as it may be now in its last act) that offers him its ways and means to transact (and possibly transition) his death. For just as a person is born into a culture and lives within it, so he dies within it.

Culture offers him: Images from popular lore, art, and religion to picture and prepare for the process of dying; examples of characters who have done so; leitmotifs to inform his own stories towards their end; and the culture's assessment of and affects about death to inform his own judgements and feeling as the certain curtain comes down on the play he took part in on this planet. Our mortal lives are very small when seen *sub specie aeternitatis*; the play and its players ephemeral when viewed from the vantage point of the Timeless. Yet each life, in its own epic/epoch, is important from the vantage point of the Eternal, and this can itself be a saving knowledge for the individual who joins his biography with a transcendental narrative. This knowledge is for most people a cultural bequeathal. Without it, one is left with Prospero's stark final reckoning of it all.

> Our revels now are ended. These our actors,
> As I foretold you, were all spirits and
> Are melted into air, into thin air:
> And, like the baseless fabric of this vision,
> Cloud-capp'd towers, the gorgeous palaces,
> \ The solemn temples, the great globe itself,
> Yea all which it inherit, shall dissolve
> And, like this insubstantial pageant faded,
> Leave not a rack behind. We are such stuff
> As dreams are made on, and our little life
> Is rounded with a sleep.
>   (*The Tempest*, Act 4. Scene 2, ll.146ff)

More consolingly but not unambiguously, the sociologist of religion Peter Berger thus reminds us that:

> Every human society is, in the last resort, men banded together in the face of death. The power of religion depends, in the last resort, upon the credibility of the banners it puts in the hands of men as they stand before death, or more accurately, as they walk, inevitably, toward it.
>   (1967, p. 53)

It will be recalled that Henderson calls the cultural unconscious 'an area of historical memory that lies between the collective unconscious and the manifest pattern of the culture'. It may include both conscious and unconscious elements. Its identity is unclear but whatever it is, it must be closely related to the archetypes of the collective unconscious for this is what it is adapting to a culture in its formation of myth and ritual, all the while that it is 'promot[ing] the process of individuation in individuals' (1990, p. 103).

Misadventures in world-historical time (or: why we lost in Vietnam)

The restorative action of the archetypal realm on the biographical realm largely occurs through the mediation of the 'cultural unconscious'. The cultural unconscious is a process of translation operating in a space between the personal and the collective unconscious. Out of their intercourse is conceived a community's foundational narratives—history and fable now melding, conceived, and issuing forth as world-historical tales. The individual finds her purpose and path in her archetypally infused biographical narrative, but largely because it is now a narrative whose archetypal energy and imagery, flush with her culture's own world-historical narratives, are vibrant with the rejuvenating power of the archetypal as she knows it in solidarity with her cultural cohort. She is 'tabernacled' with them in their shared tents on this particular world-historical field of action.

When this is happening, when the culture as a whole has a collective dedication to the Eternal as it grasps that culture and as that culture turns to embrace it, then this is a culture's apex, a *Siglo del Oro*, a renaissance, which may itself enter candidacy for elevation to mythic status in later cohorts' remembrance of it and use of it as a touchstone against which to measure their own now-corrupted, much lesser present condition.

The cultural unconscious is exceptionally powerful. It is the larger temporal field upon which most individual men and women principally meet the Eternal in Ricoeur's second type of time: world-historical time.

Cultural-narratival pathology

The problem with world-historical time lies precisely in its daunting amplitudes and expansive frequencies on the oscilloscope of history. Cultural narratives can be so temporally and ideologically vast and packed with intensity that they are easily mistaken for Transcendence Itself—not correctly apperceived as the individual's 'transitional space' towards the Transcendent (Winnicott, 1992). National and Timeless narratives conflate in the minds of a people. The State becomes the object of worship, certain of the leaders its gods because of the collective psychic energy projected onto them. This is understandable.

Nevertheless, when a national narrative is not enfolded in an eternal narrative, when the State no longer exists in the service of the Sublime (Lincoln's Gettysburg Address is an example of when it did—at least for the few minutes in which Lincoln delivered it) but only to expand its power, then the stage is set for another colonialist outrage to add to the sad annals of history.

World-historical narratives are vaster than merely biographical ones. They are often written down and housed in impressive buildings that architecturally manifest the majesty of the State. They are legitimated in displays of pomp and circumstance that the child has seen and been taught to thrill at from earliest memory. They are core in the curricula of the culture's schools. They have probably required real sacrifice, even death at home and abroad, by family members who are now themselves hallowed in family narratives; they stretch over centuries, sometimes longer. It is understandable how one can feel oneself being immortalized by incorporation in that world-historical body that is so much larger than oneself. It is understandable, but it is untenable, too.

It sets up world-historical time as a substitute for eternal Time. It tries to evade the necessity of developing an intact ego that has examined itself, not fled from itself in a world-historical narrative that has now become a substitute and an exaggerated ego-narrative. It has foreclosed the forging of the 'ego-Self axis' that is individuation. Moreover, a world-historical narrative *in place of* the Eternal, not a proper world-historical narrative *in light of* the Eternal, can only finally grow tainted (Edinger, 1973). It is Hamlet's time out of joint. It is a narratival error of sequence and precedence. And in political terms it inevitably devolves from a robust patriotism, or the celebration of and identification with a world-historical narrative in the service of the Divine, to a corrosive nationalism, or the bad faith of exalting one's ego in an inappropriate coopting of the universal narrative of the Divine to the special benefit of one's own nation's narrative. One fancies that God looks at every nation with a mixture of hope and horror.

More generally, the ideological misuse of history takes on two forms politically.

The error of the far-Left is its use of its reading of history to heedlessly attack every time-hallowed social institution and arrangement, despite its ongoing importance, even sanctity. The fault of the far-Right is the use of its reading of history to defend virtually every time-encrusted social institution and arrangement, despite its present irrelevance, even perniciousness. The far-Left recklessly attempts to discard the Eternal in its world-historical narrativizing. The far-Right impiously attempts to coopt the Eternal in its world-historical narrativizing. Both moves make it impossible for the thoughtful young soul of a student to find the tie to the sacred in the national narrative that is so key to that soul's maturation.

We will look in Part II at how the battle over school policy is often simply a question of which of these extreme and erroneous misreadings of national history will prevail, both of which, by distorting a nation's history, deprive its youth of access to the sacred through the cultural and thereby throw time out of joint for them, too—precisely the opposite effect of wedding the personal to the world-historical under the sponsorship of the visionary that schools must have if a democracy is to survive and thrive. Such was Dewey's view in any case, and this study categorially affirms that view, especially as Dewey laid it out in *Democracy and Education* (1916), which, looked at from this angle, was an attempt to harmonize the three dimensions of time in a manner that was consistent with the precepts of democracy and dedicated to advancing them. Tragically, this has become, as Bullough feelingly describes it, 'the forgotten dream of American public education' (1988).

An illustration from cinema: Full Metal Jacket

Kubrick's 1988 movie, *Full Metal Jacket*, illustrates the 'elevation' of a biographical narrative into a cultural one, with all the psychological electricity that that 'resurrection in the cultural' entails, the seemingly supratemporal status it may be felt to confer on the individual, but finally the physical and psychological carnage it can lead to when a nation's narrative is not enfolded in a higher one.

When a national narrative does not see itself in the middle as a political and cultural mediator between the individual and the Timeless but sees itself as the centre, full stop, then it is on the high road to mischief. It is dialectically 'off'. It is a failed transcendent function, in Jungian terms: Where culture should be the mediator between the individual and the eternal in creative tension, it sets itself up as the solution to the tension. Its archetypal imagery and plot lines are therefore similarly off. Kubrick catches this in this movie.

In Stanley Kubrick's masterpiece, we see how this error operates and the havoc it can wreak. We follow a fresh group of Marine recruits through their archetypal descent into hell—their gruelling months at the toughest bootcamp of them all, Parris Island: The Harvard of Horror for any new Private in the military. Through verbal humiliation, ceaseless drilling from first light every morning to well past sunset (as the dour primal darkness of the South Carolina swamplands descends upon them), combat training that pushes the now morally abased and dazed recruits to the point of both physical and emotional collapse, and draconian corporal punishment if they fail in even the minutest detail of their training (and sometimes even when they do not, just for the hell of it), their previous psychosocial identities are savaged. Their already immature, shaky biographical narratives become hopelessly fragmented and, in the case of one recruit who commits suicide, his previous biographical identity is decimated. All of this is overseen by Gunnery Sergeant Hartmann, salty to the point of sadism and in charge of this initially ragtag lot.

He paradoxically makes his programme of exaltation for them clear in his first of many verbal and physical humiliations of them: They will, if they survive this living hell, no longer be merely addled biographical beings, destined to die (he relentlessly calls them 'maggots') but will be transformed into something suggestive of the holy, deathless in its very dedication to death. They will become 'minsters of death, praying for war'. But for now, they are, in Hartmann's scathing announcement to them, just 'amphibian shit'.

Over the next months of training, Hartman works his malevolent magic with his supernatural wand in the form of the nightstick he carries almost everywhere: The wand, an otherworldly tool of the transformation of ego into the trans-egoic, the transpersonal, and therefore the trans-biographical, is here symbolically replaced with a weapon of bludgeoning the ego into conformity to the total State. The men have become killing machines—ready 'to eat their guts out and ask for seconds', as Private Joker says, his name a parody of the 'comic', heavenly narrative (as in *The Divine Comedy*) and a reference to a sadistic murderer in the Batman series, which right about the time this movie is set was airing weekly on American television.

On the last day at Parris Island before he escorts them out the gates and off to war, Hartmann tells them that they have graduated from being 'maggots' to now being Marines. Their biographical narratives, initially crucified under this modern-day Roman-Centurion's hand, are now called into existence again, even elevated, raised, as if he were the Marine messiah, to a higher narrative, the world-historical. It is false-consciousness at its most seductive. He tells them that they are no longer 'maggots'. Indeed, they are now proper Marines and, as such, are part of an imperishable brotherhood. Most of them will be shipped at once to Vietnam. Inevitably, some will not return. But what of that? They are now Marines, which, he announces with a nationalist pride that storms the gates of heaven itself and makes them—he proclaims with soteriological certainty—members of a Corps that will never die. The conclusion is simple and the implication is clear: Sacred soldiers in a sacred nation-state, it little matters if they perish in Vietnam or not. They have already attained immortality. They already dwell in 'Eternal Time'. Their biographical narratives, resurrected and transformed by the saving grace of the divine State, are of a piece with the Eternal. Or so, in an irony-saturated instance of what can only be called 'metaphysical false-consciousness', he would have them believe—as devoutly, indeed, as he does.

In archetypal terms, the young men have been ritualistically dismembered, divested of ego, torn apart limb by limb by the hounds of hell—their Gunnery Sergeant and the other drill instructors barking at them all day long like so many Cerberuses, deafening them to their individual biographies in order to re-narrativize them into complete conformity to the needs and stories of the State; to become (biologically alive or dead, it matters little to effectively immortal beings) resurrected in the State as martial-cogs in the machinery of a New Political Jerusalem.

Now turned into mechanical minions of murder, everything perfectly in world-wasting 'order', their garb both ennobling and anonymous, they are lockstep in every move, their arms like swinging metronomes on the parade field. Clocks in motion, their arms unsheathed razor-blades, they are the State-Narrative in the shape of regimented biographies. The previous personal narrative is eliminated; then a new one is bestowed on them perfectly in sync with a National Lie-cum-World-historical-Narrative about defending democracy around the world on the killing fields of Vietnam. The biographical and cultural narratives now corrupt beyond repair, all that is left to complete this narratival grotesquerie is to vulgarize the Divine.

Sgt. Hartmann, in a Black-Sabbath Christmas 'homily', lectures the recruits about Jesus as if he were just a primitive warrior-god of a savage nation, specially favouring America with license to rain down napalm-horror upon the world. The false-consciousness in all of this is stressed by the fact that the Christmas celebration will begin with a magic show. Following that, the Chaplain will preach 'the good news' of American triumphalism about how the Free World will overthrow Communism. And how will this happen? Sgt. Hartmann is clear: Through the will of God himself expressing itself in (indeed, *as*) the United States Marine Corps. Thus it is that 'God has a hard-on for Marines' as Hartmann vulgarly puts it, because, in Hartmann's troglodyte conception of Divinity as the culmination of sex-as-rape and diplomacy-as-slaughter, God is the ultimate Troglodyte King, ensconced, no doubt, in his Celestial Cave in a brute Elysium.

Elsewhere in this bizarre accounting, *Christ*, the Universal Prince of Peace, is also reduced to a nationalistic thug-god; the Narrative of Heaven is outrageously mistranslated in a foul lingo as a fake world-historical tale; and the young soldiers themselves have been terrorized into accepting a one-size-fits-all, existentially inauthentic biographical narrative as their new 'identity'. In his parodic sermon to his soldiers, Hartmann thus manages to 1) desecrate a sacred narrative, 2) subordinate it to a toxic world-historical narrative, and 3) confirm his Marines in their new (im)personal narratives as righteous monsters—pseudo-biographical gears in a mad mechanism. Hartmann's nugatory narrativizing is a crime against time.

Kubrick's movie illustrates the 'elevation' of a biographical narrative into a cultural one, with all the thrill that that 'resurrection in the cultural' entails, the seemingly supratemporal status it may be felt to confer on the individual, but also the bestiality it can lead to when a nation's narrative is not enfolded in a higher one, one that sees itself as midway between the biographical and the Timeless.

Conclusion

At an ethical maximum, the State is a cultural/political bridge between the mundane and the Eternal, the personal and the Universal—both the individual and the State 'held by' and operating under the Sign of the Timeless. When that is not the case, as is so often true when the State arrogates primacy unto itself, which States almost invariably do, then Prince Hamlet is right: 'The time is out of joint', and disorder and destruction crouch leering in the corner, poised to spring and do their wretched work. That is world-historical time at its minimum.

Nevertheless, at its ethical maximum, a culture stands between the individual and the Eternal, in a nurturing relationship with the individual below it and in a nurtured relationship with the Eternal above it. To attempt to subordinate the Eternal to the cultural is an inversion of the hierarchies of time. It is also a historical irony in that the national narrative is sacred precisely because it is subordinate to the Eternal narratives, which vary from culture to culture by means of the cultural unconscious, but which ultimately must transcend themselves in returning to their Source and Goal—not the glorification of *Cultus* but its proper use as conduit to *Aeternitatis*.

In the following quote, if we understand 'religion' to mean the breaking through and presence of the Eternal in the world and honouring the different ways that is experienced and expressed culturally, then the Existentialist theologian Paul Tillich's proclamation rings true: 'Religion is the substance of culture, and culture is the form of religion' (1987, p. 103). And, I would add, the core of religion, announced in a culture's sacred stories, is archetypal.

It is the ontological Presence of the Eternal Now of liberation and salvation—that which exists as sovereign in the archetypal realm and which, in the Platonic sense of the term, is the archetypal realm—that is the substance of religion. The cultural narratives are the forms that record and remind a culture of that overarching Presence. The Presence subsumes the cultural structures, not the other way around.

When a nation's foundational narratives exist in the service of the Universal Presence that engendered them differentially, it is to be extolled for operating in good faith and in the spirit of a globally generous patriotism. When, on the other hand, a nation coopts its sacred stories as justification for all sorts of mischief performed internally and externally in the service of anti-democratic purposes, it has devolved into self-righteous nationalism. The educational implications of this, especially for public education, are manifold.

Notes

1 Concerning the topic, which the parameters of this study do not allow me to delve into, of how foundational archetypal stories, themes, characters, imagery, and so on then inform a culture's art and humanities, the reader would do well to begin by consulting: Barnaby and D'Acierno, 1990; Philipson, 1963; Rowland, 2012; Snider, 1991; Sugg, 1992; Wheelwright, 1974). The reader interested in how foundational-cultural archetypal images find their way into the individual's dreams, gifts, complexes, and psychopathologies, the following studies provide fine analyses and sound suggestions for further research: Adams, 1995; Gray, 1996; Samuels, 2001.
2 www.poetryfoundation.org/poems/43290/the-second-coming (accessed 9/27/2019).
3 See also Brown, 1970; Fiedler, 1969; Herzog, 1967; Sovatsky, 1998 on the centrality of the idea of death and the desire to overcome it as the heart of our personal narratives.

Chapter 3

Intimately unknown

The collective unconscious

Introduction

This chapter aims to deepen our appreciation of the relationship between the archetypes and time in terms of the three-fold expression of that relationship in biographical, world-historical narrative, and sacred narrative (1985).

To summarize Chapters 1 and 2: The manner in and extent to which an individual enters into relationship with the archetypal realm and its transcendent Time (portrayed as the eternal Now) shapes her biographical narrative in ordinary time in the most consequential ways. The integrally related process of her moving into more conscious relationship with the archetypes and the collective unconscious is mediated by the cultural unconscious. The collective unconscious and its archetypes can only be known to us by means of archetypal symbols, and the cultural unconscious is the dynamic capacity that is always doing just that—translating each archetype into its many culturally specific images. It is the cosmic multiculturalist. These archetypal symbols inevitably vary from culture to culture in how they manifest the supratemporal archetype itself, how they get 'dressed up' in space and time, as it were, in terms, images, artistic expressions that make sense to a certain group of people in a specific geographical here and certain historical now.

However, the transtemporal, trans-spatial archetypes that are at the core of what these different groups of symbols represent in their specific ways remains the same—each archetype an aspect of the Collective Unconscious— a facet of the Eternal Core that is the Timeless. Each of these facets has a thematic core when it presents itself to human consciousness, which must function categorically if it is to function at all (Eisendrath-Young and Hall, 1991). That is simply the way we are hardwired (Matlin, 2012). Besides, without categories it is impossible for us to create patterns, which is the heart of narrativizing.

However, we must be mindful that in talking about the Collective Unconscious and the Timeless (which, by the view of it that I take in this study, are isomorphic) we are using very limited language to talk about limitless 'structures' and 'dynamics' that are higher and deeper, farther reaching and more deeply penetrating than anything that our discursive tools and terms could ever 'know'—except, that is, in a very tentative way—and that 'way' is the archetypal symbol. Insofar as the collective unconscious is at the heart of the production of those symbols from culture to culture, it is close to the heart of things in general. Here, again, I raise the notion of an ontology or even a metaphysics of multiculturalism that goes beyond its mere political iterations (Mayes et al., 2016).

'First' contact with the archetypes

The notion of the archetype, which we have already discussed at some length, began to take shape in Carl Gustav Jung as a young psychiatrist at the famous Burghölzli Clinic, the 'mental hospital' attached to the University of Zürich, although some of his spiritual experiences as a boy and his readings as a youth and college student had already been pointing him in that direction (Bair, 2003; Shamdasani, 2005, 2003).

One day while making his daily rounds, Jung stopped to talk with a man who was being treated for schizophrenia. Jung recounts what transpired in his autobiography, *Memories, Dreams, Reflections*.[1] It is often cited in the Jungian literature as a pivotal early moment in Jung's formulation of his notion of the archetype.

While doing his rounds, he came across a patient blinking at the sun. The patient said to Jung that Jung must also look at the sun with eyes half shut. If he did, he would see the sun's phallus. If he moved my head from side to side the sun-phallus would move too, and that was the origin of the wind. Four years after this event, Jung was studying the Paris magic papyrus, considered a liturgy of the Mithraic cult. In it, various visions of the papyrus' author are given. One of them discussed the 'origin of the wind' and consisted of a series of instructions, invocations, and visions that corresponded with an arresting exactness to what the Jung man had told Jung four years earlier about the sun, its phallus, and where the wind came from (1969a, pp. 150f).

Jung was eerily impressed by what seemed to him a highly improbable correspondence between the fantasy of a relatively unlettered citizen of a small Swiss village and the storyline, imagery, and even the theme of an ancient liturgy commemorating creation.

Jung gradually[2] arrived at the conclusion that the similarity between a contemporary individual's dreams and an ancient myth—a stunning correspondence that he, already a competent student of ancient mythologies in addition to being an up-and-coming young psychiatrist, would now discern in many of his patients' dreams—was evidence of a more ancient level of psyche than had previously been imagined in the standard psychiatric literature.

'The unknown as it immediately affects us'

Step by step, Jung came to the conclusion that every human was born with it, whatever 'it' was. But whatever it was, it was a universal feature of the psyche. And it was so deep, primordial and yet, simultaneously, somehow transcendent, that there was really no possibility of ever coming into direct contact with it. It would obliterate the mind and vacate the personality. It would be the psychodynamic equivalent of the Pauline notice that 'It is a fearful thing to fall into the hands of the Living God' (Hebrews 10: 31). Its primal power and transcendent impulsion, comprised of cosmic as much as simply psychic energy, and even more the former than the latter, or so it seemed to the Gnostic Jung (Hoeller, 1982), was so great that it would blow into shards any psychological function or formation that found its way to face-to-face confrontation with it. If it did, the result would be psychosis.

The Collective Unconscious and the mystical calculus of it as the 'integral' summation of its trans-conceptual archetypes could not be faced directly or held steadily. It could only be intuited, apperceived by engaging with the symbols it produced: Archetypal symbols. These the human could begin to register on its apperceptive radar.

The matrix (the collective unconscious) out of which those symbols emerged must forever be *terra incognita* to human consciousness. But the symbols themselves? They could be known. Indeed, they must be known, Jung insisted, as not only a psychological imperative but an ethical one. The ethics and mysticism in Jung that still draw so many to his work today cost him dearly in his professional life.

But what else could he do? Jung believed that he had discovered something of the first importance. He also reckoned that it was out of this universal substratum of consciousness that the relatively tiny circle of personal, merely biographical consciousness emerged, with its strictly personal subconscious and its 'laws' that governed its rather hydraulic mechanics. Freud felt he had found them. Jung mostly agreed with them (Jung, 1967a).

But Jung's other layer of psyche preceded the existence of the individual and his personal psyche. Somehow, at birth, it was already there in the individual, inscribed in him at and as his core. About this, Freud seemed to know or care very little, thought the idea both absurd and dangerous, and in no uncertain terms warned Jung off of such lines in his research and writing (Jung, 1973).

Jung arrived at conclusions that took him beyond what the Freudian model of the psyche could cope with, or was even willing to allow (Charet, 1993). This, despite the fact that such things were considered acceptable objects of scholarly research at the time (Douglas, 1997) and that Jung's doctoral dissertation was on mediumship. In a conversation recorded in Jung's autobiography *Memories, Dreams, Reflections* that portended the final break between Freud and Jung, Freud nervously exhorted Jung to steer clear of such things.

But Jung would not be put off. He believed that there was a collective unconscious that existed before the individual and his personal psyche even came into existence, although, when the personal psyche did form, this collective (because everyone had it) unconscious (because no one could ever become aware of its unreachable depths and heights) seemed to come with it. Accordingly, Jung called it the collective unconscious.

Jung began to note and record the tales, motifs, images, and symbols that it produced in patients' stories and images that corresponded with the stories and symbols wrought by humankind in its earliest recorded history: Stories about how the universe began, how human beings arose in it, how people should live and die, and what might lie beyond all of that. And of course, Jung made his own mark on ego psychology (Mayes, 2017a, 2005), primarily in his contribution of the terms extroversion, persona, shadow, complex, and countertransference/counter-projection to the lexicon of psychodynamic psychology.

But what of this deepest subterranean level, massive, vast, and constantly bubbling over with lava-streams of energy and imagery, and not all of it welcome, some of it even chilling or grotesque? Where was the psychology that tried to make sense out of this layer of psyche? It existed at a deeper level than conventional medical psychiatry was prone to plumb. Its eruption as dreams, fantasies, and neurotic and psychotic structures and metamorphoses exhibited pregnant but puzzling correspondences with mankind's most ancient myths and religions and art. Where was the psychology that tried to make sense out of that? There was none in the academy. What was needed (and it took no Daniel to read the writing on the wall to know it would be rejected) was a psychology of the unconscious. This would challenge the materialist assumptions of the empiricism that ruled the academy and would be either sniffed at, thrust aside or, most painfully of all, chuckled over. Jung's mission would be to challenge that, to change it, to coax the study of the psyche, psyche-ology ('the study of spirit' in Greek, after all) forward, towards its own 'self-realization'—the close examination and complex honouring of the ways of Spirit at the limits of human psychospiritual functioning. With Jung, notwithstanding his foibles and even failures, 20th-century psychology begins to individuate.

At any rate, one thing is certain. Jung—who had been publicly announced by Freud as his 'heir apparent' to take over a psychiatric dynasty that by the end of Freud's life had begun to control most medical schools' departments of psychiatry—gave all of that up, and in his mid-30s, too, when ambition is fervent—in order to make outrageous announcements about 'primal thought forms' that weren't even thoughts and some strange realm of consciousness that spun out fairytales and madmen.

But Jung had seen what he had seen, knew what he knew, and there was nothing for it for Jung but to say it. It went beyond Freud's mechanisms of repression, reaction formation, sublimation, superego, libido, cathexis, and such. These were all useful terms and tools at the level of the personal psyche. But at this newly discovered transpersonal level of psyche, they were not adequate to the task. Personal darkness, the crepuscular kingdom of the individual's subconscious, was hard enough to face.

But now to be staring into a primal darkness out of which personal darkness arose secondarily? That was to be looking into darkness itself, 'darkness visible' as Milton paints the atmosphere of hell in *Paradise Lost*. It was to put one's hand on the nakedly beating 'heart of darkness'—the metaphysical 'horror' in Conrad's story. It would be to encounter not just a psychological dynamic to be adjusted in a consulting room, but a living ethical reality that infected the world—maybe the cosmos.

There is reason to suspect that the following line would have caught his attention. In any case, it fits perfectly into Jung's later gripe against St Augustine that he did not take evil seriously enough. Paul did! Evil was no *privatio boni*, no parlour-game that reduced the vast, vicious vortex in the cosmos peopled by horrible entities into just a polite 'absence of good'. Not Paul. And certainly not Jung either. Proclaimed Paul: 'Our wrestling is not against flesh and blood, but against the principalities, against the powers, against the world's rulers of the darkness of this age, and against the spiritual forces of wickedness in the heavenly places' (Ephesians 6:12). Jung's was a transcendental politics.

The theological 'Mystery of Iniquity', the 'Problem of Pain', would be Jung's, too, and he would wrestle with it full-on, in intensely personal, unguarded rigour in his *Answer to Job* later in his career. Evil was real. Jung felt it the height of absurdity, a breach of elemental common sense, to think or say otherwise, as his inveighing against poor St Augustine bears testimony. Besides, any psychology that strove to the heights of spirit had better come to grips with the depths of darkness.

So Jung had good reason to worry about the resistance that this idea would inevitably excite in his colleagues. For he was announcing something that the terms and conditions of strictly personalistic psychology—dogmatically materialist and flat in affect when it came to such wildly disruptive announcements as he was about to make—was probably not equipped and certainly not disposed to hear, much less handle. Nevertheless, the still relatively young psychiatrist stood to make the astonishing claim that the unconscious is not one structure and dynamic but two: a personal unconscious and a *trans*personal unconscious (1967a, p. 66).

Jung was confident that in coming upon the collective unconscious, what he had 'discovered [was] the hidden treasure upon which mankind ever and anon has drawn, and from which it has raised up its gods and demons, and all those potent and mighty thoughts without which man ceases to be man' (Jung, 1967a, pp. 66f).

'Gods and demons'? Was Jung being so audacious as to suggest that he had a psychospiritual key to good and evil? Nietzsche had said he had the philosophical one. And look what happened to him. He went mad! Jung seemed to be trying to lead psychology into a Twilight Zone, inviting it to play with fire, and he might, like Nietzsche, not be all that mentally stable himself— a charge from the academy that would beleaguer him for the remainder of his days (Bair, 2003). Besides, what were these universal 'thought-forms' of humanity? If they were 'thought-forms', then they presumably were *a priori* to thought, so how in the world could we ever think of them, theorize about them, or use them in any practical way? Jung might be worse than brilliantly mad. He might be impractical!

It isn't easy for anyone to weather such responses to one's work, and it took more than Jung's rural Swiss grit to deal with it. That Jung had his personal flaws and cultural prejudices, boundaries that he should have crossed and others that he shouldn't have, major mess-ups and even sins, has by now been extensively argued with a strange fervour in some post-Jungian scholarship (Hauke, 2000; Samuels, 1997).[3] Then again, who among us does not have such things within us? But that Jung was a man of courage and conviction in announcing, standing by, and developing what he believed to be true must also be granted.

'Who knows what evil lurks in the mind of man?': the shadow

With these words began a popular radio programme of the 1930s. The answer to the question, 'Who knows what evil lurks in the mind of man?' was 'The Shadow knows!' No life-narrative can lay any claim to experiential depth, ethical completeness, or practical efficacy in which the individual has not wrestled with his own shadow. After all, a person's narrative of his life is his summative ethical self-evaluation, and this boils down to how one dealt with evil in oneself and in the world. That is the shadow. And yet for Jung the shadow is more than just the residence of evil within oneself, although it is easily mistaken for just that. A life-narrative is necessarily a study in mixed light and dark. Gnostic, it was also gnarly.

Narrativity as an ethical project

As Linde puts it, narrativity is perhaps our 'most powerful tool for creating, negotiating and displaying the moral standing of the self' (1993, p. 123). Narrative and meaning are inextricably bound (White, 1980). There is no narrative that does not have at its infrastructure, and indeed *as* its infrastructure and therefore often at an unconscious level, a set of assumptions about what is ultimately desirable and what is not. It is precisely this that drives the plots in one way as opposed to another. It is this that allows us to assess its characters along the way as having made good choices or bad, and it is this that makes some of them not only attractive but vitally relevant to us, and others as indifferent at best and sometimes even repugnant; and it is the values we hold that we hold *up* against how the narrative resolves that cause us to evaluate the narrative as either a good or bad one in the last analysis. And if the narrative is about oneself and told by oneself, its overriding (even if understated) purpose is to establish that 'When all is said and done, I am a good person.' Moreover, it is the 'evaluative component' that lies at the heart of narrative, Linde concludes, observing that this is why the most plausible and attractive narratives have a strong ethical component (1993).

We cannot live without narrativizing (White, 1980). We are human because we narrativize, but we are humane only if we narrativize compassionately. This precludes demonizing 'the other' in our narratives. Simplistic narratives are dangerous, for they hate whatever they do not understand (White, 1980) and thus they wind up hating a lot and are not only ignorant but hatefully ignorant. A hatefully ignorant person, joined with other such people, can do horribly violent things under the hypnotic sway of mass psychology. This is a point on which the conservative Freud and Jung were very much in agreement[4] and why they believed that a major function of public schooling should be to promote psychodynamic health (Mayes, 2009).

And even if a group, projectively narrativizing, does not act out this potential in manifestly violent ways, they necessarily miss out on that ethical complexity that each one of us uniquely is, and therefore support policies (they may even author them) that are morally violent and injurious to others in subtler ways that still do have practical consequences.

The Existentialist theologian Reinhold Niebuhr (1944) thus concluded: Do not look for the biblical separation of 'the children of light and the children of darkness' as an actual event that will happen at the end of historical time with one side winners and the other the goats. Rather, look for it within yourself, in biographical time, assessing yourself in terms of the ethic of Love that is timeless Time. Painstakingly, suffer the painful recognition that the war between good and evil is between impulses within oneself. For, if the Kingdom of Heaven is within each individual, so is the apocalypse that precedes it, as one at last faces up to one's inherent nature as both angelic and diabolic and as everything in between, and as one both sees this and deals with it in how he tells the story of his life. The truest narratives are apocalypses of self-recognition.

One's own narrativizing about oneself and others thus emerges as nothing less than making ethical sense out of one's life. And in doing this, our prime directive is that we not demonize others in the pursuit of our own story as demonstrating our moral superiority. For that is, given the raw facts of who we are (breaking through in the dreadful dream-dramas that wake us up at 3 a.m. and will not let us return to sleep), necessarily a false narrative. More even than false, it is unethical. It is the self-contradictory attempt to find oneself fully as a subject by reducing others to simplistic objects.

Jung cast considerable light on all of this in one of his ideas that has become standard in not only depth psychology but in contemporary culture: Projection.

Projection and the shadow

One of the most persistent themes in *The Collected Works* is the psychological and ethical obligation to examine one's shadow as thoroughly as possible. Jung believed there was no better remedy for a sanctimonious overvaluation of oneself and undervaluation of others than getting into the boxing-ring with your own shadow and going the full 15 rounds with him. You'll be lucky to come out of that ring just by the skin of your teeth. Although similar to Freud's idea of the personal subconscious, the shadow is more than that. 'By shadow I mean ... the sum of all those unpleasant qualities we like to hide, together with the insufficiently developed functions, and the contents of the personal unconscious' (Jung, 1967b, p. 66, n. 5). The evil in us has been consigned to the shadow, of course, but not so much because it is evil as because it is something we prefer not to acknowledge as belonging to us. Along with evil we find repressed memories and even simply 'qualities we like to hide'. Politics makes strange bedfellows. The shadow makes even stranger. For, not everything we try to hide is necessarily evil.

We may hide certain qualities early on in our lives because they are delicate potentialities that, even in our earliest youth, we sensed it would be wrong to submit to the insensitivities of brute competition. Hidden qualities may be gifts we occulted in a kind of mercy killing, for we knew they would be received wrongly but rewarded richly, which means we would one day use them craftily. Better to put them to sleep in the shadow's freezing machines. These are beauties we banish from awareness because our world is too unbeautiful to expose them to it, and we, of the world, might sin against ourselves one day in sinning against our own beauty. So let this beauty be a 'Sleeping Beauty'—even if it must be placed next to evil. Even more so than politics, the shadow makes strange bedfellows.

This range that the Shadow contains should not surprise us when we remember that the Shadow is itself an archetype, and every archetype has a bright side and a dark side (Jung, 1969b, p. 183). The shadow is, indeed, one of the most basic and readily identifiable archetypes and the first one that a patient must confront in therapy (Jung, 1969a, p. 208).

The 'bi-chromality' of each archetype is just the way it must be since the Archetype of archetypes Itself, God, has a light and dark side, according to Jung's theology (Jung, 1969c, pp, 124, 135).[5] How could it not, if archetypes are the templates of our lives and our lives are infinite shades of grey? What's more, and strange as it may sound, it thus emerges that we each have not only a dark shadow (true evil) but also a light shadow (positive qualities we hide).

Projection as a shadow function

The shadow is the substance of projection, and projection is the enactment of the shadow, and this is the case because we condemn most passionately in others what we most refuse to see in ourselves. This is not exactly the latest-breaking news, of course. Jesus said the same thing, and with not only the Pharisees but everyone in mind when he counselled against judgmentalism:

> How can you say to your brother, 'Let me take the speck out of your eye,' when all the time there is a plank in your own eye? You hypocrite! First take the plan out of your own eye, and then you will see clearly to remove the speck from your brother's eye.
>
> (Matthew 7: 1–5)

Not to tend to one's own darkness before presuming to enlighten another's is to play a jejune game of psychological hide-and-seek with oneself by refusing to cast the light of honest introspection on one's own discarded, repressed, and sometimes meretricious parts. It is a sort of moral maths that our judgment of others varies in direct proportion to what is bad in ourselves. What we condemn in our fellow flawed humans is often a diversionary tactic to hide from oneself. To the measure we judge, we are also judged—but by ourselves. As we have just seen, every narrative is driven by ethical problematics, and the most problematic thing of all is the person who is telling her story.

So what is the shadow?

In the first place, said Jung, let us be clear that the shadow is not just a psychotherapeutic 'issue' with its appropriate 'treatment plan' for a 'cure'. How comfortable and how wrong. 'The shadow is a moral problem', even an 'ethical quandary' (Jung, 1969c, p. 8) that demands more than just an admission that one has some nasty habits, more even than a bit of mildly tearful soul-searching. It is an ethical engagement *with* one's total being *of* one's total being in an emotional space that, like Milton's Hell in Paradise Lost, is lighted only by 'darkness visible'. And thus 'it should not be twisted into an intellectual activity, for it has far more the meaning of a suffering and a passion that implicate the whole man' (1969b, p. 208).

A 'suffering and a passion' could hardly be written by the scripturally adept preacher's son, Carl, without an accompanying image of Christ labouring down the *Via Dolorosa* or on the Cross. Jung thereby implicitly blends the patient's biographical narrative *in extremis* with the story of the suffering god whose pain is ultimately redemptive. Such reframing of one's personal narrative in transcendent terms is itself therapeutic and is, arguably, the basic 'approach' in Analytical Psychology. Furthermore, the close linkage of the personal and the transpersonal domains to achieve health in both Jungian psychotherapy and Narrative psychotherapy supports the idea that at the core of every personal complex is an archetypal symbol (White and Epston, 1990; Diekman, 1999; Kalsched, 1996; Knox, 2004; Sovatsky, 1998).

It is every person's inner Mephistopheles in Goethe's *Faust*, an icon of evil itself, who in an unguarded moment confesses in hellish agony to Faust, that he, Mephistopheles, is himself hell, which does not exist as a physical place one is sent to but is an existential condition that one is. It is 'the illness that we are' (Dourley, 1984). We are our own shadows. We can most easily locate and engage it not in someone else but inside our own s(k)ins. Jungian psychology calls this process 'withdrawing projections', and it is a *sine qua non* of individuation.

Do greed, lust, ambition, and cruelty characterize this world? They do. Therefore, the world is our mirror! For look within. There one will find evil's source. In one's own shadow one discovers (unhappy explorer!) every moral malady that besets the world (1967b, p. 183, fn 14). This is the narratival tragedy of biographical time if it has no access to sacred narratives to relieve its pain and find some purpose in it. It is one of biography's prime organizing leitmotifs. It is the doleful mask that the Greek Tragedy alternately wears with the smiling one. The only cure—so all the great religions proclaim with one voice—is a sacred narrative, written by the Impeccable Author, printed on a Peerless Press, and distributed to humanity in its many cultures and epochs in different imagistic editions but all alike in their unique power to redeem both the individual and the State from falling apart after everything else (and chiefly oneself) has been tried and found wanting.

Of course, there is social injustice, and no one can plausibly lay claim to an ethical life if he is insensitive to it (Jung, 1969b, p. 224). A constant theme in Jung's writings, however, is that we must first each face our own evil as individuals (1970a, p. 53; 1969b, p. 35; 1969c, p. 10). We must descend to the messy underworld of the human heart, where, as the religions teach, the source of darkness exists first and foremost in the individual. If charity begins at home, so does political reformation. Otherwise, all our social programmes will finally amount to self-deceptive rhetoric, floundering evasions of the corruption in our own hearts that breed social injustice in the first place (Jung, 1967b, p. 226; 1970a, pp. 154, 216, 289; 1969c, p. 233).

That the individual finds her identity in her culture is true. But it is equally true, Jung insists, that a culture is capable of performing this high task only if it is comprised of individuals who, having done their own psychological and ethical work, can withdraw their projections and see themselves and others clearly. It is only such individuals who can rise to Jung's millennial call to take the ancient religious myths and make them their own, for they no longer look for forgiveness from an external God but seek clarity of the internal Self. These are they who can lead the way in recovering religion by de-literalizing it and then re-symbolizing it.

At any rate, is it not, asked Jung, the undealt-with shadow ranging around, untamed and at will, in the back chambers of the psyche, the real reason why programmes of social salvation imposed by a political elite spawn more evil than they eradicate? Who among us is not the proverbial physician who must first heal himself before presuming that he has the political and ethical medicine to heal others?

The fruit of doing one's shadow work is that one evolves into a more compassionate, less demanding person who, having looked at his faults and weaknesses, can gently laugh at himself and is less likely to derisively laugh at others or imperiously tell them what they 'need to do' to become 'better'. In other words: 'He among you who is without sin, let him cast the first stone' (John 8: 7).

Eternal time: trial by fire

Throughout this chapter, I have advocated for and will continue to develop in what follows what I would call 'The Tenet of the Transcendent': Without a connection of the ego in the time of consensual-reality to a higher 'Self'—requiring the forging of an axis between the ego and this higher Self', and therefore without biographical time keyed into some sense of sacral Time, one may easily become another lost individual on the dispirited cityscape. Jung's principal concern both theoretically and clinically, and the title of his popular (1957) analysis of alienation, 'modern man in search of a soul', was to be a spiritual physician to the alienated human being in these terrible times we had world-historically stumbled into.

Alienation had been a topic of interest in sociology since Durkheim's first inquiries into *anomie* in 1897. These studies have concerned themselves with the idea that we have lost the emotionally complex connection to our souls in the seductive 'simplistics' of mere systematicity, the corporate cooptation of consciousness, the idolizing of PowerPoints and flow charts, and the despiritualizing of our daily work—a point which Jung makes throughout *The Collected Works*.

For although a personal narrative under the sign of the Timeless is usually a hopeful one when all is said and done and Jung's writings aimed to be in the service of a 'hermeneutics of hope', despair is real, unavoidable (though not insuperable), and must be acknowledged, even affirmed as such (Homans, 1995). The full and frank experience of despair is the precondition to any non-dogmatic, humane faith—and to any psychospiritually realistic life. Kierkegaard emphasized this in his work (1969).

For Jung, it is ultimately all a matter of cultivating a connection between agency and intuition, realism and vision as the individual cultivates a connection between her temporal and transcendent identities, between ego and Self. This will be the golden thread running through her life-narrative if it is headed towards individuation. Trying to understand what this means in terms of educational processes is the goal of archetypal pedagogy and an important topic in the second part of this study, to it we now turn.

Notes

1   Jung's friend and associate Aniela Jaffé, was instrumental in producing this book. Although it had previously been believed that she had been merely a sort of sympathetic scribe for Jung on this book, it now seems that she took a more active role than that in shaping this public picture to fashion Jung into the questing knight of psychospiritual excellence that she wanted him to be for herself and his (*their*) readers (Bair, 2003; Shamdasani, 2003).

2   'Gradually' in terms of his own internal processes, perhaps, as he began to make his own various ideas and traditions that he was already well aware of, especially certain Western mystical traditions. That Jung knew of these things from at least his undergraduate days is evident in his lectures to his fellow members of the University of Zurich's *Zofingia Club*. It was a tradition stretching at least as far back as Plotinus. It infused German and Romantic poetry, which Jung knew more than just passingly, it having had its heyday just several decades before his birth. He also knew and appreciated similar enunciations of this Gnostic and Theosophical point of view in the writings of Bachofen, von Carus, and Flournoy (Ellenberger, 1970). And finally, Jung's mother, Helene Preisswerk, was a medium and seeress of no mean accomplishments. It is wrong to minimize Jung (Glover, 1956). His stature as one of the great thinkers of the 20th century is beyond question. However, it is no less a mistake to treat his work as if it sprang full-fledged from the forehead of Zeus as an instance of unalloyed genius (van der Post, 1975). Jung stands in a tradition—one of its brightest stars in the 20th century, to be sure, but standing on shoulders before him. There is very little in Jung that one can point to as without precedent. Yet, this is true of all of us. I often think of Jung as Hamlet did his father—not as a god but as a most extraordinary mortal: 'He was a man. Take him for all in all. / I shall not look upon his like again' (*Hamlet*, Act I, Scene ii).

3   I am not necessarily attributing such opinions to either Hauke or Samuels, who are reporting these and other views in their welcome and rightly celebrated surveys of post-Jungian theory.

4   See, for example, Freud, 1957, pp. 172–177, 194–198; Jung, 1966b, pp. 5, 107.

5   The idea that God is the author of evil as well as good is not without its scriptural warrant, for example, in the *Book of Job*. See also *Isaiah* 45: 7; *Matthew* 5: 45.

Part II

Towards a unified depth-educational psychology

Mending the Freudian-Jungian rift

Chapter 4

Foundations of depth psychology in education

Before commencing upon a primarily archetypal approach to major pedagogical issues, it will first be necessary to look at the psychoanalytic roots of the whole endeavour of applying depth psychology to education. These roots are in the psychoanalytic tradition—both Freudian and post-Freudian—of pedagogical studies. The depth-psychological study of educational processes was launched in the early 1920s mainly by certain psychoanalytic theorists who had previously been teachers or were involved with teaching. We owe a great debt of gratitude to Freud, Jung, and Adler for their preliminary work in educational issues but an even greater one to Anna Freud, Melanie Klein, Maria Montessori, Susan Isaacs, August Aichhorn, and Oskar Pfister for all they did to establish the psychodynamics of educational processes as a field of inquiry, although it is still under-appreciated in psychology and educational psychology.

In Chapter 1, we briefly looked at the military-industrial roots of educational psychology obsession with the 'secondary' processes that are virtually the sole focus of educational psychology currently and its scant concern for 'primary' processes of the subconscious at the personal level and the collective unconscious at the transpersonal level. This is a sin of omission since a conscious thought is merely the tip of the iceberg that rests upon much deeper psychic structures and hidden forces that shape cognition at every point. Those deeper dynamics can either impede or enhance cognition, depending upon how carefully they are honoured and how skillfully they are handled.

In this chapter, I look at some of the major psychoanalytic statements about this because, in addition to the disciplinary importance of understanding the ideological genealogy of any theory that a discipline concerns itself with, I will draw from various ideas and terms from psychoanalytic pedagogy in the archetypal analyses of educational issues and processes that will follow this chapter, and many of these terms remain the same as when they were introduced to psychology a century ago. Also, I will attempt to model how psychoanalytic theory and archetypal theory can be brought together and not remain in the sterile but still fraught schism that the Freud-Jung break began. It is now high time, these 100 years later, to get over that and to move on, arms linked, in common cause. To work towards that end is one of the primary purposes of this study.

Depth psychology in the schools: high hopes, scant results

Psychoanalytic theory has not had nearly the effect on the American curriculum that it seemed destined to have in the opening years of the 20th century, when there were great expectations that teachers, through adequate psychological training and (ideally) the experience of their own psychoanalyses, would be able to deploy psychoanalytic insights in teaching and interacting with students (Cremin, 1964; Kliebard, 1986; Watras, 2002). This would empower them to teach in ways that not only conveyed knowledge but would also be emotionally beneficial, even therapeutic, to the students in their charge.

In the terms introduced in Part I, this represented nothing less than a crusade to enrich personal narratives by digging deeply beneath the surface machinations of the ego to mine their students' and their own existential profundities for affective and imagistic gold. Although clearly a biographical project wedged into consensual linear time, it also showed signs of reaching beyond that in its fascination with symbolism, affect, and the timelessness of the subconscious, where all dynamics are experienced as going on in a constant present. This was not the eternal Present of eternal Presence. But it was a reach in that direction, an intimation of our status as the *sub specie-aeternitatis* creature.

As it played out in educational processes, the core psychodynamic idea was that the teacher, although certainly not a therapist, should nevertheless learn enough about psychoanalysis to know how to guide students in their interactions with each other, with the curriculum, and with the teacher herself so that students' unhealthy inhibitions could be overcome and, at the same time, their libido could be harnessed in socially constructive ways.

In her *Four Lectures for Teachers and Parents on Psychoanalysis* (1930), no less a personage than Anna Freud echoed this sentiment when she noted that the educator, like the parent, should always have before her the fact that 'the task of upbringing, based on analytic understanding, is to find a middle road between ... extremes—that is to say, to find for each stage in the child's life the right proportion between drive gratification and drive control' (Freud, 1930, p. 128; see also Zachry, 1929, p. 3).

Only a psychologically healthy and therapeutically savvy teacher could truly help the student achieve that balance in school matters between the instinctual id and the unforgiving superego. At least, she was best positioned to do that if only she would. Furthermore, the psychoanalytically wise teacher would know how to draw those students who had fallen into the underworld of juvenile delinquency back into the less stormy environs of sociocultural normalcy and productivity. This notion of 'mental hygiene' in the schools was elaborately presented in such classic studies as Oskar Pfister's (1922) *Psychoanalysis in the Service of Education*, August Aichhorn's (1925/1951) *Wayward Youth*, Susan Isaacs' (1932) *The Children We Teach*, Caroline Zachry's (1940) *Emotion and Conduct in Adolescence*, and most powerfully of all in Redl and Wattenberg's (1951) masterpiece, *Mental Hygiene in Teaching*.

Nevertheless, as Hilgard (1987) concluded in his magisterial study of the evolution of academic and clinical psychology in the United States, there was at most only an 'indirect influence of psychoanalysis on elementary education[;] the direct influence was meager, at least before World War II' (p. 688). In secondary education, where social expectations, economic demands, and academic stakes were higher, attention to the student's inner life was even sketchier, which the psychoanalysts would continue to lament in the following decades.

In 1951, for instance, Redl and Wattenberg expressed surprise that, despite its potential to create more joy in teaching and more excitement in learning, the mental hygiene movement had still not made a noticeable impact on school policies or practices (p. ix). Sixteen years later, Kubie's observations were even more dire: 'Self-knowledge, which requires the mastery of new tools of psychological explanation, is wholly overlooked throughout the entire scheme of "modern education", from kindergarten to the highest levels of academic training' (1967, p. 62; see also Jones, 1968 and Laux, 1968).

Louise Tyler picked up the same complaint in the next decade, declaring that 'psychoanalytic theory has been in existence for a half-century, yet no attempt has been made to utilize it in any systematic way for curriculum development or for understanding curricular effectiveness' (1975, p. 55). And as late as 2002, Barford could still rightfully bemoan the fact that in teacher education, 'it is behaviourism, cognitivism, and humanism that are studied, completely overlooking what psychoanalysis has to offer both the prospective and practicing teacher' (2002, p. 42), a conclusion I also reached in a 1996 study (Mayes, 1996).

The attempt to fortify biographical time with deeper personal significance and higher world-historical purpose seemed a doomed campaign. This was due in part to some popular misconceptions about psychoanalysis.

Misconceptions about classical psychoanalysis

Freudian psychology is often seen as being exclusively about sex. Certainly, there is an extraordinary emphasis on sexuality in Freud's writings. However, as early as 1914, with more than 20 prolific years still before him, Freud allowed and would go on to develop the idea that there were 'various points in favour of the hypothesis of a primordial differentiation between sexual instincts and other instincts, ego instincts ...' (1914/1957, p. 106). There is no doubt that sexuality is the sun around which the Freudian psychic system revolves. Crucially, however, his allowance for a 'primordial differentiation' between a sexual instinct and an ego instinct is, although stated *sotto voce*, thunderous in its implications.

There is, Freud implies, uniquely in the human being the emergence of the ego and then its establishment and maintenance as a realized 'instinct', not-too-distant in overall psychic impact from sexuality. It is the other necessary key, Freud was stating, to opening the double-bolt door that hides the full spectacle of what a human being is.

This represents a giant step up in Freud's picture of the human being as not just another sexually driven animal with some higher cognitive abilities thrown in as a sort of evolutionary bonus prize. No. The human being now 'has' that endopsychic structure called an 'ego' as a *sine qua non* of his identity. Indeed, it *is* his identity. He thereby becomes capable of 1) awareness of a self in relationship to other selves and 2) generating and sustaining long strings of memories that he can weave together with other strands of memory in order ultimately to be a biographical narrative. Psychoanalysis is, indeed, the critical interrogation of that narrative when it gets stalled, freeing up the patient 'to love and to work' in Freud's famous phrase. Therapy is largely narratival rewriting (White and Epston, 1990).

In other words, the ego carries with it the mixed bag of awareness that it will one day die. This sets the stage for self-awareness in the context of the Eternal. *Memento mori.*

More: in the last phase of his theorizing and practice, Freud would expand the notion of libido, which he had previously seen as merely sexual energy but now reflective of a much larger force to which he ascribes an almost cosmic significance. He called it Eros, depicting it as a sort of generalized life-instinct, which was constantly doing battle with a death-instinct that he called Thanatos—or the desire of every creature to return to a state of eternal rest in the primal womb/tomb of Being—the archetypal Great Mother (Jung, 1967b, p. 228).

The picture that begins to take shape in Freud is of the human being as driven by two universal forces in dialectic opposition on a stage whose backdrop is the eternal and whose dramatic conclusion is return to the cosmic mother. We are moving into archetypal territory here that is not so very distant from the territory that Jung 'discovered', and it operates under the sign of the Timeless. It is governed as well by the chronology of biographical time and has horizons—distant but discernible—that give out onto realms where cosmic periodicities hold sway. It is thus inaccurate and unfair to portray Freud as obsessed with simply the primal rhythms of feral pulsations, consumptions and metabolisms. The human being lives in the middle of an almost cosmic war, Johannine in its scope, between two archetypes, life and death, and their archetypally imagistic avatars, Eros and Thanatos.

In Freud's classically tragic parsing of the human narrative (not for nothing is he best known for a complex named after one of the most tortured characters in the Greek drama) death must inevitably triumph. 'The goal of all life is death', declared Freud in a volume tellingly entitled *Beyond the Pleasure Principle*, for 'the inanimate was there before the animate' (1923, p. 160). Here in his 'hermeneutics of suspicion' (Ricoeur, 1991) is where Freud primarily differs from Jung, whose hermeneutics are belief and hope (Homans, 1995). But that is a difference of tone, not of substance and scope. Freud's work is not only beyond-merely sexual. It is, in its best moments, within sight of Jung's archetypal realms—and Jungians err in assessing it anything less.

The evolution of psychoanalytic pedagogy since the 1920s

The psychoanalytic pedagogues whom I have already mentioned registered at once that Freud's use of the term 'sexuality' referred to more than just the raw mechanics of intercourse. It was what it was, yes. But it also reached beyond itself as all great ideas do. Sexuality was emblematic of, even a symbol for, something that bespoke more than just coitus.

We see this as early as 1925 when August Aichhorn, addressing teachers in his book *Wayward Youth* (1925/1951) (which contained a foreword by Freud himself), insisted that he would often use the word sexuality 'in the broad psychoanalytic sense [so that] it must not be confused with genital sexuality' (1925/1951, p. 216). In so doing, Aichhorn, along with his pedagogical cohort in the early psychoanalytic movement, laid the groundwork for exploring a wide range of questions and offering a host of powerful answers about that finally unfathomable complexity that is teaching and learning.

Oskar Pfister, a Protestant minister and one of Freud's primary disciples, even understood the term sublimation in its literal sense—that is, as a process of making something more and more sublime. Somewhat like Plato in *The Symposium*, Pfister (1922) saw in infantile sexual energy and later, in adolescent and adult genital sexuality, the basis for what would finally evolve into an integral love of God.

Over the last century, since the first major statements by psychoanalysts appeared on the scene and were hungrily consumed by educationists in the psychological wing of the American Progressive Education Movement (Cremin, 1964), there have been several sea-changes in how psychoanalytic theorists in various post-Freudian camps have come to understand 'libido'(Mayes, 2009). This range from picturing libido at its energic core as the desire for meaningful relationships with other individuals (Winnicott, 1992) to the striving towards eternal relationship with a 'living God' (Rizzuto, 1979; see also Meissner, 1984).

When 'the desire for mastery' and 'the urge to efficacy' are seen as something that the *sub specie aeternitatis* creature does, as a matter of high importance and as a 'universal human need', to deal with that creature's self-awareness of its finitude against the backdrop of the Timeless, then reading libido in terms of the acts of learning emerges as the spiritualizing of pedagogy itself (Britzman, 2003, 2001, 1999; Field, Cohler, and Wool, 1989; Redl and Wattenberg, 1951).

This ethical heuristic allows us as Jungians to explore, osmose, and deploy both classical-Freudian (Britzman, 2001) and post-Freudian models of the structure and dynamics of psyche (Field, Cohler, and Wool, 1989) with gratitude for its searching inquiries and humane revelations about what goes on within the individual psychodynamically and biographically when she is in a learning situation. It even tentatively offers ways and means to redeem biographical time and make it a site of the Sacred even in the most ordinary educational venues.

These models proffer important insights into a student's interiority that can help the teacher teach with a maximum of psychodynamic care and finesse. Highly nuanced pictures of the pedagogical psyche, these models cast light on those 'primary processes' that are the affective and epistemological bedrock upon which cognition lives, moves, and has its being as it approaches a wide variety of analytic, aesthetic, and ethical tasks. They intensify the I-Thou relationship between the teacher and the student and are thus distinctly ethical (Buber, 1965). All of this works to restore education as an eternal principle, an archetypal constellation, and an ethical reality that ham-fisted human capital pedagogies and even enlightened humanistic ones cannot approximate with their non-transcendent assumptions.

Thus, instead of the erring enmity that has existed over the last century between 'Freudian' and 'Jungian' camps in theoretical warfare, we as Jungians can begin to appreciate the spiritual, even archetypal core of Redl and Wattenberg's (1951) counsel that 'one of the universal human [and therefore archetypal] needs is a feeling of adequacy, of self-respect' (p. 188, emphasis added; see also Symonds, 1951, p. 184).

The great child analyst Lili Peller, employing classical Freudian terminology, observed that when ego, id, and superego are in harmony because of successful sublimation, 'the desire for mastery' becomes the directing impulse, not the sexual urge (1956/1978, p. 93). Peller built upon the insights of the physician and pedagogue Maria Montessori to conclude that of at least equal importance to sex are various 'component drives': 'curiosity, the desire to explore ...' (Peller, 1967/1978, p. 116). It was and remains the essential psychoanalytical message to parents and teachers that 'above all, infants, like older children and adults, get gratification from being a *cause*, from making things *happen*, [leading to] "effectance pleasure"' (Basch, 1989, p. 779; emphasis added). One's biographical narrative is immeasurably enriched thereby; for, it is one of my major contentions in this study that our life-narratives as existential beings are inseparable from our narratives of ourselves as learners.

Life is a ceaseless educational project. We are teaching and learning on a non-stop train-ride throughout the day. Indeed, I suspect that if one could somehow magically 'partial out' that part of one's narrative that is involved in some type of teaching and learning broadly conceived, there would not be much of that day left to talk about. From the second we draw our first breath to the second we give up our last one, we are teaching and learning in practical, cultural, ethical, and even ontological 'structurations' of interrelationship (Giddens, 1990, 1991; see also Fairbairn, 1992; Winnicott, 1992).

The revision of libido as primarily 'knowledge- and wisdom-seeking' defines libido in ethically robust and intuitively attractive terms and places it at the service of the other two types of time—the cultural/world-historical and the Timeless, which come bearing lessons for us at every stride and turn of experience. Indeed, it places what I would call the 'relational-epistemic libido' at the heart of our existence as creatures *sub specie aeternitatis*, ideally taking in and metabolizing the lessons of life to become a sagacious person in biographical time, or not doing so in an existential failure to grow in a life of learning, a life that *is* learning. Libido as learning is in touch with the Timeless and reaches toward the archetypal.

Psychoanalytic pedagogy and its sociocultural dimensions

There is an erroneous notion that psychoanalytic theory and therapy are all about unleashing feral drives and finding ways to give them free rein to satisfy themselves—or at least score as much satisfaction as the sexual market will bear. A close look at what the psychoanalytic pedagogues from within the profession of psychoanalysis have said about this, however, reveals it to be a mischaracterization of their work.

'Making the world safe for democracy'

From the inception of psychoanalytic pedagogy in the writings of psychiatrists in the 1920s until those of psychiatrists today, the child's social adaptation is a prime *desideratum*. Aichhorn certainly overstated the case in the pronouncement that 'in general, to be social means to have an ego which can subordinate itself to authority without conflict' (1925/1951, p. 214). Yet, even Aichhorn understood well enough that the real goal of psychoanalytic pedagogy was not to make the child's libido a slave of society but, rather, to find ways that libido and ego could jointly function in a fashion that was individually satisfying but also culturally conserving.

Caroline Zachry, a leader of the psychoanalytic wing of the Progressive Education movement, outlined the school's social responsibility, which was to increase adaptation to existing political structures: 'The happiness and social usefulness of the individual' could only be accomplished if the teacher understood how the child's psyche worked, in order to help the child fit into 'life as it is' (Zachry, 1929, pp. 61, 78). Anna Freud registered similarly conservative observations in her *Four Lectures for Teachers and Parents on Psychoanalysis*. And a mere two years later, perhaps the greatest of all child analysts, Melanie Klein—who often openly disagreed with Anna Freud about whether or not the child's libido should be 'schooled' in quite so stark a fashion as Anna Freud believed—nevertheless admitted that

> one of the results of early analysis should be to enable the child to adapt itself to reality. If this has been successfully achieved, one sees in children, among other things, a lessening of educational difficulties as the child has become able to tolerate the frustrations entailed by reality.
>
> (1932/1975, p. 4)

This theme would prove to be key in the writings of major psychoanalytic theorists over the next three decades. In the middle of the 1940s as soldiers returned from war, its horror sketched in stark, jagged lines across their faces and what is now identified as post-traumatic-stress disorder branded into their central nervous systems, some who had dismissed psychoanalysis as a self-absorbed hobby for the wealthy began to affirm how deeply psychological pain can run and how necessary its treatment was. The Cold War also contributed to a heightened valuation of psychoanalysis. The nation perceived itself under subtle siege by the Red Menace of Communism. It was felt that we needed psychologically strong children to resist its blandishments and seductions (Cremin, 1988).

Peter Blos, for instance, a leading psychoanalytic theorist and practitioner in the 1940s, counselled that 'it is in the power of education to supply the experiences which can satisfy [libidinal] needs and, at the same time, modify them in terms of social and cultural values' (1940, p. 491). In this way, schools could perform the vital function of helping the student find 'values and standards acceptable by society yet distinctly his own' (1940, p. 498; see also Fenichel, 1945, p. 583). Pearson (1954), a child psychoanalyst with a special interest in school issues, was quite explicit about the need to dispel the popular misconception that psychoanalysis aimed to give maximum latitude to the child's desires, insisting that it was the goal of psychoanalytic pedagogy to fit the child into society.

Even during the tumultuous 1960s in the U.S., many psychoanalytic pedagogues resisted the permissiveness that characterized that decade, continuing to champion what they saw as the ethical imperative for the teacher to represent an 'ego-ideal' for the student (Grossman, 1975, p. 67). As they saw it, their overarching mission was to help the student achieve a healthy balance between ego-constraints and libidinal energy so that he would grow up to be neither a 'Dull Jack' nor a 'Playboy' (Piers, 1969, p. 105).

Psychoanalysis and the 'expansion of time' in educational processes: From nation to salvation

Not only did psychoanalytic theory envisage itself as the best approach to encouraging emotionally rich biographical narratives; it was now ideologically linking its work to the even higher plane of a world-historical project. That was American democracy and what it perceived to be its almost-messianic role in establishing a *Pax Americana* so that it could spread its governmental gospel to any nation that would receive this political evangel. Although American psychoanalysis was mustering its forces to bring a novel set of concepts and practices to this cause, the cause itself was not new.

An excursus on the history of teaching in the United States

Almost 300 years earlier, the American divine Jonathon Winthrop, taking Matthew 5:14 as his text, said that 'You are the light of the world. A city that is set on a hill cannot be hidden', preached that 'wee must Consider that wee shall be as a Citty upon a Hill, the eies of all people are uppon us'. The notion that America must be 'a righteous empire' (Marty, 1970) was the subtext of virtually every history text in the schools. Thus, in what was undoubtedly a conscious reference to his fellow New Englander's sermon centuries before (Kennedy was perhaps the most historically educated of American presidents), President Kennedy's words resonated in the popular mind when he declared in his inaugural address in January of 1961 that 'The energy, the faith, the devotion which we bring to this endeavour will light our country and all who serve it—and the glow from that fire can truly light the world.'

One finds a similar faith in the writings of the psychoanalytic pedagogues, some of whom—Bruno Bettelheim and Viktor Frankl are two of the most notable examples—were survivors of the Holocaust and treasured the ethnic diversity and ideological freedom they felt they were now able to live and work in on the security of American soil.

The aim that virtually all the psychoanalytic pedagogues shared was the promotion of democracy. Indeed, in general the history of teaching in the United States cannot be separated from this conviction. It is on full display in the words and works of Horace Mann, the father of American public schooling in the 1830s on, who dedicated himself to the then-fledgling cause of public education—or 'common schools' as they were first called (Messerli, 1972). Joining him were such vigorously idealistic, religiously minded women of the early 19th century as Catherine Beecher. Beecher was the daughter of the well-known Protestant social reformer, the Reverend Lyman Beecher, and sister of Harriet Beecher Stowe, author of *Uncle Tom's Cabin*, and another adherent of the 'Social Gospel' that her father preached (Sklar, 1974).

Mann and Beecher can be largely credited with getting public schooling underway as a going concern in the United States. Mann and Beecher worked under the assumption that democracy is the mind and will of God in political form, the apotheosis of history, and that democracy depends on schools to shape young people into adult citizens who held the knowledge and were held by the vision of the sacredness of democracy. But schools, of course, relied on teachers. It was on them, in the last analysis, that the fate of this whole endeavour would rise or fall.

In an archetypal analysis of this history of teaching in the United States, I identified the role of the teacher as having been invested in full measure then and still being influenced to some degree with the archetypal energy and imagery of the teacher as a 'federal prophet of democracy' (Mayes, 2011). Biographical, world-historical, and sacred narrative interact, meld, and operate as one towards an apotheosis in the lives of these most idealistic of teachers in American history.

To be sure, the history of teaching in the United States has a more painful side in terms of sexism, racism, and the perpetuation of socioeconomic inequalities over the last 150 years or so as I and others have pointed out in historical analyses of the development of colleges of education and historical reconstructions of teachers' classroom practices (Mayes, 1996; see also Cuban, 1993, 1989; Clifford and Guthrie, 1988; Popkewitz, 1987). Yet it is too cynical to ignore the light as well as the dark that comprise that *chiaroscuro* painting that is the history of teaching in the United States. It is easy enough now, and certainly not without some justification, to deconstruct that endeavour as having been false ideological cover for colonial purposes (Zinn, 1990). However, things being what they are, a mixture of dark and light, there was also a sense of high collective purpose and national destiny that must be reckoned into the equation.

By revealing the depths of the biographical narrative and then linking that to a compelling historical narrative that claimed heavenly paternity, psychoanalytic pedagogy was hitting on all three temporalities, generating those three narratives in mutual influence. It was fully engaged in a project of not only school reform but spiritual renewal.

The inadequacy of a merely cognitive approach to learning

To return to the early days of psychoanalytic pedagogy: The first principle of any psychologically sensitive view of learning was that what we learn or sometimes for good reasons resist learning—how we learn, that is, and with what degree of authenticity, passion, and commitment; and the uses to which we then hopefully put that conscious, cognitive material in humility and solidarity with our fellow beings—all of this is constantly being coordinated by subconscious and unconscious factors. In other words, it is primary processes that orchestrate how we will interpret and assess incoming information and ideas and what we will then do on that basis.

It is axiomatic in depth-psychological pedagogy that a student's emotional and intellectual development are so intertwined that 'success in one is contingent upon success in the other' (Zachry, 1929, p. 272). It is not the mechanics of linear, anonymous, conforming time that can claim priority in what educational processes, in essence, are. It is multiple currents of roiling subjectivity— from the brute force of the feral subconscious to the otherworldly, archetypal draw of the collective unconscious—that set the stage and direct the drama of educational processes.

In 1940, Blos made the subjectivist/phenomenological point that 'no two children in a classroom are having exactly the same experience'. This is because 'the past and present experiences of the individual', having shaped his psyche, will necessarily determine his emotional response to subject matter, 'the meaning it will have for him, his ability to accept it, and the purpose it will serve in his total development' (p. 492). 'The child does not react solely with his intellect to mental operations but needs to reinforce them with personal meanings and urgencies which are related to them ...' (p. 494).

Peller (1945/1978) amplified Blos' theme five years later. It was a volatile compound of a student's 'deep and contradicting emotions [with] his intellectual power', she pointed out, that would manifest as the attitudes and aptitudes in his observable 'performance' in the classroom. To consider and measure only the student's empirical performance would be to see only half of what was going on and to miss the total picture of this vulnerable creature who had been placed in her care—a care which would be quite influential in effecting her student's global sense of himself as a learner in many contexts and for many tasks throughout the rest of his life.

To appreciate and work with the student as a learner in his entirety—head and heart, conscious and subconscious—was the role of the humane teacher, and this required that she take into account the paradox of the student's 'ability for keen observation as well as for denying unpleasant facts' (Peller, 1945) p. 54). It was not an easy task for a teacher but it was an ethical imperative that, if she attended to it, would lend her vocation a dignity that would ennoble her life and would exert an influence that would invigorate her student's life for the rest of that student's life. Since one's narrative of oneself as an educational being is inseparable from and determinative of one's narrative of oneself as an existential being, then it must be clear to the teacher how ethically vital it was for her to regard the student at both cognitive and emotional levels.

The need for a sense of efficacy

This growing appreciation of the psychodynamic complexity of learning and its role in the student's total psychic economy led in the psychoanalytic literature of the next decade, the 1950s, to the increasing presence of the term 'self-esteem' (Symonds, 1951, p. 189). This term was and remains an idea that many dismiss, even ridicule, as mere sentimentality and coddling the student.

But that critique is as wrong as it is callous, and finally it is just bad pedagogy to disregard a student's understanding of herself as a learner.

Anyone who cares to actually look into the matter will find straight-away in the research literature and hear from veteran teachers what simply consulting his common sense would have revealed in the first place, and that is that children with high self-esteem tend to be the most intellectually creative because they have the courage to risk being creative (Brophy, 1994; Pearson, 1954). Creativity is a difficult and uncertain business. It involves plenty of embarrassing stumbles along the way and discouraging blunders before one arrives at a novel and elegant solution to a problem. Children with low self-esteem are not likely to tough it out through that process. Children who believe that they can solve the problem eventually are much more likely to actually do so than students with low self-esteem, for whom making oneself even more vulnerable than one already is is not an acceptable emotional bargain.

The student is not just a biographical being, even in the fullest sense of that term. She is perforce a world-historical being, too, as we saw in Part I. Without a sense of self-efficacy, she will soon enough despair of herself as having anything to contribute to a great world-historical venture and would lack the self-confidence to do it even if she had a contribution to make. She is diminished thereby and democracy itself is put at risk. Her sense of poor self-efficacy may actually reach to the high heavens, where she feels that someone as weak as she could never hope for anything but rejection from on high. What one often finds in pastoral counselling is that some parishioners project bad object-relations with parents onto Divinity and are at the same time so consumed by a sense of personal unworthiness that they are doubly insulated against any operation of grace in their lives. Their religious convictions may or may not be 'correct'. That is not the issue. The point is that they are so wounded biographically around matters relating to self-worth that they are spiritually frozen. At any rate, those who cavalierly dismiss the importance of self-esteem in a student's life across the narratival board—from the personal to the transpersonal—may wish to consider the importance of schooling in the individual's total psychic economy.

In the terms of the preceding chapters, the 'time' of the classroom must be measured not just by the progress of the hands on the clock from 8 a.m. to 3 p.m. The psychoanalytic genius was to assert that it is the quality of the student's biographical narrative and the viability of a nation's world-historical narrative that are finally at stake in the richness or poverty of the 'temporalities' that obtain in the schools. And as I have contended in other studies (Mayes, 2017b, 2015, 2012), it is also the question of whether a student will have experienced an archetypally heroic journey or simply a lockstep march through an emotional, political, cultural, and spiritual wasteland in his years in school.

A curriculum that attends to the psychodynamic and psychospiritual elements in the student's delicate chemistry as a learner will produce beneficent chain-reactions in her that synergistically spark the engine of a political, psychic, and spiritual venturing forth. A curriculum that ignores such things must, to some degree and at various levels, cause the student's life as an existential being, not just a student, to stall. Learning is a complex process, both in how it happens and in the effects it has throughout one's emotional and ethical systems.

The passions of cognition

In the 1960s, Kubie, a well-known learning theorist of that decade, accentuated the complex subjectivity of educational processes in pointing out that 'even when a scientist is studying atomic energy or a biological process or the chemical properties of some isotope', he is still engaged in various levels of emotional activity. Consciously, of course, the scientist deals with his subjects 'as realities'. However, 'on the preconscious level (the transitional area between waking and falling asleep), he deals with their allegorical and emotional import, direct and indirect'. Then, at the deepest unconscious levels of his psyche, the waking realities of 'biological processes, chemical properties, and isotopes' become even more enmeshed in the scientist's own complex emotional dynamics. 'On an unconscious level, without realising it', the scientist's unconscious mind translates his subject matter into its own symbolic language, which will invariably 'express the unconscious, conflict-laden, and confused level of his own spirit, using the language of his specialty as a vehicle for the projection of his internal struggles' (Kubie, 1967, p. 63).

Lest one doubt this, one need only consult personal experience. Have we not all had the experience of being almost asleep and then being awakened by something? We come to, realizing that we had been thinking about something even then, but in a bizarre way. A thought about a dinner appointment the following night had morphed just before dropping off to sleep into a fantasy about travelling through an ancient African city, an outpost of the Roman Empire, one's life in grave danger. One realizes that the phantasmagoria is somehow related to that simple dinner engagement tomorrow night. But how?

The point here is simply that that kind of semi- and unconscious process is always going on in parallel fashion while we are conscious. What we might be conscious of is a 'feeling tone' to the conscious thought that we can't account for. Why this feeling of anxiety mixed with a small rush of excitement (and possibly even a flash of a memory of something that happened once during a class in college) at a certain conscious thought? If one accessed the unconscious processes going on at that moment, one would discover the reason. There is probably no conscious thought that does not run in parallel fashion to a complex dream drama going on at the same moment in the unconscious. Little do we realize that we live this dual life from the moment we open our eyes in the morning (and 'exit' the dream world) till the moment we close our eyes again that night (to go back into it full tilt).

In his important study *Fantasy and Feeling in Education*, Jones (1966) poetically declared that the whole student is involved in learning, not just his ability to conceptualize, for his imagination may well be involved in picturing 'how to conceive a squared root, a declined verb, a balanced equation, the plural of "deer"; or the harshness of the Arctic environment, or the nature of myth, or the varieties of human conflict regulation—or the meaning of infinity' (p. 82).

Barford in 2002 would sum up the progress of psychodynamic pedagogy over three decades later—decades in which he judged that the psychodynamic, psychospiritual roots of education had remained unwatered by any serious public or policymakers' attention.

Joining forces

The pity in this is that although the research had with the new millennium extended its boundaries to 'the imaginal domain' (Barford, 2002), that domain where archetypal images prevail and where archetypal pedagogy dwells, this progress went and continues to go largely unnoticed by Analytical Psychology and Psychoanalysis alike, not to mention the rest of the scholarly world. The purpose of archetypal pedagogy in political and cultural terms is to help create spaces for Spirit in educational processes—public no less than private. However, it will take even more concerted effort among depth-psychological pedagogues of every stripe to put differences aside, except where they fuel mutually respectful dialectical progress in our research and practice, and cultivate those fertile but sleeping fields where we have so much in common.

This is a difficult task but not impossible; and difficult or not, it is what must be done if a combined depth-psychological pedagogics is to begin to be more visible in the literature and more often used in classroom practices. For, as is the case with psychoanalytic theory and archetypal psychology in general as both have evolved over the last century, so it is with psychoanalytic pedagogy and archetypal pedagogy: That which unites the two is now much greater than that which divides them. It is time to forget Freud's and Jung's ill-conceived and frankly neurotic contentions, to renounce the myth among Jungians that Freud was somehow more guilty of them than Jung was[1], and join forces and resources in exploring the depths and heights of psyche, and to do so in the service of our students.

In the remainder of this chapter, therefore, I would like to draw the attention of other Jungians, especially those involved in education, to just a few of the riches that post-Freudian theory has offered over the last seven decades or so. It is past time that we pay it its proper respect and go about the business of metabolizing its prodigious insights simply because it is the right thing to do and will ground our theorizing, and also because its fate and our fate hang in the same balance. Theoretically and strategically, we have much to gain by establishing ties with psychoanalytic pedagogy, which has a rich history of almost a century now (Mayes, 2009).

Post-Freudian theorists

In this section, I would like to present two important post-Freudian theorists because their work has provided the foundation of a good deal of subsequent theorizing in psychoanalytic pedagogy over the last three decades. Although they retain much of Freud's endopsychic modelling of psyche in terms of its structure and dynamics, they, like post-Freudians in general, reject the idea that sexuality powers psyche. They insist instead that it is the need for an integral ego in relationship with others that is the prime motivator of psychodynamics.

Heinz Kohut (1913–1981)

For Kohut, an ego that was stable, powerful, and able to enter into fruitful relationships enjoyed a healthy 'primary narcissism'. Here, narcissism does not carry the negative connotations it does in ordinary usage. It means simply that an individual has a salutary sense of self-worth and can confidently yet also compassionately interact with other such individuals in the most intimate to the most simply obligatory situations. The individual has attained this state of wellbeing primarily because he was appropriately affirmed in his infancy and youth by his primary caregivers, the most important one, of course, generally being the mother. She is the infant's most important 'selfobject' of the circle of selfobjects—traditionally, this has been father and siblings—that surround the infant as he is being introduced to the world.

The term 'selfobject' is an unfortunate one, for these people are anything but mere 'objects' for the infant. Indeed, they are the individuals who are closest to him—the *objects* of the infant's earliest attention and affection, through whom the infant learns about its *self* by the way they interact with him. Hence the term 'selfobject'. If their interaction is loving and appropriate, he learns that he is a valuable being and that the world is essentially safe and trustworthy, which is the core of his healthy primary narcissism. The selfobject is not, in the final analysis, actually the other person but is the *image* of that person that the infant has introjected. When the infant's and then the child's inner world is populated by positive selfobjects, the basis for a healthy, lifelong primary narcissism has been established (Kohut, 1978, pp. 430ff). This happens in two ways.

The first way is called the 'mirroring transference' and the second is the 'idealizing transference'. In the former, the child learns who he is in the way the mother—and, of course, other selfobjects—reflect back to him their feelings about him. It is primarily in the mirror of the mother, however, that he learns who he is. In the second, the child learns what is good, true, and beautiful in what he sees in the mother—and, again, other selfobjects. Writes Kohut: The 'idealized parental imago ... is gazed at in awe, admired, looked up to, and [is that] which one wants to become ...' (Kohut, 1978, p. 430). This dynamic establishes the child's value-system.

Jung notes that beyond—or rather, at the core of—this interaction with the two most primary of selfobjects, mother and father, are the archetypal Great Mother and Great Father as the Cosmic Parent-Gods of the universe. The infant begins to form its idea of the archetypally male and female principles that govern the cosmos (as in the Yang and Yin of Taoism) by extrapolating from the biological parent onto the cosmic parent/principle (Jung, 1969b, pp. 67–68). This happens at the same time as the growing child unconsciously begins to measure its parents' actual performance as parents against an idealized image of what it should be on the basis of the archetypal Great Mother and Great Father (Jung, 1969c, p. 18, 1954, p. 45).

The former syndrome—projecting one's actual parents onto the arche-typally masculine and feminine aspects of the Divine—often presents a tremendous problem in pastoral counselling because, if the parent or parents were cruel, inaccessible, abandoned the child, or were in some other way inadequate and even inappropriate in their parenting, that child, now an adult, may assume that God views her in the same way. Needless to say, this engenders a wide range of negative responses in her to God—from a cringing sense of guilt to a firebrand rejection of any evidence of grace. Disaggregating those emotions is a necessary step in the person coming to a conclusion about what she actually believes about the Divine, not what she ascribes to Divinity on the basis of early object-relations.

Educational implications of Kohutian object relations theory

Along similar lines, it is, I think, possible to speak of teachers as positive or negative selfobjects for their students. In the teacher's response to the student's comments and products, she is always sending all sorts of somatic and subconscious messages to the student—not to mention the explicit messages—about how she finally assesses him as a learner. She is his mirror. And from the earliest years of preschool until the day she defends her dissertation, a student will look to her teacher to catch a vision of what it means to be a person who is a capable, ethical, and passionate learner. The mirroring and idealizing transferences are in full force in the classroom. A good deal of the teacher's success lies in how well she can harness that force to use it in her student's psychological, ethical, and spiritual service.

Of course, we have been assuming so far that all will always go well in the infant's early object-relationship formation and that she operates in the world on the strength of a healthy primary narcissism. Obviously, that is not so. Many children receive the message that they are not welcome in the world, that they are a burden, and a fit object for punishment, ridicule, or—worst of all—indifference. Such children suffer what Kohut calls a 'narcissistic wound'. As an adult, the person will still try to get the basic existential affirmation we all need, but now, of course, he must do it through neurotic means. These comprise the 'narcissistic personality disorders' and they evidence a toxic 'secondary narcissism' that is the result of the person's 'primary narcissistic' needs having gone unmet. They can range from being excessively demanding of one's partner in a relationship to exposing oneself to 60,000 people in a football stadium and streaking across the field naked. Given how closely one's 'educational narrative' is tied into one's larger 'existential narrative', the teacher as a good pedagogical selfobject for the student can do a lot in building the student up and can do just as much harm as a bad pedagogical selfobject. As we have already seen, teaching is not therapy. But a teacher almost invariably has a therapeutic effect, positive or negative, and usually both. Armed with the understanding of the psychodynamics of learning, the teacher may do her best to insure that that effect is positive.

D. W. Winnicott (1896–1971)

For Winnicott, as for Kohut, the goal of therapy is the construction of a flexible but stable ego in realistic and creative communion with others. Like Kohut, too, Winnicott sees how indispensable the child's earliest months and years will prove in either forming a basis for it or not. And again, like Kohut, Winnicott sees the mother-infant/mother-child as being at the very heart of the matter.

The 'holding environment' and 'good-enough mothering'

For Winnicott, psychological health entails that the infant experience its first world as a good 'holding environment'. Primally, this is the mother's womb, then her arms, then her presence, then her loving gaze from across a room, then a weekly telephone call during the child's first year away from home in college, then a call when he needs money. It is a 'space'—both literal and symbolic—in which the child feels essentially safe and therefore free to explore the surrounding world in increasing measure as it matures. Occasionally, the child will err in its explorations. There will naturally be a consequence. But the mother, who allows these degrees of freedom in and for the child, also makes sure that the new environment is sufficiently safe and is, in this sense, an extension of the original holding environment, so that neither the error nor the consequence will be grave. This is what Winnicott calls 'good-enough mothering'.

Like the term 'object', the term 'good-enough' can be misleading. It is not meant to suggest an indifference, insouciance, or ineptitude on the mother's part. Rather, it is meant to indicate that 'perfect mothering', in which the child is absolutely safe (as if such a thing were possible) and never exposed to a situation with a potentially negative consequence (as if such a thing were desirable), is an unrealistic, frightened, and thus neurotic one. It communicates to the child that the world is perilous at every turn and that a mistake is catastrophic.

A second thing it communicates to the child is that to love someone (as the mother does him) is to be hypervigilant of them and never to have needs of one's own outside of caring for the beloved. That is not relationship, however. That is bondage. It is imprisonment in the needs of the beloved. It is the mother's forfeiting of her own identity. For a child to make a remediable mistake in a new world it is exploring is not a problem. It is an opportunity. It is the nature of creativity. It is regrouping and faring forward. Most importantly, it is the foundation of humour and humility. Conversely and catastrophically, for the child to learn that love means forfeiting, even crucifying, all of one's legitimate needs, however, is more than a problem; it is a 'double-bind' that is a prelude to collapse (Bateson, 1972; see also Feige, 1999). The irony, then, is that 'good-enough mothering' is much better than 'perfect mothering'. Good-enough mothering establishes and then nurtures a flexible, open-ended, and positive narrative in the child. 'Perfect' mothering delimits the child's narrative to just the 'one correct way' and imagines draconian consequences if it is not followed. It is, in fact, the psychopathological root of the standardized curriculum.

As the foundation of standardized testing, on which the perfect 100 per cent score and utter adherence to the prescribed path are at a premium, both 'perfect' mothering and its pedagogical outgrowth, standardized testing, are neurotic. All too easily can they can deform the child into an emotionally twisted adult, consigning him to either an emotionally closed-down, unadventurous life or one that is ceaselessly in futile pursuit of an inhuman perfection. Both types of mindsets and behaviours will require considerable therapy to recovery from their 'perfect' origins.

The transcendent function and mothering

In educational terms, the child of the good-enough mother enjoys another advantage over the child of the perfect-mother. The former has learned to face opposition, negotiate it, and move to a higher plane of being in order to find, rest in, and then operationalize a higher solution than it probably would have previously imagined. In other words, the infant is learning the ins-and-outs of the quintessentially educative processes of the transcendent function. This is education that takes risks in the name of growth and freedom. The 'perfection' of the standardized curriculum, on the other hand, 'trains' the student out of her native spontaneity and genius and, crucifying her on the cross of conformity, prepares her for that life of 'quiet desperation' that is, Thoreau said, the lot of most people. They learn to live that li(f)e in the classroom as the deeper curriculum that the State imposes on the child, imprints in the child's central nervous system after the child's 12-year subjection to its scholastic conditioning program has come to an end and the State is now well pleased at having another worker-citizen to carry on with its devastating world-historical project of eliminating the individual by neutralizing his intellectual and moral courage in the service of the 'perfect', socially engineered state.

The transitional object in education

Another educationally important idea that Winnicott has given us is that of the 'transitional object'.

As the infant matures, there will be more and more moments when the mother is absent, and those moments will increase in duration as well as frequency. Because of the infant's total physical and emotional symbiosis with the mother, it is literally 'the end of the world' when mother leaves the child. She is not just the most important thing in the world to the child. She *is* the world. Everything lives, moves, and has its being in her. She is the context of everything. When she leaves, the world also folds up into a suitcase that goes out of the door. The infant is left in a cosmic void and the terror is total. For, as Jung points out, not only the biological mother but the Mother of the Cosmos, the female aspect of God, and therefore the universe itself flickers out in a flash and the infant is left cosmically bereft. Looked at in this light, the Existentialist dread of the universe as a cosmic absence may be, at least in some instances, a later edition of the infantile terror at the death of the archetypal Great Mother—the death of the Feminine Aspect of God.

When all goes well, however, and with increasing separation, the infant, and then the older child, comes to sense both physically and emotionally the existentially necessary but terrifying lesson that there is a grand divide between the world of Me and Not-Me—the Not-Me world first being experienced by the child as the withdrawing and sometimes even absent mother. To first simply endure and then more skillfully negotiate the space between the world of Me and Not-Me, the infant will come to rely upon a *transitional object*. Through it, the child learns that the world is not our oyster, but it can be a field for our creativity. The key is the transitional object. Why is this? It is because

> a transitional object is a psychologically living symbol, a replacement self-object whose significance and power lie in the fact that the child's imagination invests it with the power to satisfy at least some of its needs. A favourite blanket becomes the child's substitute for the mother when she is away. Through creative fantasy, the child turns the blanket into a transitional object that is now not just a blanket or a mother but a 'poetic' fusion of both … As the child develops, it chooses more complex transitional objects to symbolically express and deal with the existential gap between its inner and outer realities. In a sense, therefore, all of our philosophical and artistic products, our concepts and images, are dauntingly

articulated transitional objects through which we express our fundamental existential need to interpret and interact with external reality,
which otherwise would disintegrate into nothingness. In this sense, every
educational act and product is a transitional object in search of an absolute knowledge that must forever evade education. Perhaps the university
is the ultimate intellectual transitional object.

(Mayes, 2017a, pp. 32f)

The transitional object is so named because it is a 'transit' between the world
of 'I' and 'Not I'. Before she began to leave the scene periodically, the mother
was both the ground and extension of 'I' for the infant. With her absence, that
ground falls out from beneath him; without her, what he sees in front of him
now is not an extension of himself filling space that is safe because she rules
over it. Rather, he sees space filled with people and happenings that he does
not understand and that may be bent on destroying him—what Melanie Klein
called the infant's 'paranoid position'. Both his very self and the protection of
that self disappear in the moment she does.

As the child's cognitive capacity grows, it naturally devises increasingly
complex transitional objects to deal with an increasingly nuanced sense of the
world but with the same root-terror, one that was expressed about our basic
existential condition by A. E. Housman, in his cry: 'I, lonely and afraid, in a
world I never made' (http://holyjoe.org/poetry/housman1.htm, accessed 9/2/
19). It is the transitional object that both assuages that fear, or at least makes
it productive, not paralysing, and that may even offer hope. This is, finally, the
hope that, beyond the fear and confusion, there is a fundamental goodness in
the universe that abides and will at last take us back and take us in. The transitional object is the seed of metaphysical hope.

Kohutian and Winnicottian psychology as spiritual projects

Our acts of creativity may then be seen as a manifestation of that hope—
however one expresses one's creativity. It may be in a heavy-machinery mech-
anic at sunrise who came into the shop early, as he often does, contemplating
a malfunctioning diesel engine over a cup of coffee in order to fix it as effectively and efficiently as possible; a CEO of a small but promising firm brooding
late at night over her desk in an empty building after everyone else has gone
home about the best way of marketing a product that she deeply believes in;
a major league baseball player watching hours upon hours of himself at bat
to learn better how to anticipate that 'high and inside' pitch that fools him
every time into swinging at empty air—he doesn't want to let his fans down;
or a novelist sitting with a cup of coffee and staring at the blank computer
screen before she takes the tremendous gamble of writing the first sentence of
her new novel—one that she hopes will be her best, one that she hopes will do
good for other suffering souls.

When these acts are done in good faith as one's best expression of who one is and what one can do to negotiate that otherwise exasperating, terrifying gap between oneself and what is finally the nature of things—that which one is always straining to apprehend, intuit, and then contact through one's creativity—then one is engaged in the production of a transitional object.

Indeed, in the final analysis, is not a life-narrative itself a transitional object, maybe even the ultimate transitional object? It is the sense that a person makes of her life through a story that stands between her and the cosmos as chaos. It is the best expression of what she most values, what for her constitutes Ultimacy. *In this emphasis on ultimate matters and its implicit hope that one's central values have standing in the universe, Kohutian and Winnicottian Selfobject Psychology emerge as an essentially spiritual project— or at least, paving the way for one—* as is anything that leads one to authentically engage with one's existence as an individual amongst other similarly constituted beings, living individually (the biographical narrative) and collectively (the world-historical narrative) *sub specie aeternitatis* (the narrative of Time beyond time).

This is clear in Winnicott's model, with the engagement of ultimate questions as the project that stimulates psyche into creating transitional objects in their most mature forms as approaches to a Presence on the other side of the Existential terror of non-Being. But the spiritual dimension is also discernible in Kohut. The idealizing transference rests on the assumption of ethical values that the individual finds embodied in an admired selfobject and that he desires to find in himself in the mirroring transference. Having an ethical core and operating from it is the implicit hope and demand of Kohut's psychology. This is not just Jung's 'modern man in search of a soul' but is man *always* in search of a soul through creativity in action and courage in the cosmos.

There is another aspect of Kohutian and Winnicottian psychology that lays the foundation for a spiritual life. It is their shared goal of creating an individual who, as an individual, can rise to his full stature as a responsible and empowered agent in life and thus move through it with character and commitment. To be sure, this is not in itself necessarily a spiritual project, but no spiritual project is authentic if it lacks it. And in the following passage, we find Jung asserting just this in terms that resonate with the three narratival modes that we have been considering throughout this book.

Individual self-reflection [at the biographical level], return of the individual ... to his own deepest being [at the spiritually foundational level], with its individual and social destiny [thereby joining the individual and the worldhistorical narratives to the individual's divine narrative], here is the beginning of a cure for the blindness which reigns at the present hour.

(Jung, 1967b, p. 5)

Without the psychological cohesiveness and moral creativity of the individual—the upshot of Kohutian and Winnicottian psychology—it is impossible to achieve what Jung is urging us on towards in his constant call for the individual to live in 'integrity' in both senses of that term—that is, in self-contained unity and ethical commitment, the very things that it is Winnicott's and Kohut's goal to help the individual find and then build upon as the governing orientation of his life.

Kohut, Winnicott, and Jung: political and educational implications

It is the narratival *re*-creation of the individual in the three temporal dimensions in which he moves that must be the precondition for the massive social change we saw Jung calling for in Chapter 2; there, he declared that any valid and durable cure for the ailments of the world must begin with the reformation of the individual (Jung, 1967b, p. 226). To say that Jung felt a sense of urgency in all this would be inadequate in conveying the almost apocalyptically imperative tone Jung uses in discussing these matters. It is why he is always imploring that 'special attention ... be paid to this delicate plant "individuality" if it is not to be completely smothered' (p. 155).

Jung understood that to accomplish this would require sea-changes in how modern Western society educated its youth. But there had to be a major reorientation in schooling, Jung believed, from its thralldom to corporatism and the ensuing neglect of the individual. The question for Jung was not how we could manage to make such changes but how we could afford *not* to do so. Fully half a century before, Lawrence Cremin (1988) prophesied the imperilling of democracy in the collectivizing of its schooling; Jung in 1934 was issuing similar warnings.

The profound need to break the stranglehold on education of socialist collectivism on the Left and corporate capitalism on the Right was clear to Jung even in the 1930s. He charged both the Left and the Right in this regard with being breeding grounds for 'immorality and blind stupidity' that any kind of groupthink bred in groups of people because 'individuality [is] inevitably ... driven to the wall' when it is not the constant object of our most punctilious care (1967b, p. 153). 'Society, by automatically stressing all the collective qualities in its individual representatives puts a premium on mediocrity, on everything that settles down to vegetate in an easy, irresponsible way.' And to stress again and leave no doubt about how this happens, Jung unequivocally declared: 'It begins in school [and] continues at the university ...' (Jung, 1967b, p. 153).

In terms of the curriculum, Jung did not presume to suggest what specifically should be taught. He was adamant, however, about what should *not* be the focus of public education: 'It cannot be the aim of education to turn out rationalists, materialists, specialists, technicians and others of the kind who, unconscious of their origins, are precipitated abruptly into the present and contribute to the disorientation and fragmentation of society' (1958, p. 345). However, this is precisely what modern education was doing, in Jung's estimation, which is what makes modern education 'morbidly one-sided' in favour of technical rationality (Jung, 1970, p. 153).

The fault largely lay in the colossal influence of the United States (a country with which Jung had rather a love-hate relationship) in the first half of the 20th century. Its global reach was not proving to be especially salutary, at least in educational terms; for, the international effect of the seductions of American materialism was to breed technical education agendas in schooling worldwide (Jung, 1970a, p. 266). Such education did little but confirm the common man in his plight as a cog in the 'sorting machine' of education (Spring, 1976a), training him to be an obedient 'worker-citizen' (Spring, 1976a, b) and depriving him of a liberal education, which alone would ultimately prove much more empowering to the ordinary citizen than technical training ever could (Ravitch, 1983).

Personally disempowering, culturally destructive, and spiritually denuded, modern education failed all three narratival tests for producing a vibrant and visionary subject who would refuse every blandishment, nagging, coercion, or temptation to become an object of the State or industry. What could one expect such education to produce but the 'mass man' (Jung, 1966b, p. 148)—awash in anonymity, crazed to conform, and narratively naked? What was necessary was a classroom that was both psychodynamically and psychospiritually attuned to the student as a potentially rich individual, cultural, and spiritual being. Post-Freudian pedagogy and archetypal pedagogy, forces united—the former grounding the latter and the latter spiritualizing the former—are positioned to bring that sea-change to pass. Now is the time. Let us begin.

Note

1   This is a naïve misconception that even a cursory reading of their letters dispels, for Jung was as petulant as Freud in them and, truth be told, even more so more often than not (Jung, 1973).

Chapter 5

Notes towards a 'unified depth-educational psychology'

A primer of the classroom as a historical-cultural and socioeconomic space

When we walk into a classroom, we enter a zone that is an aggregation of various symbolic 'spaces'. As when viewing a Cubist painting, we must regard the classroom from multiple conceptual angles in order to begin to get an adequate sense of its many meanings.

It is important that a study of the classroom as a psychodynamic and psychospiritual space enfold into its account these other material, historical, and cultural influences on what goes on in schools if for no other reason than that those things will impact what is psychodynamically and psychospiritually going on there—and what is not.

Without at least considering those sociohistorical factors in our researches into schooling,[1] an exclusively psychodynamic and psychospiritual approach can get lost in the clouds. Like the Laputans in Swift's *Gulliver's Travels*, we as educational researchers will find ourselves engaged in abstract studies that have no positive effect on what will actually happen in the classroom. We will therefore be limited in whatever good we might do for students and teachers, which must always be uppermost in our intentions as educationists. What follows is a thumbnail sketch of a few of the most salient factors that 'shape' the schools.

To begin at the beginning, the space of a classroom is literally that—a physical space; and yet, its very physicality is symbolic. Its architectural design speaks volumes about how the physical complex of a school reflects the sponsoring society's views about what education means, who will get what kind of education (depending on the specific school they attend, for they will vary dramatically in attractiveness, activities offered, and prestige), and the uses to which those different kinds of education gained at those different installations will be put. The physical spaces of a school make up a many layered text (Ellis, 2001).

An interesting case in point is the American urban classroom of the late 19th and early 20th century. This is a relevant example for the purposes of this book; for, it is that classroom a century ago that has evolved into the typical contemporary American public school classroom (McLaren, 1998). As such, reading the earlier, prototypical classroom as a text reveals a good deal about the basic cultural-historical and socioeconomic assumptions that current classrooms encode in brick-and-mortar.

Photographs of these classrooms are often visually dominated by squat, no-frills, workmanly desks, each the same, each bolted to the floor, aligned in rank-and-file precision, and all pointing in an inerrant geometry toward the front, where the teacher presides as the sole arbiter of what will go on in this space according to a strict schedule and uniform curriculum, to which he in turn is subject in a chain of command. His performance in delivering this curriculum is monitored just as closely as the students' in consuming and then reproducing it on uniform tests. As with any standardized test, the ability to memorize and the disposition to conform is what is required and rewarded, not the intuitive use of information to fashion compelling ideas and then to make rich connections among a spectrum of ideas. The design of the room makes it clear that taking bold imaginative leaps is not what the curriculum that will be enforced in it is about.

The reader may be reminded of bootcamp as portrayed in *Full Metal Jacket* and discussed above, and rightfully so since public schooling has at many sites become a kind of political bootcamp to induct children into a hyper-rationalized system where, through standardized testing and psychometric assessments, it will be determined where a child 'belongs'. This will generally reflect to a considerable degree the social positioning of the family from which the child comes. There is no more accurate predictor of whether or not a child will go on to college and what the status of that college will be than her parents' combined income (Berliner and Biddle, 1995). In this sense, schools 'reproduce' extant power structures in a society, and, in reproducing, serve to legitimate (while they also camouflage) that reproduction as a strictly academic matter. This deflects attention from the fact that the child's academic performance is at least as much a political, cultural, and socioeconomic matter as it is a function of the child's intelligence (McLaren, 1998).

To return to the classroom of 1900, it was identical to the other classrooms in the school, and in some schools each classroom was just one node of a spoke of many spokes that radiated around a hub in which the principal, a sort of plant manager, sat, installed at the centre, in his 'panopticon'. This referred to the command-headquarters of any institutional site from which everything (*pan-*) could be seen (*optic*) and directed.

In *Discipline and Punish* (1979), Foucault observed that not only schools but other institutional structures at the beginning of the 20th century followed the same federal architectural template. Hospitals, orphanages, charity homes, and psychiatric facilities—those agencies that over the next century would accrete into the American social welfare system—architecturally encoded the enhanced rationalization and secularization of Western industrial political-economies that Weber first identified as such at the outset of the 20th century. Yet, Marx had identified this social-rationalization at the service of capital two decades earlier in *Das Kapital*, naming it as the reason modern man was alienated from his work, from others, and therefore from himself. Durkheim, contemporaneously with Weber, pinpointed this 'anonymity' as a sociological explanation of suicide.

Despite the different services offered to (and in some cases, imposed on) citizens, all of these physical/symbolic spaces manifested the new centralization of power, and the ethos of uniformity that it required. And it was all laid out for the manager in F.W. Taylor's influential *Principles of Scientific Management*. Appearing in 1911, it outlined for policy makers, chief executive officers, and site-based managers in the new 'order of things' how to go about their business with the utmost precision, pragmatism, and above all, profitability, deploying all the latest technologies of the new psychological and social 'sciences' and compliant to the exigencies of the rapidly expanding State.

Education was becoming a 'sorting machine' which students enter at one end and come out at the other as uncritical 'worker-citizens' (Spring, 2006, 1976). The schools could be seen as another industrial plant, where corporately approved knowledge was the commodity and the students were paid in grades that statistically both portrayed their comparative performance and erased their identity. Paolo Freire (1970) named this 'the banking model of education'.

Interestingly but not surprisingly, it is about this time that teachers stop writing prose reports to parents about their student's particular challenges and strengths. Instead, report cards with few, if any, personal observations made about the student become the order of the day. The child is shrunk to a set of statistics that can be parsed to resolve the equation of where he can most profitably be situated in 'the military industrial-educational complex' (Cremin, 1988). The bell-curve becomes king, and where the student fits into its depersonalized range will determine what, if any, further education he receives, what the nature of that education will be, and where all of this will ultimately place him as a socioeconomic unit in the political economy in which, after all, schools are wedged (Bowles and Gintis, 1976; Morrow and Torres, 1995).

More: this is implemented differentially. Due to funding algorithms in American schooling and tax structures that favour the wealthy, children, although equal *de jure* in the eyes of the State, are managed *de facto* quite differently depending upon their parents' socioeconomic and cultural 'positioning' in a society, what the sociologist Pierre Bourdieu (1977) calls their *habitus*. The more empowered the *habitus* from which a child comes, the more architecturally attractive the school, the more richly appointed its classrooms, the more varied and current the technologies in the classroom, the more exciting and consequential its extracurricular activities, the more experienced its teachers, and the more cognitively rich the curriculum.

All of this communicates to well-positioned students that they are loved and valued and that the future has great things in store for them—the quintessential feature of any healthy and energetic biographical narrative. On the other hand, students from unfavourably positioned groups attend schools that are poorer in every respect, including the curriculum they study and the extracurricular resources available to them. This sets students up for academic failure and a biographical narrative that is often wounded regarding themselves as educational beings. These personal narratives confirm and perpetuate their families' larger narratives of who they are as a group, and those narratives are often grim.

And with this we have two more dimensions that comprise the classroom space—the interrelated economic and cultural spaces, both of which, to be sure, are much more complex than this brief discussion of typical educational spaces allows (Kozol, 1991; Pai and Adler, 2001; Thompson and Mayes, 2020). For our purposes here, I would mention, as I and my colleagues have written elsewhere (Mayes et al., 2016) that:

> There is no such thing as 'culture-free' teaching or learning. Not only is education central to most societies; cultural norms are central to how teaching and learning are practiced and what is seen as appropriate material for students to learn. Culture and education are inextricably related—so much so, in fact, that, in a sense, they 'define' each other.
>
> (Pai and Adler, 2001)

> [S]ince classrooms are embedded in a society whose norms they reflect, students from cultures other than the dominant one(s) may be more or less primed for academic success, depending upon the degree of 'cultural continuity' between their culture and that of the school.
>
> (Mayes et al., 2016, p. iv)

Of course, teachers—many of whom come from the dominant culture and all of whom are more or less required to teach a state-mandated core curriculum—must attend to the normative values of the society in which the school is embedded. There are institutional, district, state, and federal requirements—all of which embody cultural norms—that teachers simply cannot ignore. Nor should they ignore them. It would be disempowering for minority students if the teacher did not teach students the dominant bodies of knowledge and the official 'languages of success' that will ultimately allow these children to have increasingly vibrant and influential voices in the ongoing cultural conversations about how we all choose to define ourselves as a society (Ravtich, 2000).

I follow Macias (1987) in his study of Papago children on the reservation in Tucson, Arizona, in concluding that a politically and culturally responsible and responsive pedagogy should aim at 1) teaching the 'official curriculum' that constitutes the 'language of power', 2) being as consistent as possible with the students' culture in how it goes about doing this, and 3) including the struggle of the students' culture *vis-à-vis* the topics under analysis in the curriculum so as to invite all the students to politically and ethically interrogate the dominant culture.

A room with a view: the classroom as psychodynamic and psychospiritual spaces

What I attempted to show in the previous chapter and would like to expand upon in this chapter is the tremendous need to pay a great deal more attention than we presently do to the psychodynamic space that a classroom is, and that we need to start paying any attention *at all* to its psychospiritual dimensions and possibilities, as we did in the preceding chapter in the discussion of Kohut and Winnicott. I would like to continue in that direction in this chapter.

The roots of teaching and learning as psychodynamics space: 'where id is, there shall ego be'

In his 'New Introductory Lectures on Psychoanalysis', Freud in 1933 famously declared that 'Where id is, there will ego be'. It was a simple-enough sentence—deceptively simple, in fact. For, what it represented was a clarion call, crisp, insistent and defiant, playing in the key of the Age of Enlightenment to sound out its message: The triumph of man's reason over his irrationality. Where id—the repository of all that is irrational, driven by blind instincts, and ultimately destructive—is, there will ego—that which is rational, moved by higher intellectual purposes, and socially generative—be. Freud's statement might be read as the psychodynamic motto of the Enlightenment, a mission statement for Western culture, a proclamation of purpose. All in the human animal that made man a terror to man—rapaciousness and bloodlust—had to be corralled and kept in the ornate symbolic pen of society if that animal were to survive; for, it was only in social order that man could find refuge from himself.

It was also his refuge from nature, which Freud, as originally a natural scientist, admired, but which, as a philosopher of sorts, he must also look at with terror. Rapt in admiration as he observes teeming nature and its laws in the service of Eros, the 'life-force', man is ultimately gripped, both mentally and physically, by cold horror at nature's ultimate nullity, *Thanatos*, the death-force, and the extinction of all of man's passion and reason, in the grave.

As we saw earlier, Freud was finally a pessimist, his life stoic, and his hermeneutics seeped in suspicion, for 'the goal of all life is death. The inanimate was there before the animate' (Freud, 1923/1957, p. 160). Although a son of the Enlightenment, Freud did not share its faith that reason could rough off all man's edges, that it could perfect that slightly more-evolved simian called man—who not that long ago had been running around jungles and forests in constant search of food and sex, its fur matted with mud and faeces—who would now become the citizen of the secular New Jerusalem. And besides, death always had the last word.

The popular image of Freud as the man who, not a little devilishly, opened the sexual Pandora's box and thus let loose a century of sexual licence has it all wrong. As Philip Rieff's groundbreaking study established over a half-century ago, Freud's was 'the mind of the moralist' (1961). It could hardly have been otherwise. Young Sigismund Schlomo Freud grew up in a patri-archal home, presided over by his father, Jacob. Although Jacob Freud had strayed from his Hassidic roots that included rabbis, he was well known for his assiduous and adept Torah study. That it was a conservative environment in which Sigmund was raised is clear. Add to that the fact that the Freud home was situated in the Victorian milieu of Catholic Vienna and one has a clearer view of 'the moralist'.

Equally, Freud was a pragmatist. He knew there would always be a chthonic surplus in the human being despite all of psychoanalysis' best efforts and that, after all, psychoanalysis could not recreate man from a clean slate. Only God could do that, and there was no God. That did not, however, deter Freud from trying to tame the beast or at least bring his most feral passions under some semblance of control so that decent society and good order would prevail. That was Freud's goal. Like Jung, Freud was a conservative.

Man would always be neurotic. That was man's lot; so long after Eden, that had not changed, nor would it. Freud's father's teachings took firm hold in his son, at least regarding the compromised condition of the human being, who must therefore, in turn, compromise in order to go on existing. The question was not: 'Will man be neurotic?' The question was: 'What kind of neurotic will man be?' Would he be functionally neurotic? Could psychoanalysis provide him ways 'to love and to work'—Freud's therapeutic goal. The stakes could not be higher. For if psychoanalysis could not make good on its promise that 'where id is, there will ego be', then two equally disastrous fates awaited the human animal: 1) to explode under the pressure of too many unfulfilled feral desires and thus destroy himself, others, and (as things now stand) the planet in the megalomaniac triumph of the id, or 2) to implode under the depressive, excessive weight of an imperial, hyper-pious superego.

The trick was to balance the id and the superego so that deeply flawed man could somehow survive—his limitations carved into his very neurology by the moral acid of the symbolic apple that he had somehow consumed or been consumed by. God alone knew how or why man's plight was so difficult and contradictory, and, again, God did not exist, only a religious fable, which had nevertheless subtly taken up residence in the after-all Jewish Freud. But what-ever the cause of Freud's worldview—and they include other world-historical determinants (Gay, 1998) which it is beyond the purpose of this book to examine—the task that lay before him as, in a sense, the archetypal Hebrew prophet, was to let the people know of their lamentable condition but also to offer a saving message: 'Where id is, there will ego be' (Kirschner, 1996). To miss the prophet in Freud is to miss Freud.

As we saw in the previous chapter, certain psychoanalytic theorists—some retaining the first model that Freud presented but interpreting and using it in a much more optimistic way, others reworking it considerably in terms of selfobjects—have had a lot to say about education, and we will explore that further in the rest of this chapter. But we must do so in sober recognition that this is where the whole psychoanalytical-pedagogical project began.

The possibilities of teaching and learning as psychospiritual space: 'when an inner situation is not made conscious, it happens outside as fate'

Freud's statement came in 1932, when he was 76 years old. In 1951, Jung, also 76, made what seems to have been a similar statement: 'When an inner situation is not made conscious, it happens outside as fate.' The set-up appears to be the same in both cases. Consciousness is being threatened by something that is not conscious and that may therefore undo consciousness if that threat is not dealt with.

In Freud, the adversary, General Id, whose command centre is in the subconscious, must be routed out or else he will wreak havoc on consciousness, emblemized and actualized as the ego, which now rouses itself to do battle against the id.

Freud's war of the ego on the id is not just a defensive manoeuvre to protect the homeland. It is an expansionist, unapologetic, psychic-military campaign, or rather an unending series of assaults on the darkness of the id, constant deployments of luminous conscious psychic energy until the job is done and the id is disassembled and defeated. In archetypal terms, it is the Promethean triumph of Logos over Eros, spreading the stolen fire of consciousness around the gloom and horror of the jungles and forests human beings had emerged out of and still carried within them. Its mission is to vanquish id, for wherever id was, ego-consciousness will push back its primordial gloom. Where id was, now ego will plant its flag, establish a field-headquarters, and construct new settlements of awareness. This is the ego-militant against any inner force that would becloud the Light of reason.

As we have seen, Freud the pragmatist understood that this would never happen entirely, but he was committed to a constant state of war, no prisoners taken, against the id, for the id's very existence represented a potential terrorist's threat to the triumph of ego, and the terrorist-id might strike anywhere, anytime. Constant vigilance, the price of democracy, was even more the price of consciousness in the first place.

Jung seems to be similarly calling the forces of consciousness to deal with 'an inner situation'. It also must be handled so that it does not 'happen outside as fate'. In both Freud's and Jung's brief statements, the order of battle seems to be to muster and deploy the weapons of awareness to neutralize the enemy within so that it does not have a chance to work its black magic 'outside'—in the conscious world.

Despite these apparent similarities between Freud's statement and Jung's, however, those similarities turn out to be more apparent than real.

For, Freud presents us with id as a rampaging beast, salivating and screaming, raw, frenzied for more blood and sex, which it can never get enough of. And that animal-energy, entirely within us, must be controlled by ego-reason, the human being's zookeeper of its own lower realms. Otherwise, its energy, bursting all the boundaries that ego-reason has set, will demolish our fragile social structures and nuanced psychic boundaries and leave us in the helter-skelter of psychosocial disorientation. Our debasement would be terrible to behold and our extinction might be lurking just around the next world-historical corner. Indeed, psychotherapy might be seen as a means at the level of personal biography to preserve democracy at a world-historical level. However, the absence of a sacred narrative in Freud's project is a fatal partiality that has been addressed in some later post-Freudian theorizing (Epstein, 1995; Meissner, 1984; Rizzuto, 1979). This is an area where Jungian psychology could be of great service to post-Freudian theory, as exemplified, for instance, in Ulanov's (2001) *Finding Space: Winnicott, God, and Psychic Reality*, which nimbly bridges the gap between the Jungian and post-Freudian approaches to religious issues.

At any rate, Jung, in speaking of 'an inner situation', is referring not only to a personal subconscious within us but, as he puts it more open-endedly, to something not yet 'made conscious'. Tellingly, for Jung, that which is 'not conscious', although it may be active in the personalistic realm of the subconscious and the id, is not by any means primarily that. By describing it as that which is 'not conscious'—that is to say, 'unconscious'—Jung is using a phrase that, significantly, avoids the use of 'subconscious', which is presumably the term he would have used if that were all that he was referring to. The implicit use of the term 'unconscious' almost certainly is meant by Jung to signal the reader that he is referring us to the Collective Unconscious.

In one sense, of course, the Collective Unconscious is 'inside us'. It is an 'inner situation'. However, the Collective Unconscious cannot finally be limited to some space inside the head, or indeed to any space at all. For, in what I take as one of Jung's most defining declarations, we must keep ever before us his insistence that 'the unconscious is not this thing or that; it is the Unknown as it immediately affects us' (1969b, p. 68).

As 'the Unknown' what Jung is alluding to as an 'inner situation' has more than just a psychodynamic range and depth. Rather, Jung's idea of the Unconscious is replete with all the mysterious valences, the paradoxical (al) chemistry, the astonishing appearances and equally enigmatic disappearances, and, in short, the multidimensionality and polysemy of the Divine itself, and his use of the adjectival 'not known' moves us ineluctably in that direction. The most profoundly inner situation is also precisely where the supra-spatial, supratemporal resides in its communications with the individual human being. It is thus only secondarily an 'inner situation' and primarily a ubiquitous one.

This is a tremendous narratival difference between the Freudian subconscious and the Jungian Unconscious. For Freud, the subconscious is the foreclosing of any possibility of the Sacred—both because we are so dark and also because the subconscious dies with the individual. Not so Jung's Collective Unconscious, which, although containing darkness, is preponderantly spiritual, and which sweeps the human being up in its eternal dynamic, carrying him heavenward again.

Like the element and the archetypal figure of Mercury in alchemy (he who was, indeed, the governing Spirit of the whole project as Jung saw it), the Divine—Mercury as Its icon—is transcendent, inexplicable. True, one could ascribe certain characteristics to it, but they were so paradoxical that their very incongruity left one stunned in silence and more mystified than before. Primarily, one could say that it was bivalent, Light and Dark blended (but always under the ultimate pull of the Light—these were Christian alchemists, after all, whom Jung was talking about)—and therefore paradoxical, which means unpredictable and inscrutable, unlocalizable, which is a universal feature of any 'definition' of the Godhead. This 'inner situation' was thus archetypal because, as noted at the outset of this study, the archetypes were the 'site' where God spoke to human beings. Jung's idea of the archetype rested on an ontological, perhaps even metaphysical one, since, as we also just saw, he insisted on his core essential and essentialist intuition, that 'God has made an inconceivably sublime and mysteriously contradictory image of himself, without the help of man and implanted it in man's unconscious as the archetype' (1977, p. 667).

This idea, heavy in allusions to Genesis 1:27 with Jehovah making man in His image, clearly was not just an incidental one for Jung. It was a governing precept, one that was so dear to him that it was (allusive now to the inscribing of the Decalogue in Exodus 20: 17) carved in stone on his tower at Bollingen, the medieval tower, strategically erected not too close to his home and from which much of his *Collected Works* came forth to meet the largely puzzled and often-disapproving scrutiny of the medical and academic community of his day—something that naturally was always an irritant to him and often painful. Nevertheless: *Vocatus atque non vocatus Deus aderit.* 'Bidden or unbidden, God will appear'. The Unconscious as the Unknown, which went beyond the spaces of the personally puzzling and landed one in the transpersonal hyperspace of the cosmically mystifying, is the core and perpetual 'inner situation' for the human being. It will manifest itself in our external lives when least expected as it is taking up another unpredictable, ephemeral season of residence within us in the deepest reaches of our psychospiritual economy. Indeed, the Unconscious as the Unknown is the Unknown largely because of its sovereign spontaneity—the unpredictable but inevitable action of the Eternal on us. To Thorndike's 'All that exists, exists in some amount and can be measured',[2] we confidently respond, on the basis of the Collective Unconscious, that 'What ultimately exists does not exist in some amount and could never be measured.'

The Unknown is within us, yes, but it is around us, too—above us and below us. It is nowhere to be seen but everywhere to be felt. It is impossibly distant from us and closer to us than our next thought. It is ontologically the most radically other 'Other' and also our most intimate Self. It may thus be registered as 'an inner situation', but it is not only that. It can just as easily constellate as an outer situation, as 'fate'. Jung's statement must be taken more philosophically than psychodynamically, then, to be referring to the Mystery in action, to the Unknown in its paradoxical bilocation as both 'an inner situation' and an outer constellation, which in turn is key to the idea of synchronicity, of course (Jung, 1969a, pp. 417–519; see also Cambray, 2009; Main, 2004). That which abides in Eternal Time, that which will, one way or another, break through into our merely biographical narrative and make Itself known as a perpetual possibility in a cosmically pregnant moment—that is Fate.

Quite unlike Freud, then, Jung was not talking merely about the need to face the subconscious lest it subvert consciousness—all of which is strictly 'internal', psychodynamic stuff. What Jung is talking about may involve that. Jung wrote volumes on that and offered to 'Self-Psychology' important terms: persona, complex, shadow, the midlife crisis, complex, countertransference.

But the Collective Unconscious and its archetypes took the Western Psychological Project to the transpersonal climes, where what matters most is the individual's response to the operation of the Timeless on her. To the degree that she will go within to seek that place that is beyond within or without, a place that resonates to the call being issued to and also now issuing from the individual in this ontological and ethical moment both in and out of time, she has moved that much closer to her eternal identity. This is the upward-spiralling process Jung called individuation, towards the discovery of what he called the Self, one's sempiternal identity in a perpetual 'Now'. The ego, in its feeble transitory condition, is the mere foam of a chimerical 'now' on an endless ocean that undulates forever and ever as an eternal 'Now'.

This process presents itself as an 'inner situation', for it is within the individual as one of its aspects. Yet it is greater than she. That is what makes it salvific. Presenting itself in her biographical timelines and giving them purpose, it is able to do so precisely because it transcends those biographical timelines, transmogrifies them in the celestial engines of the Divine. At the same time as it affirms her life in its Existential specifics, it also leaves paltry particularities behind. As she folds this knowledge into herself while folding herself into it, she is responding to her fate—a fate that lies in her very response to this ongoing Annunciation of the Timeless in time. That is the one response, and it redeems the biographical by transfiguring it in the trans-biographical.

The other response is that she may, yet again, deny it, maybe only doubt it, but in any case deflect and defer it. In this manner, we, like her, consign ourselves to another round of suffering in unassuaged time (perhaps even karmically; Jung was fascinated by Yoga and Buddhism) through what seem to be our aeons of agonies in merely mechanical sequence. But 'Fate' will present itself to us again and again, as yet another opportunity of redeeming our merely egoic 'time', and we may, this time, reach out to that Time beyond time as it is reaching out to us, and thus redeem the time by recognizing and reorganizing ourselves as immortal beings in mortal transit and temporal probation.

There are many inner situations that will require the incursion of fate that calls out to us and that calls us out of mere animal-nature to clarify them and thus to realize the Self. They will be hard. We will sometimes weep. But all is not lost. It is never lost. Indeed, the loss in that fire—as we stand helplessly by and watch our existential and lifeworld attachments and enchantments be burned to nothingness—is the gain. For what, post-holocaust, vanished in the fire is what had to be relinquished, detached from—mourned for, yes, but finally let go of.

Vocatus atque non vocatus Deus aderit

It can happen in a classroom, too—in any classroom and in various ways but always with the curriculum pointing beyond itself, the teacher and the student, re-formed in insight that takes them, still in this physical and conceptual space but also lifted beyond it, into zones of revelation, into redemptive apocalypses, even in restorative repentances in which they meet each other, the curriculum, and indeed themselves as something wholly, and holy, new (Huebner, 1999).

The subjective curriculum: the sixth dimension

Freud's statement juxtaposed against Jung's reveals—ironically, because of their surface similarities—a fundamental difference between the two men and the pedagogies that flowed from their theories: Freud, intent upon the enrichment of the biographical within inescapable mortal limitations; Jung, aiming to link the biographical with the trans-biographical to transcend those boundaries; Freud, the hermeneut of suspicion, Jung the hermeneut of hope (Homans, 1995; Ricoeur, 1985). And yet, in the work of the post-Freudians, on one side, and in that of psychoanalytically minded Jungians, on the other, there has opened up a middle ground where dialogue is possible in the theory and practice of psychotherapy.

Is this possible as well in educational psychology? Is there territory in educational theory as it is presently constituted from which such a project might launch and attain orbit? I believe there is. It is what I call the sixth dimension of the taxonomy of the curriculum. What is this sixth dimension? Therein lies a tale.

Notes

1   For the most widely referenced studies of the history of U.S. education, see: Cremin, 1988, 1964; Gelberg, 1997; Kliebard, 1986; Ravitch, 1983; Spring, 2006, 1976; Tyack, 1974; Violas, 1978; Vinovskis, 1985; Watras, 2002.
2   In fact, it was one of Thorndike's students who added 'and can be measured', but it has become something of a convention to attribute the whole quote to Thorndike.

Chapter 6

The subjective curriculum

The sixth dimension of the 'imaginal domain'

Introduction

In 1985, Elliot Eisner offered a taxonomy of the curriculum that divided it into five dimensions (Eisner and Vallance, 1985). They are the official curriculum, the operational curriculum, the hidden curriculum, the null curriculum, and the extra curriculum.

In a study examining 100 years of teaching in public schools in the U.S. from about 1890 to 1990, Cuban (1993) observed that as a teacher becomes increasingly expert in her work, she takes with a grain of salt the official curriculum mandated by the State. This is the operational curriculum.

Whereas the novice teacher will shape her curriculum almost entirely around the state's dictates, the experienced teacher will have learned within several years and under the advisement of veteran teachers at her site to design her curriculum much more according to what she, in her context-sensitive view of what her students really need, determines. This is the reworked official curriculum according to her best judgement, not what a state board of education says, many of whose members have traditionally not been teachers but upper- and upper-middle-class male lawyers—not a group that has been particularly sensitive to women and children (Apple, 1990, 1987). By the end of her career, Cuban opines, the teacher will have come to draw only about five per cent of her curriculum from what the State demands.

Eisner calls the teacher's personal adaptation of the official curriculum the operational curriculum. As an act of political resistance or simply because of deeper personal wisdom that she has picked up along the way and now wants to share with 'her children', she will include this in her curriculum: The operational curriculum.

In the operational curriculum, it is raising her students' consciousness— what Freire (1970) called *conscientización*—that she sees as her primary ethical and political purpose as an educator and guide to the children under her almost pastoral care (Joseph and Burnaford, 1994).

The hidden curriculum is comprised of implicit messages that are sent by the official curriculum. A simple example of this is pictures in textbooks. One searches in vain in a textbook in physics of the 1950s for a picture of a girl involved in anything but being lost in rapt admiration for the boys who were always building things and solving problems involving physics. The implicit message was that being a female meant not being a physicist but being married to one and supporting him in his work. That is, of course, a legitimate choice. The point is that at that time there was not much choice about it.

The null curriculum is significant because it is what has been excluded from the curriculum—sometimes for good reason, sometimes because something is not developed or significant enough to merit inclusion in the curriculum, but sometimes because presenting it would offer information, ideas, and personal examples that would get students thinking about things that might prove threatening to existing power structures in the sponsoring society.

Thus, the films in civics classes of the early 1960s in the U.S. about 'How a Bill Becomes a Law' featured legislators who were all white and male. That people of colour and women were not among those legislators was not mentioned. They were the null curriculum, and their absence spoke volumes.

The extra curriculum is what happens at a school that is not what goes on in the classroom but in clubs, athletic programmes, student newspapers, student involvement in community programmes, and so on. Some studies and surveys estimate that the extra curriculum accounts for as much as 90 per cent of why students like to go to school—mainly because the extra-curriculum offers them subjects and activities that they enjoy and find relevant to their lives.

The phenomenological primacy of the subjective curriculum

In Learning and Education: Psychoanalytic Perspectives, Field, Cohler, and Wool (1989) published a collection of essays just four years after Eisner's study by some of the most important psychoanalytic pedagogues in the 1980s in that still undercelebrated subdiscipline of educational psychology that had evolved over the previous almost-seven decades—depth-educational psychology (Mayes, 2009). This 1,000-page volume was a significant event in the history of psychoanalytic educational theory.

In addition to containing work by the best of the *neo*-Freudians in educational theory, it introduced a new generation of *post*-Freudian theorists in education who were beginning to centre their inquiries in selfobject psychology (Mayes, 2009). Until that time, the psychoanalytic exploration of educational processes rested almost entirely upon expansions of classical Freudian endopsychic models but not any significant challenges to them (Mayes, 2009). One of contributors to this study, Barbara Cohler, also one of its editors, wrote a chapter entitled 'Psychoanalysis and Education: Motive, Meaning, and Self'. As far as I can determine, she was the first person to use the phrase 'the subjective curriculum' (1989, p. 52). Its importance as a sixth category in Eisner's five-part taxonomy of the curriculum proposed just four years earlier can hardly be overstated. Indeed, it is arguable, as I do argue, that the subjective curriculum as the sixth domain of the curriculum may also be its most important one. Why do I make this strong claim about it? To answer this will require a discussion of Jung's psychological idea of a complex—and Dewey's political idea of complexity.

The sixth domain: of complexes and complexity in the curriculum

'The subjective curriculum'—what I am now calling the sixth domain of the curriculum—refers to how the student experiences the official and operational curricula (along with its three other domains, the hidden, null, and extra, but it is the first two that I wish to underline here). In highlighting the cruciality of the student's experience in the classroom, we move towards the psychoanalytic notion of primary processes, which was introduced above.

The primary processes are in fact not only processes but also subconscious and unconscious structures that are pivotal in filtering what will reach the conscious mind as a person surveys a situation, what feelings or 'affective tones' those secondary formations will be suffused with as they emerge into ego-consciousness. These primary influences are so potent that they will continue to drench the person's now-conscious 'knowledge' of that thing and what that individual will want to do with that knowledge although the primary function determinants lie outside of conscious awareness.

The primary processes are the womb out of which the concepts of the secondary processes are always emerging, and those primary processes can either enhance or undermine secondary processes. They will, in any case, leave their originary signature along with its stamps of approval or disapproval all over those secondary, cognitive formations.

'The unconscious', wrote Jung, waxing poetic, 'is the ever-creative mother of consciousness' (1954, p. 115). Although the traditional notion in classical Jungian psychology was that concept formation was a function of the archetypally male—that is, Logos and the Great Father (Jung, 1967a, p. 186, 1970c, pp. 96, 247, 253; 1978, p. 243; Gray, 1996; p. 171; Kast, 2006, p. 118)—it is the Great Mother under the Sign of Eros who plays the more 'seminal' role in engendering the embryonic core of a concept and therefore how that concept will gestate into openly conscious form.

Furthermore, and contrary to the general notion in our 'technical-rationality' societies (Schön, 1987), an individual's subjectivity does not represent the lapse of cognition, the decay of reason's high orbit. Subjectivity is the spiritual 'engineering' that launches cognition on its every mission and will continue to do so over a lifetime of such adventures in intellectual space Subjectivity is the fuel which powers objectivity. It is not cognition's *ornament*. It is its mother. Archetypally, it is the Great Mother at the genetic core of thought. Eros engenders cognition to a much greater degree than we are aware, if we are aware of it at all, that is.

Without teacher and student interest in the curriculum, there will be a failure to properly launch, resulting in errant trajectories in its flight: Boredom, obsession, hostility, or even irrationality regarding a topic or theory because an individual's core subjectivity was not first openly and adequately dealt with from the beginning of that individual's forced participation in a field, theory, idea, or practice (Mayes, 2017b, 2019a).

For now, it is enough to note that it is subjectivity—that which the sixth domain of the curriculum caters to—that may make or break the actual success of a curriculum at official and operational levels. Why is this?

It is because if a curriculum is strong for a teacher and student at the subjective level, they will find a way to prevail in the face of the most onerous circumstances at the other five levels. But if a curriculum fails to meet the test of subjective richness and relevance, it will little avail at any other level—at least for very long. Messiaen managed to compose symphonies in his head in Nazi concentration camps. Yet, many students in contemporary classrooms couldn't come up with a creative thought to save their lives in an utterly boring classroom—even in the architecturally sleekest classrooms overflowing with a half-million dollars of computers and another half-million dollars spent to buy the latest pre-packaged curriculum on the market, which will turn out to be another pricey exercise in pedagogical futility because it is boring.

All of this stems from the phenomenological primacy of the subjective curriculum. For, out of the range of plausible answers that a student may come up with for a question being posed in class, we must ask why she chose a certain explanation and not another equally defensible one, how she did this, and what she will then do or not do in her lifeworld with all of what she 'learned' in class, or rather what little she remembers of it. How subjectively resonant a particular curriculum is, will, as a general rule, determine how well it plays out in objective reality (Dewey, 1916; Freire, 2001, 1970).

Here, indeed, is the psychic and phenomenological wisdom in Dewey's message that interest is the prime motivator of all deep and durable learning. And what has caused an individual student to have her unique interest in a topic or activity is a matter of terrific complexity, which, although it may bear some resemblance to another student's interest in the same item, is, at the end of the day, very much her own. Indeed, could anything be more complex than the mysterious landscapes of a person's interests? They are not a checklist on a dating survey, although that is how they are advertised and monetized.

One's subjective interests are the manifold and idiosyncratic motivators and determinants of a human being's very existence. They are the existential ground on which she stands. They are the difference that she *is*. They are her life-narrative expressed as core orientations, subjective *leitmotifs*. To ignore them is precisely what standardized curricula must do to be 'standardized', which is by definition the management, minimizing, and even obliteration of difference. This ignores the individual. And with that, student disaffection will surely follow.

What the student is interested in or can be invited to be interested in is what she will truly learn. What she is not interested in, or not helped to become interested in, is something that she will perhaps memorize for a test but then forget the moment she hands her test in, for that is the only sane thing to do. To perseverate in perfectionism with something that is of little or no interest to oneself is not so much an intellectual achievement as a psychological problem, an emotional subjugation, and a cognitive self-mutilation. It is a narratival toxin at the biographical level that will ramify in unpleasant ways, eventually into the political, cultural, and spiritual levels. The academically perfect student is much more likely learning for love than loving to learn (Ekstein and Motto, 1968).

So thought Melanie Klein (1932/1975, p. 103) and a generation of psychoanalytic pedagogues after her. Such intellectual obsessiveness in the child manifests the pathological compulsion of 'learning for love', to gain someone else's approval, to live the life of a 'false self' (Winnicott, 1992) or to be 'possessed by one's persona' (Jung, 1971). It is decidedly not a healthy 'love of learning' that motivates the student (Ekstein and Motto, 1968). In Existentialist terms, it is living 'in bad faith' (Sartre, 1956).

For, at base, such self-alienating 'knowledge' is specious, a bitter fruit from an addled curricular tree. It has no relevance to the student's lifeworld. It is not a part of those primary processes that fuel her being-in-the-world from her existential core. Addressing that core is not a matter of 'pampering' the student as it is sometimes ungenerously caricatured—typically for conservative political aims to show how tough one is (and thus under the archetypally pugnacious sign of Mars), not deeply educational ones (under the impassioned signs of Eros) (Mayes, 2012). To seduce a child into learning for love, not love of learning, is a crime against the integrity of the child's still-forming biographical narrative, and it will skew her narrative for the rest of her days short of deep therapeutic work, and even then irreversible damage has been done.

To care about what the student cares about is an ethically beautiful pedagogical act. It is, notwithstanding one's limitations, to have the compassion and the courage to stand before the student in her potential fullness as a human being, which is to say a subjective being, and to ask her sincerely and to ask within oneself prayerfully, 'How may I serve?'. It is an axiological matter of dealing with the student as a multifaceted 'Thou', not a pedagogical 'It' who is required to simply and superficially absorb and reproduce information regardless of its relevance to her as a being of worth and a spectrum of potentials (Buber, 1985, 1965).

And, finally, it is a practical matter, for, in the classroom as in life, we only learn deep lessons when we are poised to learn them and not a moment before. This does not mean catering to a student's whims with a mess of watered-down, empty intellectual-calorie curricular junk-food. It means credibly lifting a student—because of the credibility of one's own love and knowledge of a field, one's own good faith and (com)passion—to a plane where, seeing the intellectual feast to which she is being invited, her being resonates and accepts. Then wearing the archetypal prophet's mantle lightly but earnestly (Mayes, 2002), the teacher in love admonishes her students in prophetic tones (Bullough, Patterson, and Mayes, 2002) to:

> Come, all you who are thirsty, come to the waters;
> And you who have no money, come, buy and eat!
> Come, buy wine and milk without money and without cost.
> Why spend money on what is not bread, and your labour on
>   what does not satisfy?
> Listen, listen to me, and eat what is good,
> and you will delight in the richest of fare.
>
> (Isaiah 55: 1–2)

To issue this invitation is both the exhilarating privilege of the teacher—and also the daunting (and sometimes dangerous) intellectual, emotional, and moral challenge. For a teacher to do this successfully is to link the student's biographical narrative with the Divinity that invests a classroom when matters of spiritual import (and these may range for any given student from learning how to repair an auto to pondering the Gettysburg Address) touch the student biographically—that is, with her life as it is forming for her at that moment, in that automotive classroom or in that lecture in a university library's history museum, or anywhere the acts of learning meld the individual and the eternal in the saving fires of education *impassioned.*

Certainly, information can be forced into us and we can be punished or rewarded into obedience. For such things, the cognitive-behavioural therapies do the job well and get paid handsomely in the balance. There is only one problem with such solutions. They do not promote learning because they are not about 'learning'. They use the child as human capital (Moe and Chubb, 2009). This turns the child into a monetary object. That is unethical. They do not love the child (Noddings, 1995, 1992). They are about 'training'— fitting the student into its 'place' in a 'military industrial-educational complex' (Cremin, 1988). Ultimately, this is not education. It is training to live in a total State—little matter whether the purposes are ideologically on the Left or Right. All that matters is obedience; for, conformity, not creativity, is the goal. 'This process', as noted above, 'begins in school, continues at the university, and rules in all departments in which the State has a hand', and 'the bigger the organization, the more unavoidable is its immorality and stupidity' (Jung, 1967b, p. 153). And, not incidentally, the more total the state, the greater its insistence upon standardized education. What better prepares a child for the totally controlled State than the totally controlled school? What more efficiently neutralizes her biographical narrative and assassinates her eternal narrative, and replaces it than the wickedly conjoined trauma and trivia of a specious national-narrative purveyed by a pedagogically poisoning State?

As Dewey (1916) saw, the destiny of America depends on the liveliness of its educational system, its attentiveness to the individual student in his complexity, its dedication to honouring the student's unique and multifarious interests. Thus, how much and how well the schools honour the teacher's and student's subjectivity is a measure of its success as a school—just as a democracy is a success exactly to the degree that it honours and protects such richness in the individual citizen. It is not, I think, putting too fine a point on it to argue that the standardization of education is prophetic of the death of a democracy—a point made by McMillan in her (2013) groundbreaking study of Kierkegaard's educational views and his unwavering focus on 'that certain individual'.

It all boils down to the difference between, on one hand, a curriculum that a student can appropriate in her narratival growth as an intellectually and spiritually adventurous agent or, on the other hand, a curriculum that appropriates her as a hapless political object whose soul has been squeezed out by the ironclad fist of the State.

Jung: the creative complex in educational processes

In psychodynamic terms, the student inevitably brings to a topic of study in the classroom her already existing *complex* of ideas, feelings, experiences, associations, and even somatic responses regarding that topic. This is what is meant by the 'subjective curriculum' and it is never the same for any two students.

As with any psychological complex, much will come into play in how a student sees a curricular point. It will involve a student's hopes and fears, attractions and repulsions, successes, and failures. Her sense of the item's relevancy or irrelevancy to her lifeworld will come to bear on her engagement with a curricular item, and this will be organically tied into her family's and culture's feelings on the topic, the political and ethical voltage the item has for them. In general, the question always arises about what symbolic associations and other subconscious processes Topic A might set off in the student from the very start. All of these factors, and so may more, all put together, account for the extreme importance of the subjective curriculum. They explain why a 'simple thought' in the classroom is never simple, just as it is never simple in a consulting room. It is complex. Indeed, it is *a complex*. In fact, every thought is. There has probably never been a completely objective thought since our specie started having them. For this reason, we must come to see that cognition is not a cold affair of simple ratiocination. Cognition is 'hot'—heated by many passions, commitments, fears, ideals, historical traumas, and future hopes (Pintrich, Marx, and Boyle, 1993).

A child who has experienced the ravages of war in his early years in a village under threat of ethnic cleansing will have a very different concept of the idea of a 'treaty' or a picture of a 'rifle' in a textbook than will a child who has grown up in the uneventful quiet of a wealthy suburban neighbour-hood. A unit of study on the ecological threat to certain types of fish off the Japanese coast will constellate quite different apperceptions in a student if his family is a poor one that depends on fishing as opposed to the child whose father is a corporate executive and the family's exposure to fish is in the form of expensive sushi rolls at a nearby pricey Japanese restaurant. If a student's holistic apperception of an idea as simple as a fish or a gun can be so varied in intensity and articulation, we can be sure that it is even more varied, even more labile, regarding more suggestive items and ideas. Every thought is a complex.

Does this mean, then, that every thought is pathological? Not at all. The notion that a 'complex' is something we 'have' that indicates an underlying 'illness' is not what Jung, who coined the term, primarily meant by it, although it is what it has become in the popular mind. 'I am ... inclined to think that autonomous complexes are among the normal phenomena of life and that they make up the structure of the unconscious psyche' (Jung, 1969a, p. 104). Elsewhere, Jung, understanding of course the morbid potential of a complex, wrote that a complex

> Only means that something discordant, unassimilated, and antagonistic exists, perhaps as an obstacle, but also as an incentive to greater effort, and so, perhaps, to new possibilities of achievement. In this sense, then, complexes are nodal points of psychological life which we would not wish to do without; indeed, they should not be missing, for otherwise psychic life should come to a standstill.
>
> (1971, p. 529)

One does not have a complex because one is ill. One has complexes simply because one thinks at all. Regarding educational issues, complexes may grow pathological when they become so potent, involuted, and negatively charged that they undermine the student's healthy engagement with a concept and may, indeed, create utter confusion in the student at the conscious level.

In therapeutic settings, a complex may look like a cognitive issue to be 'cured' through talk therapy and drugs but it is often even more fundamen-tally a psychodynamic and psychospiritual issue to be explored in educational settings in terms of the student's biographical, world-historical, and spiritual narratives through 'holistic narratival reconstruction', as I have called it else-where (Mayes, 2019, 2017b, 2017c). For, consciousness, as a secondary pro-cess, rests on the personal subconscious and collective unconscious as primary processes. This accounts for what I take to be the unavoidable fact that con-sciousness can either be raised to rare heights or diminished, even disabled, by the action of the subconscious/unconscious mind on egoic consciousness depending on how well or poorly the complexes surrounding a conscious item are handled (Jung, 1968b, p. 30).

Much rides on the teacher's sensitivity to these facts. This does not require that the teacher have a specific understanding of the many components of a student's complex surrounding the item under analysis in the classroom, although the teacher may gain a sense of what some of those components are as her work with the student develops. However, simply having a sense that an 'idea', or any 'item' in the curriculum, is not for the student what it may seem to be on the surface at the levels of both the official and operational curricula is already for the teacher to take a large step forward in being alive to the emotional colouration and conceptual transformations that will be part of the student's engagement (or resistance to engage) with the item.

In this manner, the teacher becomes the student's psychodynamic ally and, thus, a positive pedagogical selfobject for the student, who will grow, not wither, in what we may dub the 'curricular holding-environment' that the 'good-enough teacher' creates (Winnicott, 1992). In this way, the teacher also sets in motion mirroring and idealizing transferences that allow the student to see herself, in the mirror of the teacher's compassion and esteem, as an empowered and loved educational being (Kohut, 1978).

In this, as in virtually any educational issue of psychodynamic gravity, there are archetypal parallels and penetrating archetypal dynamics. Archetypally, it invests the teacher with the energy and imagery of the Good Cosmic Father and Mother. Moreover, the classroom rises to its full ethical stature and pedagogical realization: It becomes the space that contains individuals engaged in I-Thou communication that is devoted to the biographical enlivenment, world-historical vision, and spiritual evolution of all involved. It is a space that—whether peopled by an itinerant preacher speaking to fishermen on an early morning Judean shore about the Kingdom of God or whether it is students excitedly searching the web in a high-tech classroom in pursuit of creating a virtuous and just society—even in this pedagogical 'now', is enfolded in that greater Now of transcendence. The biographical and world-historical space of this particular classroom thereby constellates as the sacred space of the Archetypal Classroom—what Moffett has so charmingly called 'The Universal Classroom' (1994).

This considerably increases the chances that the student will process the curriculum in a manner that will help her surface and unify the complex surrounding the item so that the item may be engaged with in a more robust, confident, and conscious way. Her primary processes—now recognized and honoured by the teacher—existing in an empathic 'holding environment' (Winnicott, 1992) that the teacher provides, and in many senses *is*, the student can now strive towards more integral secondary conceptualizations, not aggressively resist or anxiously distort them in defence of her neglected and therefore dishonoured primary processes.

This marriage of primary and secondary processes in a classroom leads to learning that is lively, organic, and usable in the student's lifeworld. It contributes to the formation of an ever-more-felicitous biographical narrative in the student through her educational experiences that now are reinforcing her self-concept as an efficacious being, not an academically hobbled one. This is the goal of social-learning theory as well (Bandura, 1986) and thus a welcome point of intersection between depth psychology and even something as different from it as a socio-cognitive-behavioural theory.

In all of this, the subjective curriculum need not be limited just to the student's experiences but will unquestionably include the teacher's experiences, *her* primary processes, for they will come to bear upon her ways of importing and imparting curricular items. The subjective curriculum becomes even more psychologically and ethically capacious; for, it now emerges as being 'the invention of both teacher and students. Each one projects distillates of his own inner perceptions and experiences, past and present, onto the subject under study, be it mathematics, reading, history, or literature' (Field, 1989, p. 853).

The great Jewish ethicist and educational theorist Martin Buber (1985) gives an exquisite example of this in his essay 'On Teaching'. He speaks of a young substitute teacher entering a classroom full of boys at the beginning of a geography class. The boys in the classroom are noisy, rude, and maybe even a little contemptuous of a mere 'sub'. The teacher already begins to hunker down to defend himself—to let these students know who's boss, and this means he must be prepared

> to say No, to say No to everything rising against him from beneath …. And if one starts from beneath one perhaps never arrives above, but everything comes down. But then his eyes meet a face which strikes him. It is not a beautiful face nor particularly intelligent; but it is a real face, or rather, the chaos preceding the cosmos of a real face. On it he reads a question which is something different from the general curiosity … And he, the young teacher, addresses this face. He says nothing very ponderous or important, he puts an ordinary introductory question: 'What did you talk about last in geography? The Dead Sea? Well, what about the Dead Sea?' But there was obviously something not quite usual in the question, for the answer he gets is not the ordinary schoolboy answer; the boy begins to tell a story. Some months earlier he had stayed for a few hours on the shores of the Dead Sea and it is of this he tells. He adds: 'And everything looked to me as if it had been created a day before the rest of creation'. Quite unmistakably he had only in this moment made up his mind to talk about it. In the meantime his face has changed. It is no longer quite as chaotic as before. And the class has fallen silent. They all listen. The class, too, is no longer a chaos. Something has happened. The young teacher has started from above.
>
> (Buber, 1985, pp. 112–113)

When 'the relationship between the teacher and student is one of pure dialogue', then classroom discourse is aesthetically and ethically life-giving
(Buber, 1985, pp. 112–113). It becomes a Genesis-site. It is phenomenologically full in freedom, but not simply freedom-in-itself, not just liberty in ethical lassitude, unlinked to a purpose, a place holder for a sad or bad nullity.
Crucially, it also 'starts from above'. A divine narrative ('as if it had been
created a day before the rest of creation') is married to a biographical one
('The boy begins to tell a story') that is set in a place that is alive with collective national narratival richness for a group of Israeli boys, the Dead Sea.
This triple-narrative—of self, society, and the eternal—is, as I have argued
throughout this book, *salvific*, for 'the young teacher has started from above'.

For consider: In the student's present biographical 'now' coupled with the
eternally present 'Now', both of them linked to a cultural narrative (that the
Dead Sea invokes here)—all of this fulfils the purpose of archetypal pedagogy. It is the reclamation of a culture's narratival past, the commitment to
the present in relation with others in mutual biographical fullness, all under
the aegis of heaven's archetypal narratives. It is an apotheosis of archetypal
pedagogy.

In sum, it is in this sixth domain of the curriculum, the subjective curriculum, that the psychodynamic and psychospiritual pedagogies dwell and
passionately meld. It is the teacher who is aware of these deep educational
processes in the first place, and even more a teacher who can deftly handle
them in a nuanced fashion through her own study and *praxis*, who will
almost always be that blessed educator the student remembers all of her life
as the most influential in helping her, the student, finally view herself as a
empowered, impassioned, and integral educational being—narratively complete, balanced among the three narratival dimensions of education. The
student has, in a sense, come home—the teacher having been the archetypal
wise elder who was never far from her student's side in this hero's/heroine's
cycle of calling, adversity, adventure, and completion in personal and cultural renewal. Campbell's (1949) heroic cycle that he descried in scouring the
mythologies of the world, the 'monomyth' … in maths class! It happens every
day courtesy of that unsung but valiant one—the ordinary teacher with extraordinary heart and a vision vouchsafed her by the eternal Teacher, whose
students we all are in this 'Universal Schoolhouse' (Moffett, 1994).

The therapeutic classroom

From the outset of psychoanalytic theory in education in the early 1920s,
there has been concern that teachers might use psychoanalytic theories
and practices in uninformed, dangerous ways with students in the classroom. Teachers might overstep their bounds as teachers, try to play analyst
to their students, and thus turn their students into their 'patients'. All sorts
of difficulties could arise from this, of course, including 1) an even greater

power-differential between the teacher and student, 2) excessive emotional intimacy that might lead to sexual involvement, 3) the teacher's inadequate grasp of psychodynamic theory and with no practical internship, and 4) the absence of parental- and student-consent for the teacher to assume the role of psychotherapist. 'Practicing without a license' might also be thrown in for good measure. These were considered important and legitimate concerns, the 'shadow side' of the subjectively focused teacher.

At the same time, it is also true that how a teacher interacts with a student during any given class may set the emotional tone for that student and indeed for many of the students in it for the rest of the day. For the student who was the focus of her response, if the response was caring or at least courteous (assuming the student's original statement merited that level of reply) or if the response was appropriately firm (assuming the student's statement was unnecessarily negative), in either case, its emotional soundwaves may spread for quite some time. Why?

First, as in the Buddha's counsel regarding right speech, right intention, right action, right livelihood, the teacher's response should provide a model of 'rightness' for the student to shape his own life by. A teacher teaches concepts. Equally, she teaches by example. The 'correct' factual and conceptual response to the student's comments and queries matter, of course. What matters just as much and often even more is how that response was given. Kierkegaard said he admired much more the individual who devoutly believed in an 'erroneous faith' and passionately tried to live its principles with a singleness of heart than he did a person who only half-heartedly believed in a 'true faith' and whose actions were correspondingly tepid (McMillan, 2013).[1] Similarly, a teacher who gives a wrong or perhaps only partly-right answer but is willing to admit it and happily seek out the correct answer is to be admired more than the Nobel Prize winner who gives the right answer in a chilling arrogance that sours the student to any further interest in the subject-matter.

Second, the teacher, as typically the student's pedagogical selfobject, affects the student through the two Kohutian transferences. In an appropriate response to the rude student, the teacher models for the student the general parameters of what would be an acceptable response to her (activating the mirroring transference) and continues to affirm her belief that the student has it within him to rise to the occasion (activating the idealizing transference). Ideally, the student will respond well on both counts; the class itself will have benefitted from witnessing this successful transferential exchange; and the classroom as a psychodynamically viable holding environment will have been preserved and even enhanced. All would have registered and been psychospiritually deepened by the archetypal drama of the teacher/student and master/disciple played out on the stage of the classroom, for few are the relationships that are as potently archetypal as the teacher-student relationship (Mayes, 2005a). Indeed, all of the students, as both participants in and witnesses to the divine comedy, like the onstage chorus in Greek theatre, come out of such a potentially explosive and destructive experience intellectually and spiritually enlarged, particularly if the teacher, aware of the psychodynamic and archetypal nature of it, handles it with an informed ease.

Of course, there is no guarantee that the student will respond productively. This being a school and not a consulting office, there are limits to how much of this sort of exchange the teacher can engage in without it wearing her and her class' patience thin … and finally rending it. At that point, vice-principals and school counsellors move in to do their work on their terms on their turf and in their offices and it is sometimes not a pretty sight. But even in this worst-case scenario, the situation was handled gracefully and instructively as possible for all concerned and all learned a crucial lesson in productive emotional transactions surrounding conceptual interchanges that day.

There is the other side of this problem, however, and it is more difficult. It is when the teacher is acting hurtfully. Although there is no easy answer to this problem, one hopes that this sort of difficulty would occur less and less the better informed the teacher is about her own inner life as it relates to her as a teacher. It is to promote such 'teacher reflectivity' with both teachers-in-preparation in colleges of education and teachers-in-the-field in professional development activities that books such as mine and my colleagues' *Reclaiming the Fire: Depth Psychology in Teacher Renewal* (Mayes, Grandstaff, and Fidyk, 2019), other texts, and seminars and workshops have been offered over the last two to three decades (Bullough, 1991; Bullough and Gitlin, 1995; Clift and Houston, 1990; Mayes, 2001, 1999).

Skillful or maladroit as the case may be, however, that teacher's response to that student on that day, if of sufficient emotional amperage, will inscribe itself on the student's heart, soul, and mind for years afterwards and not uncommonly for the rest of that student's life. Our responses to students may even have somatic effects on them. They may wind up being our physical signature on a student of how we teach. Insensitive to this, we may wind up having played a role in creating—terrible artistry!—the slumped shoulders, downturned eyes, and dull shuffle of a student who walks out of our classroom feeling that we made him feel a failure at learning, and thus a failure at life. If we are not careful, not *full* of *care*, if we are not ready to rise to 'the challenge to care in schools' (Noddings, 1995), then we have used our sacred trust wantonly, and the moral weight will be great. For, it is impossible to sit and listen to thousands of individual's narratives over several decades of pastoral counselling and not be gripped by how deep and wide a parishioner's wounds, or how high and mobile their hopes, depending to a considerable extent on the strength of how their self-narratives were formed in their school years. Our power as teachers to do good or ill must give us all pause to create space for deep moral reflection on our craft.

This is true of all those in professions that entail intimate interaction with their client. We need to understand either how upbuilding or destructive our effects on someone can be, depending upon whether we see that other person as a divinely endowed *Thou* or as simply a means to an end—an *It* (Buber, 1965). To see a child merely as capital is morally odious and inimical to a democracy (Moe and Chubb, 2009). We must resist it for their sakes at every turn. That the world may misunderstand us in this—misunderstand us in general in our art, our craft, our calling—is lamentable. It is not, however, new. We have it on good authority from a master teacher that 'if you belonged to the world, it would love you as its own. As it is, you do not belong to the world ...' (John, 15: 19). As teachers, we are in the world but not of it. How is this true of 'the called teacher'? (Stokes, 1997)

We are in the world. We are in the thick of it. As teachers, how could we not be? One half of our task is to help our students forge forceful and sane biographical narratives. We cannot do this if we are just pie-in-the-sky dreamers. We are in the world.

But we are not of the world. As teachers, how could it be otherwise? The other half of our task it to help our students work out narratives that are world-historically significant to them, and that, in turn, are tempered according to the influences of the Timeless as it touches each student uniquely. Our students will descry these higher patterns and purposes in their profession as their capacities develop. These are capacities we dare not underestimate or underserve. To do so is to miss the psychospiritual possibilities of education. This emphatically includes public education (Kniker, 1990, 1985; Nord, 1995, 1994).[2]

Fordham and the entire 'Developmental' School of Jungian psychology (Samuels, 1997) have shown that from birth the neonate is involved in tasks that are in the service of individuation, redolent of the archetypal, and that even at the tenderest ages shows signs of stirring and reaching—tendrils to the sun—towards that which is Timeless, in the very simplest of ideas and activities. Children are capable of being present, at least in some smaller measure, to curricular topics and activities that promote their individuation.

Here is an area where Jung seems to have gotten off on a wrong track in eventually asserting that individuation-work should not be attempted in therapy until the patient is in a midlife transition—roughly around 35 years old (Jung, 1978, p, 16). Shamdasani has shown, in fact, that the idea that one cannot begin to individuate until around midlife was not part of Jung's original thinking on individuation and only appeared around 1921 with the publication of *Psychological Types*.

Hence, in the very early tasks at school at Piagetian pre-operational levels, there are ways that are developmentally congruous, pedagogically innovative, and legally unobjectionable that establish early linkage of the youngest student's proto-ego formations with her intuited, intuiting Self. The students' waxing cognition offers educators at every level ways to 'educate for individuation' as the child matures (Mayes, 2017b). Indeed, Piaget himself thought it inevitable that at some point cognitive-developmental psychology and psychoanalysis would merge because they had so much to offer each other and simply because cognition separated from emotion fatally compromised both (Anthony, 1989). The plausibility of this project—that is, bringing Jung and Piaget together—is indicated by the fact that Piaget was generally positive about Jung (Shamdasani, 2009, p. 288).

Some research has begun to point out correspondences between, say, Piaget's notion of accommodation/assimilation and archetypal patterns of transformation (Knox, 2004). More broadly, this all bears witness to still unexplored territory where Jungian psychology can enter into conversation with (post-)Freudian psychology, on one hand, and with the cognitive sciences, on the other hand. In doing this, Analytical Psychology would be doing academic discourse in general a service in the recent movement to loosen up the lines that divide disciplinary boundaries, to make them more fungible, and all in the service of promoting a 'Transdisciplinarity' (Sommerville and Rappaport, 2000) that must enhance creativity in any and every field. This was something that Jung always wished for Analytical Psychology (Samuels, 1997).

Those who worry about the possibility of mischief and harm from the teacher who vaunts herself as a therapist are right to do so and we do well to heed their warning. But the cost of ignoring how psychologically consequential a classroom is and of not helping teachers learn to teach in a therapeutically wise manner—that is irresponsible.

To recap: although not a therapist, the teacher, in her cognitively consequential role, will be much more likely to fill that role effectively if she approaches it in an emotionally skillful manner. In this, her goal is not to do therapy but to create a therapeutic classroom environment in which thought and feeling are wedded. This makes cognition emotionally relevant and sturdy. Conversely, it makes emotions wise and efficacious through thinking clearly and courageously about them. These are the finest fruits of the subjective curriculum.

Psychoanalytical and psychospiritual approaches to transference in the classroom

One of the most rewarding and perplexing issues in depth psychology is that of the transference and countertransference, which is no less inevitably present and paradoxical in the classroom's subjective curriculum than in what goes on in the consulting room—and holding great possibilities in both settings.

Oskar Pfister (1922), a Protestant minister and a member of Freud's early inner-circle of disciples, pointed out that since teaching and learning are markedly emotional processes, it is essential that the teacher possess at least some knowledge of emotional dynamics in the classroom. Pfister, as a clergyman, was no doubt aware not only theoretically but personally of how transferences are particularly strong when one person holds more power in the relationship than the other does—as in the asymmetrical relationship between doctor and patient, lawyer and client, minister and parishioner—and, of course, teacher and student (Wiedemann, 1995, p. 175). Blos (1940,

p. 505), a psychoanalyst whose research focused on educational questions, argued that psychoanalytic knowledge should be part of teacher education curricula in order to help teachers understand their students' general developmental issues and at least some of their present behaviours that might otherwise disorient and even derail the uninformed teacher.

In a similar vein, I have pressed for including units on transferential dynamics in teacher education curricula on not only psychodynamic but also archetypal grounds. I have also laid out ways for teachers to engage in what I call 'archetypal reflectivity' (Mayes, 2019b, 2012, 2004, 2002, 2001, 1999).

For, the transference occurs at not only the level of the personal subconscious but also at the level of the Collective Unconscious. A student may therefore not simply be projecting issues regarding, say, his father onto the teacher. He may (and I argue, inevitably will) simultaneously be transferring archetypal energy and imagery, in this case of the Great Solar-God Father, that is at the core of that personal issue. This is really just to say that every personal issue occurs not simply as an individual affair but also a universal one. Each personal issue touches and is touched by the fact that the individual is that creature who perforce exists *sub specie aeternitatis*. There are perforce connections between the biographical and trans-biographical in the psychic economy (Sovatsky, 1998). 'Archetypal reflectivity' helps teachers see how students may be transferring archetypal issues onto them. Even more, it helps teachers see how they may be projecting their own archetypal issues about being a teacher onto their students in both personal and archetypal transferences.

For instance, a student whose father is demanding and emotionally unavailable is not only likely to project the specific image of that father onto a male teacher along with all the conflicting emotions that the father evokes in him. He will also be projecting the imagery and energy of the archetypal parallel to (or as I would prefer to put it, the psychospiritual source of) this personality type—in this case, the Senex, who, as the aged, grizzly, pinched, and loveless bad father/grandfather caricature of the good-father (Logos, the source of divine reason, balance, and enlightened conversation), raises associated images of the evil Sorcerer and the Dictator.

As another example, take the female teacher who is known for her nurturing style of teaching. Put into the mix a student whose mother struggles financially and thus rarely sees her child and is also addicted to a substance that further truncates any meaningful time together. In the nurturing female teacher's class, this student may transfer his needs onto the teacher on a 'personal wavelength', the nature and intensity of which the teacher now understands and can 'handle' whereas, without such knowledge, the ardency of her young student's devotion may be a puzzle—and a disquieting one, too.

However, the student may also be transferring onto the teacher the headier imago of the cosmic 'Great Mother', who has been rendered artistically in forms as diverse as the primal earth mother statuette in Neolithic stone called

'The Venus of Willendorf' to the delicate Jewish maiden in Giotto's The Annunciation. If the teacher is finding herself being covered with projections that seem all out of proportion to the empirical situation (and what teacher of many years of experience has not had students whose adoration or enmity is simply too much given the facts of the situation?), she may reasonably surmise that not only a personal but also an archetypal transference has constellated in the student.

Unaware of this, the teacher may be lured into an overidentification with the Mother archetype. The problem here is the excessive focus on just one aspect of the 'complete feminine' as envisaged by Irene de Castillejo (1973) in *Knowing Woman*. De Castillejo envisaged the archetypally integral feminine as a synergy of four aspects that she presented as a square with four quadrants. In Jungian psychology, this is called a 'quaternity' and has enormous significance when it appears in dreams and artistic products.

In De Castillejo's quaternity, one axis has 'Mother/Hetaera' as one of its poles; the other, 'Prophetess/Amazon'. According to De Castillejo, the integral 'female psyche' balances these elements. If the teacher in our example is led by the power of this and undoubtedly other students' archetypal projections onto her to identify with them overmuch, it may be at the cost of the teacher's psychic balance. She will lose touch with the other aspects of her psyche (whether or not it is under the aegis of a putative 'integral feminine' psyche) and the other aspects of her holistic power (Mayes, 2019b).

Such quarternary chi-square figures (i.e., boxed cross) as De Castillejo deploys are important in classical Jungian psychology, in which numbers carry psychologically symbolic weight. Indeed, Jung saw numbers as 'an archetype of order which has become conscious' (Jung as cited in Von Franz, 1991, p. 268; see also Robertson, 1995). The psychospiritual heft of a number was the primary thing for Jung, a number's functionality as the means of counting concrete items vitally important, of course, but still secondary to its archetypal function as an aspect and image of archetypal 'order'. Pauson, in her 1988 study of Jung as a philosopher, mentions Jung's interest in numbers in esoteric philosophy as spiritually vital symbols, which, important in alchemy, was also key in Jung's crowning studies in that area (1970c, 1968a, b).

All of this and more is implicated in the student's archetypal projections onto the teacher. The teacher who is familiar with such things, in concert with the related vision of her role that psychoanalytic pedagogy provides her, enjoys a more profound view of her role as a teacher. This is knowledge she can use in garnering from her work a psychospiritual energy that galvanizes her biographical narrative and links it to Sacred Time as archetypal realization—the perpetual Now immanent in the transitory now (Tillich, 1963). This is the nature of any sacrament—the embodiment of the Eternal in the temporal object or situation (Eliade, 1959, 1954).

It is in this sense that the classroom can become a site of the sacramental, whether what is being studied is art history or auto mechanics and without a word having been spoken about 'religion'. Many students will feel this and at least a few will answer to it with an ever-deepening love of the subject-matter and love of learning in general because their teacher is fully in touch with herself as a psychodynamic and psychospiritual being.

Lest one be tempted to accuse Analytical Psychology—and, by extension, archetypal pedagogy—of being overly subjective and therefore apolitical, it is important to bear in mind that although Jung privileged the personal dimension over the social one, as we have seen throughout this study, there is no doubt that he felt deeply and even insisted on the indispensability of the social dimension in the psychic economy. Individuation was not an airy-fairy escape from one's social life-tasks, and one could not credibly claim to be engaged in the process of individuation if one had not responsibly risen to one's role as a political being (Jung, 1967b, p. 224). In fact, not to realize oneself as a social and historical being must result in a neurosis (Jung, 1966b, p. 24), which is why in general therapy must see the patient in his sociohistorical circumstances, not just as some hermetically sealed and therefore solipsistic creature.

The political dimension is an indispensable aspect of the subjective curriculum in pedagogical terms because our political convictions are very important to our subjectivity in general.

Echoing the political passions of many educationists in the 1960s, Kubie (1967) felt that because 'the next goal of education is nothing less than the progressive freeing of man', the teacher could best reach this liberatory goal 'through psychoanalytically rich education' (p. 70). To accomplish this would also entail the teacher knowing 'how to cultivate and deploy aroused imaginations, and their attendant emotions' in order to help free the child both intellectually and politically—but to accomplish this in his legitimate capacity as a teacher, not a feigned one as a therapist (Jones, 1968, p. 85).

Two decades later, the same call for psychoanalytically informed educators was still being issued. For, 'the teacher, if he or she is to be successful, must function as a psychotherapist, not in the formal sense of conducting therapy sessions with the students, but in the practical sense of being alert and responsive to the psychological needs that students evince both by what they do and what they do not do' (Basch, 1989 p. 772).

At the archetypal level, helping the student find the Promethean energy that burns with such pure ardour in her burgeoning vision of herself as an actor in the world-historical drama of democracy strengthens that second striation of narrative within her and builds her up in this existentially pivotal respect.

Jung on teaching

Jung had a great deal to say about the teacher's role. He was insistent that, because of the variety and importance of the teacher's influence on the individual and culture, the teacher needed to gain a high degree of self-awareness. The role of a teacher is perennial and potent, central to the human experience—and this makes it, by definition, archetypal. Besides, Jung took it as given that the child's most influential relationship after her relationship with her parents was with her teacher (Jung, 1954, p. 55). The relationship with the parent—being primal, immediate, and extending over an entire lifetime—perhaps the most important of all archetypes and the reason humans have, time immemorial, pictured divinity as a Father and/or Mother God (Jung, 1969a, p. 156).

Because the relationship with the teacher stands right next to the parental one, it was inevitable that the teacher would be bathed in archetypal light by the student's projections of the Great Cosmic Mother and the Great Cosmic Father—those two gendered faces of the Godhead—onto him and her.[3] But … *Caveat, Magister!* Every archetype has a dark side to match the light. The teacher might also be streaked with diabolical shadows in the student's eyes.

For now, suffice it to say that the Teacher-as-Saviour ought to be prepared to be seen as also the Tempter, the Seducer, even the Devil by students from time to time. Indeed, the figure of the teacher is an especially inviting 'hook', as Jungians put it, on which others can easily 'hang' all sorts of archetypal images and roles. It can be emotionally exhausting work to be a teacher, in other words, and it wanted real psychodynamic and psychospiritual acumen in the teacher, Jung believed, to know how to handle all this psychic energy being focused on her at virtually every moment that she stood in front of the class.

She was the receptacle of their primary-process issues and projections and, as we have just seen, that is an even more embattled territory, riddled with complexes like landmines. Her effects on the student are thus colossal. That they also be wise and life-promoting was therefore a matter of great moment, and the more study and *praxis* she devotes to understanding her role, the better the chances that she will exercise her power in psychically and ethically salutary ways.

That is why it is pedagogically and psychically crucial that the teacher be conscious of the role he is playing—a consciousness that does not come easily and only through study of the psychic dynamics of teaching, reflections on one's actual *praxis* in the classroom, and consideration of one's own psychic issues that, stimulated by the student's projections, could all too easily result in the teacher's countertransference back onto the student with all its terrible range of intensities and enmeshments that would do no one any good and might well do someone great harm (Jung, 1954, p. 55). This necessitated more than just passing awareness of psychology for the teacher (Jung, 1954, pp. 51, 68, 74, 112, 132, 138), and it should be the business of teacher education programmes to make sure that the prospective teacher got what she needed (1954, p. 150).

It would be a mistake, however, to conclude that the teacher's role was powerful primarily because it was carried on contiguously to the parents'.

True: *In loco parentis* certainly raised the stakes in the dyadic interactions between teacher and student. But part of that was no doubt due to a late-19th century, industrial-society arrangement in which children were taken from parents for long stretches of time each day and placed into an educational machine that was even then beginning to fit them into their ultimate roles in the scientific-management model of society (Jansz and van Drunen, 2004). Furthermore, it was (and still is) also true that maternal transferences by the child on to the teacher were most active in the K-3 years especially, when the child was experiencing the first real separations from the mother.

But if these considerations were the most important in explaining the psychic valence of the teacher-student relationship, it would make the teacher-student dyad derivative. And that would be to miss the point. It would be like saying that the Warrior archetype is important because it is derivative of the Father-archetype or the Warrioress because derivative of the Mother-archetype. It would, in short, deprive the Teacher and Warrior/Warrioress archetypes of their independent status *qua* archetypes.

In other words, *the teacher-student relationship is not finally an epiphenomenon of the parent-child relationship. Rather, the teacher-student dyad is inherently an archetype, and one of the most compelling and autonomous ones, too.* Where could you look in the world's most foundational cultural narratives and not find the teacher-student configuration as a *leitmotif?* And what are the world's most spiritually foundational documents other than discourses between an anointed teacher proclaiming the curriculum of heaven in the schoolhouse of mortality to students both responsive and recalcitrant?

As a psychotherapist, it was evident to Jung that '[p]sychotherapy has taught us that in the final reckoning it is not knowledge, not technical skill, that has a curative effect, but the personality of the doctor. And it is the same with [the teacher]: It presupposes self-education'—which is to say: education about the self, self-reflectivity (1954, p. 140). On the strength of this notion, Caroline Zachry, a leader of the psychoanalytic wing of the Progressive Education movement, argued for the need of every teacher to undergo a psychoanalysis. That was a draconian suggestion, of course, but it did highlight the need for the teacher to be psychodynamically self-aware. Like psychotherapy, teaching revealed itself in the last analysis to be more of an art than a science. To be a psychotherapist or to be a teacher was at its root an ethical undertaking. Only secondarily (if at all) did it require mastery of a set of pre-packaged professional 'skills' and never should it foster uncritical 'dispositions' as in the corporate, 'technist' type of teacher education on display at many colleges of education today.

Indeed, current teacher education, obsessed with technical skills in the teacher that will lead to the highest scores on standardized tests for her students when she finally is in charge of her own classroom, has been the order of the day in most colleges of education for at least the last half-century

(Borrowman, 1965; Bullough, 1991; Mayes, 1997). Colleges of education would do well to push the pause button on their mad rush to find the newest and glitziest pre-packaged teacher education curricula, take a breather, and try to muster the moral equilibrium to consider the simple ethical wisdom and pedagogical commonsense in Jung's reminder that 'if the personal relationship of the child to the teacher is a good one, it matters very little whether the method of teaching is the most up-to-date. Success does not depend on the method', for its goal is 'to make real women and men', and this is done by honest encounter, person-to-person, authentic and invested, not through pre-packaged routines (1954, p. 150).

Educational problems with emotional roots

Cohler noted that although 'psychoanalytic inquiry regarding education should focus both on factors interfering with learning [as well as] those contributing to enhanced learning', it is nevertheless the case that the psychoanalytic educational theorists over the last eight decades have concentrated mostly on educational problems (1989, p. 66).

Obviously this book argues for a greater focus on the subjective curriculum than is presently the case. However, as with anything else, it must be admitted that such a focus also comes with a price. It is that teaching becomes more complex. Nothing is easier than sticking to the minute-by-minute lesson plan of clearly defined, instrumentally measurable 'learning objectives'. It minimizes the messiness of human communication. The only problem here is that very little that is of great ethical worth or emotional abundance can be communicated in this way; for, this is a matter of the subjective curriculum, and where there is subjectivity, there is complexity; and where there is complexity, there can be problems.

Thus, Melanie Klein held that Oedipal neuroses in children 'show themselves, among other things, in excessive educational difficulties and it would be more correct to call them neurotic symptoms or characterological difficulties [than educational ones]' (1975 [1932], p. 100). Concurring, Redl and Wattenberg (1951) outlined neurotic 'mechanisms' that 'inhibit learning', categorizing specific dysfunctions in a nosology of 'mechanisms of denial', 'mechanisms of escape', and 'mechanisms of shift and substitution' (1951, pp. 51–70).

Pearson (1954) saw learning problems as essentially a conflict between the ego and superego or between the ego and id.

An example of an ego-superego learning problem would be a child whose perfectionist father expects so much of him academically that he develops severe performance-anxiety and cannot perform well, or even perform at all. An ego-id problem might manifest as a child who is oedipally enmeshed with his mother and projects his conflicted feelings about that situation onto his teacher—sometimes 'performing' in seduced and seducing complicity with the teacher-mother in his obedience and excellent grades, sometimes symbol-ically manifesting resentment at the enmeshment with his mother by peri-odically lashing out at the teacher and purposefully failing at occasional but important classroom tasks, leaving the teacher mystified at this rare but distressing bad show.

Breastfeeding issues might also lie at the root of certain so-called 'learning problems', according to Eckstein (1969). After all, as I have noted elsewhere, do we not often speak of learning in terms of ingesting food?

> One devours a book, consumes information, chews on new ideas, tries to get the flavor of an argument that somebody has cooked up, takes time to digest facts or concepts, and sometimes is even required to regur-gitate knowledge on tests. Surely these colloquial parallelisms are not gratuitous but reflect a fundamental tie between taking in abstract pieces of knowledge cognitively and taking nutrients physically. Considering how much a baby learns of its world in its first feeding encounters with its mother—whether the world is safe, full, and soothing or whether it is unpredictable, unsatisfying, and meager—helps one appreciate Ekstein's surprising suggestion that 'the first curriculum struggle ever developed does not take place in school but rather ensues between mother and infant as she is nursing her baby. The full breast is the first curriculum the baby must empty and digest in order to meet the goal and require-ment of satiation'.
>
> (Mayes, 2015, p. 112)

From an archetypal angle of analysis, these gustatory issues gain even greater depth and immediacy if seen as having at their core the archetype of the Great Mother, symbolic of an ontological nurturance which, if the growing child is developing in psychospiritually rich environments, will lead to a basic, irrepressible courage and optimism in the adult. However, if this is not the psychic and ontological ground on which the child develops, it can cause depression and anxiety disorders intra-psychically, mistrust and avoidance of others and other social disorders interpersonally, and a pes-simism philosophically.

With such a blended approach ready-to-hand for the clinician, her diag-nosis and treatment of the analysand would be more variegated and more full-bodied, certainly more energetic, and therefore more likely to result in broader and more creative forms of healing in that client.

The educational psychologist, approaching a student with parallel learning problems—disengagement from the curriculum, flat affect or even animosity towards the teacher, self-alienation from classmates, and an overall picture of herself as an inferior learning-being—would also be more global and effective in helping the child develop a love of learning and a burgeoning faith in her-self as a learner (Bullough, 2001).

An integrated psychodynamic and psychospiritual approach would also be responsive to Cohler's insistence that the main topic we as educational researchers must pursue and the most important findings we can communicate to teachers are how to instil and nurture the 'courage to try' and 'courage to learn' in students (Cohler, 1989, pp. 49, 53). Bernstein echoed this sentiment: 'No matter how great the opportunity, motivation, or innate capacity, no learning will occur unless the individual finds within himself the courage to try' (Bernstein, 1989, p. 143).

Anthony brilliantly summed it all up in his notion of the 'learning ego' (Anthony, 1989, p. 108). This ego is a determining factor in the general structure and dynamics of the composite ego. In the same year, Salzberger-Wittenberg (1989) in her adventurous study *The Emotional Experience of Teaching and Learning* reminded psychoanalytic pedagogues that '[t]he many drive-determined aspects of learning—for example, conflict, anxiety, defence, repetition, regression, specific and nonspecific transferences and counter-transferences, and the like' can short-circuit even the best teacher's best efforts if she does not have at least some understanding of how the psyche responds to learning situations.

Barford introduced an exquisite idea—'the imaginal domain.' This is that 'unique domain of learning where objectives ideas and subjective emotions are joined together' (2002, p. 57). This is similar to Winnicott's 'transitional space', by the way, and key to a Jungian epistemology, which I will pick up later. Handled poorly by the teacher, this conjunction of emotion and idea in the student can lead to destructive outbursts and pugnacious face-offs with other similarly inflamed students as well as with the teacher. The psychoanalytically wise teacher, however, can canalize that energy in students and use it to impassion, elevate, and intensify classroom inquiries.

Conclusion: in praise of imperfection

Melanie Klein, in the language of classical Freudian drive theory, wrote of an 'instinct for knowledge', which she wished to encourage so that it would 'turn freely in a number of different directions, yet without having that character of compulsion which is typical of an obsessional neurosis' (1975 [1932], p. 103). One saw this obsessiveness most clearly in students 'whose defensive specialty is that of excessive intellectualization' (Jones, 1968, p. 230)—children whose neurotic strategy consists in 'the frequently defensive use of the purely intellectual act' (Piers and Piers, 1989, p. 202). When this is the case, then 'knowledge itself may be a defence against learning' as Deborah Britzman, a psychoanalyst and currently the premier interpreter of Freud to educationists, points out (Britzman, 1999, p. 10).

From a Jungian vantage point, I have advocated for what I have called 'education for individuation' (2017b, 2005a, 2005b) over the last 20 years. Although a difficult term to define and one that must be approached from many angles, it is clear that 'individuation' is the centrepiece of Jungian psychotherapy. It is never 'attained' once and for all. There are no 'Achievement Awards' for it. True, those who specially develop toward a realization of their eternal identity in their individuating processes here and now constitute a 'natural aristocracy' (Jung, 1967b, pp. 116f; 148) but only in the sense of a spiritual hierarchy of the humble. These are they who seek and speak deeper inner truths in order to find God and themselves in an upward spiral, always striving to its own apex in its idiosyncratic revolutions but realizing it will never fully complete that journey, at least not in this life. That is individuation.

Perhaps individuation's most salient marker lies in the individuating person's dedication to resolving opposites within himself, to integrate all of who and what one is in order to harness the energies those antinomies generate.

Individuation is to discover one's opposites, understand them better, and bring them into realistic and humane contact with each other—for one's own good and for the good of the world. Through it, the individual may 1) find better balance within himself, 2) develop greater realism about himself as precisely the being who carries all moral light and all moral darkness within himself, 3) inflict fewer judgements upon himself and others since he has discovered himself capable of being and doing just about anything along the clines of the dialectical poles that power his psyche, and 4) do some lasting good in the world that is now based on the foundation of melded psychodynamic and psychospiritual self-knowledge.

This moral pragmatism is most efficacious in the world when the four aspects of a total intelligence are blended in the individual. In *Psychological Types* (1971), Jung named them: thinking, feeling, intuition, and sensation and suggested ways of bringing them into dynamic interrelationship. Of course, no one is equally good in all four domains, and very few are those individuals who excel in more than two. But each intelligence can be enhanced and brought into an individuated orchestration of all our experiential capacities.

Education that promotes this in the child—that is to say, education that is holistic; education that combines the best that psychoanalytic and psychospiritual theory and practice have to offer—results in healthier adults who, joined in a democracy, keep this delicate world-historical project moving forward. It is 'education for individuation'. And it is this which—dedicated to the integral health of the individual, the maintenance and expansion of the noblest of world-historical projects, and the vision of the individual in communion with the Divine and thus being transformed into eternal beings—*this* is the antidote to the pathology of the 'perfect'—which is to day, 'the model neurotic'—student.

In such a pedagogy lies the synergy of the four functions, the honouring of the three narratives of teaching and learning, the harnessing of two dialectical poles, and the operation of it all under the Sign of that Divinity which, in religions East and West, is acknowledged as One.

Notes

1 McMillan (2013) has teased out the educational implications of this Kierkegaardian notion, among a broad array of others drawn from his major works, deftly and in depth in *A Pedagogy of Liminality: Kierkegaard's Challenge to Corporate Education.*

2 In surveying the major camps into which Jungian psychology had evolved in the 20th century, Samuels in 1997 concluded that there were three. First was the Developmental School, headed by Michael Fordham, which, disagreeing with Jung, said that archetypal psychology in general and the idea of individuation in particular applied across the lifespan, not just post-35 years old as Jung finally drew the line. Second is the classical Jungian view, with variations from theorist to theorist, of course, but pretty much taking Jung on face value and looking to archetypes as providing some sort of connection to an ontological reality. Third is the archetypal, which avoids any general statements about the nature of the archetype, seeing each person as generating his or her own highly idiosyncratic 'system' of archetypes that are key in the individual's 'soul-making', as the leader of this movement, James Hillman, puts in (or, rather, takes it from John Keats).

3 Taoism's picturing of the Divine Feminine and the Sacred Masculine as Yin and Yang in constant creative dialectic tension beautifully exemplifies an ontology of gender.

Part III

Jung, the symbol, and education

Chapter 7

The politics of the symbol as an educational project

Jung: the conservative radical

We have had several occasions to look at the difference between a hermeneutics of suspicion (Ricoeur, 1991) and a hermeneutics of hope (Homans, 1995). The former looks at a person, thing, or state of affairs and centres its attention on what is problematic in it, the latter on what is potentially constructive, even redemptive. Jung was a hermeneut of hope. It is not perhaps sexuality as such that was the cause of the breach between Jung and Freud as it was Freud's idea that every dream symbol was reducible to a covert sexual meaning. Jung felt that dream symbols, even those that had overt sexual content (and far from all of them did) were messages from nature—or at least from the individual's spiritual nature—about what was keeping the individual from becoming an integral, creative, and compassionate being, and what to do about it so that the individual would become one. That is hope. Hope is spirit. Despair is spirit denied. It is reduction. Jung was ever in search of amplification (Jung, 1970a, pp. 169–170). That Jung's was a hermeneutics of hope does not mean that he was a constant optimist, however, who went around keeping the sunny side up all the time ... or even most of the time. It meant simply that he tried, often against great odds, to discern a positive purpose in what might otherwise seem to be an irredeemable situation.

No matter its degree, a position of hope could not have been an easy position to maintain at a time when intellectuals and artists across Europe were succumbing to an all-pervasive disillusionment, precariously poised as they were on a dreadful fulcrum of history between two world wars and in a cultural moment when the modernist programme of finding a grand scheme to live by was seriously in jeopardy. Not for nothing were they called 'The Lost Generation'. Jung was part of that world-historical cohort, making it all the more remarkable that he created a picture of psyche in primary colours painted with the brush of psychospiritual possibility.

T. S. Eliot was probably more typical of his generation in echoing its nihilistic tone in 1924—when Jung was 49 years old and thus very much in the thick of it all—in his poem *The Hollow Men*. At the very end of the poem, Eliot gave voice to the *ennui* mixed with anxiety that the fear of the demise of

Western culture was breeding in his cohort. Eliot predicts that the world will end not without a glorious 'bang' but a pathetic 'whimper' (Eliot, 1971, p. 59).

It is in this *fin de siècle* context, thick with 'the sense of an ending' (Kermode, 2000), that we must understand what Jung was up against in maintaining a hermeneutics of hope.

From the vantage point of the hermeneutics of hope, Jung called for revolution in response to the crisis of Western culture. The reader will remember that this revolution was paradoxical, like most of Jung's greatest thoughts. In a move that was conservative and progressive, the Jungian revolution would entail inventing and experimenting with one's entire life. The focus would be preponderantly on the individual and not on the 'saving institutions' of *ecclesia* and state that had sustained the human being from time immemorial. That was its radical aspect. On the other hand, it would require a return to the narratives and symbols of a 2,500-year religious tradition of Western culture. They would be descried, teased out of dreams, wrestled with, and elaborated on in the therapeutic setting using a system that Jung called 'active imagination' (Jung, 1969a, p. 68; Jung, 1970a, pp. 169, 170, 172, 530–531, 653, 799–800).

This reliance upon time-hallowed foundational Western mythologies, from Zeus to Christ, was a conservative move. We will turn to this particular paradox—Jung's appeal to foundational religious narratives in a consummately idiosyncratic manner—in just a moment. But first it is important to note that Jung's work is in general riddled with paradoxes that exasperate many readers and lead them to declare him 'unreadable'. Jung was aware of this.

'Wholeness is perforce paradoxical'

He explained it by pointing out that his writings were filled with paradoxes for the simple reason that life itself is filled paradoxes. Is it not the case, he asked, that, unless we are fanatical ideologues (something Jung despised [Jung, 1969c, p. 86]), we are met with contradictory truths no matter where we turn—or even just competing truths, each of them equally compelling? Few things are black-and-white. 'Nothing is ever just one thing.'[1] Any psychotherapeutic or educational programme that wished to cover the spectrum of human experience, as any deeply meaningful psychotherapy or educational programme must—any psychology or pedagogy, that is, that wished to be complete and true to the varieties of human experience, that aimed not at being theoretically elegant but at being experientially rich, would necessarily be chock-full of paradoxes. 'Wholeness is perforce paradoxical in its manifestations', Jung wrote (1969c, p. 145).

There are two other reasons that Jung believed that to be a human being required living in paradox. They have to do with 1) the nature of language itself, which in turn has to do with our inherent epistemological limitations.

As language reaches its limits in the confrontation with the Limitless, it, like a particle in a thought-experiment reaching the end of any law that could possibly 'account for' Infinite Space, bifurcated into contradictory elements darting off to opposite ends of the universe in a split second, as if to highlight, in the languages of the laws of physics, the final paucity of any mathematical formula in the face of the Incomprehensibility that is God who, as the Author of physics, preceded physics and will outlive it, too; and 2) Jung's view of God as containing all Good and all Evil within Itself: the root paradox in Jung's dualistic theology (Jung, 1977, p. 682, 712). We will return to these points in the next chapter when we get into the ontological assumptions in Jung's understanding of symbols and its educational consequences. For now, let us pick up once more the paradox at hand: Jung's idea of a revolution.

On one hand, the revolution of which Jung spoke was etymologically just that—a 're-*vol*-ution', a 're-*volv*[e]-ing', a 're-*turn*-ing' to older truths, to ancient truths indeed. This quintessentially conservative act would require not the disruptive political action of a group of ideologically driven fellow-travellers, which we generally associate with the idea of revolution. Rather, Jung's revolution was a mostly quiet and supremely individualist act of self-scrutiny, rethinking, and reform. That is the conservative part. But for what purpose? It was to clothe ancient truths in entirely new garb, not the corporate uniform or doctrinal uniformity of an institution but the idiosyncratic apparel of one's very own fashioned on those truths in the way that served one's deepest and highest purposes best (1967b, p. 5). That is the revolutionary part.

Jung's diagnosis of therapy and education: the state of the symbol

Jung wrote that we should always closely question and test anything that is new, for it may well 'turn out to be only a new disease' (1954, p. 145). Great care must be taken in the critique of culture that the roots of a culture be maintained with an equal rigour to preserve their perennial flowering. Dispossessed of this, we are without moorings and without perspective, 'defenceless dupes' of the latest fad (Jung, 1954, p. 145).

Let us by all means critique our culture with unsentimental clarity, but let us revere at the same time the symbols, narratives, and other collective connections that a people has with higher vision—connections that that very culture has in its foundational narratives provided us and upon which our critique depends in the first place. Here, as throughout in Jung, it is the renewal of sacred symbols through personal reinterpretation and appropriation of them, not a wanton disregard for them, even a peevish enmity against them, that is key. It was crucial that education fulfil both of these functions: The responsible preservation of foundational images and narratives and their radical reinterpretation.

About their future in the remainder of the 20th century and into the 21st century, Jung mustered all his intellectual and ethical resources to avert what he feared would be their pitiable end in the times into which he had been born, a century of two World Wars—unprecedented conflagrations, almost apocalyptic—with slaughter on a scale and with a frigid monstrosity that history's most sociopathic tyrants did not imagine.

Yet even worse than all this (if such a thing were possible) were the subtler attacks on the human spirit that were spreading like squid's ink throughout the roiling waters of a profoundly perturbed European culture in the 20th century. It was all churning globally into a tsunami of history, indeed a tsunami to wash away history, leaving us, the unfortunates who would remain, shipwrecked on the horrible shores of cultural collapse. Looked at from a certain angle, Jung's work is as much cultural as psychological—a lifetime focused on salvaging the integrity of Western history and the individual psyche that now fragilely swayed on point of collapse—and rescuing his culture by pointing it a way forward.

Jung ... and Ricoeur's three narratives in the classroom and the consulting room

In the narratival terms of the first part of this study, Jung was attempting to reconnect modern man in search of a soul with the eternal wellsprings of Spirit, transcendent Time, and thereby redeem our disintegrating historical narrative while throwing a lifeline to countless individuals adrift in alienated personal narratives in which they exhaustedly stumbled towards the chasm of personal and political extinction.

What Jung was setting out to do, according to two of depth psychology's most astute interpreters, Philip Rieff (1987) and Henri Ellenberger (1976), was to balance the need for a rootedness in the symbol systems of the past (the sense of which was being lost, or rather tossed with a frightening speed and reckless abandon) with a historically nuanced direction for the future (which was now being envisaged, indeed socially engineered, in superficial political terms merely) that was coordinated by a vision of the Divine (which Jung hoped to help make personally credible to modern man in search of a soul at a time when institutional religion was falling into a historically unprecedented disfavour).

It should not be surprising that Jung's concern with and assessment of both therapy and education shared so much. Their social history was and remains almost identical. In my experience, one can teach a course in the social history of psychology and another in the social history of education and follow about the same outline headings in both (Jansz and van Drunen, 2004; Cremin, 1988). But their parallelism runs even more deeply than a sociohistorical parallelism.

For at their root and at their best, education and psychotherapy both concern themselves with thoughts and emotions at foundational levels of the student's and patient's existential makeup and situation. Hence, those two persons who were to serve as the guides in these parallel processes, the therapist and the teacher, had better make sure that they were in tune with themselves as well lest they wind up being the blind leading the blind into a ditch. It would need considerable 'archetypal reflectivity' on the teacher's and therapist's part (Mayes, 2005b, 2004, 2001, 1999, 1998; Mayes, Grandstaff, and Fidyk, 2019). Recall above how Jung said that it was not technical skill but knowing herself that made a doctor or teacher great (Jung, 1966b, p. 140). This, he insisted, requires 'self-education'.

The decaying orbit of the symbol since the Enlightenment

Jung was, in the tradition of his professional icon, the 16th-century Paracelsus, above all a physician of the *individual* soul. However (or better: therefore), he was a perspicuous observer and nimble analyst of the culture and the world-historical moment in which the individual was born, suffered, and would die in his 'being-towards-death' (Heidegger, 1964; Herzog, 1967). Despite uninformed charges against Jung that he was apolitical, he was manifestly political in every volume of *The Collected Works*, almost every essay in every volume; for, he was interested in the patient as a world-historical being who could not be understood, much less treated, apart from her world-historical situatedness. Jung knew very well that a person's truths are inextricable from the Gordian knots of ideologies, power-structures, historical wreckage, cultural complexes, and horizons of possibility and impossibility of the world into which she was born—her symbolic and literal place(s) in it (Gadamer, 1993; Jaspers, 1986).

To be sure, Jung despaired of political solutions to our most persistent questions and incurable agonies as human beings (Jung, 1970a, p. 289). It is the individual who must be the alpha and omega of all theorizing and *praxis*. That is axiomatic in Jung. The essential features of the human condition *sub specie aeternitatis* is never altered very much by a new bill, policy, or law. Jung inveighed against the naïve notion that we could craft a social utopia that would make much of a dent in the most poignant and abiding forms of human suffering. He called the attempt to do so 'the rationalist and political psychosis that is the affliction of our day' (as cited in Frey-Rohn, 1974, p. 61). Far from solving our problems, this political psychosis had become one of their major causes in modernity as everything—no matter how deserving of reverence—was reduced to its lowest common political denominator.

The Enlightenment's overvaluation of reason had led to our present obsession with rational empiricism. In this, Jung anticipated by several decades what would become postmodernism's principle critique of modernity: The riot of functionalism and the reduction of all questions to political ones (Foucault, 1980, 1979, 1975, 1972). Yet, although Jung never missed an opportunity to argue against political solutions to the existential problem of being a human being (1969b, p. 289), he also fully recognized that a therapist or teacher could not adequately understand the patient or student in her charge without considering the political constitution of that individual's life (1967b, p. 20).[2]

Jung's view of the individual was related to his view of the course of Western culture in general. Western culture had taken a wrong turn in the 18th century (Becker, 1966) because it was then that reason had divorced itself from faith, and what made it even worse was that reason had won the divorce settlement lock, stock, and barrel. Religion was left a poor thing and decreasingly relevant to the average person. Religion could now be seen only out of the corner of one's eye so as not to have to meet her pitiful stare as she homelessly roamed the streets like a pauper to sell artificial flowers as curiosities of the past. That religion is now a dead item is an idea known as the 'secularization hypothesis' in sociology.[3]

By Jung's reckoning, this massive cultural shift was an ethical error of the first order. It might even be a metaphysical one. And it was certainly a world-historical catastrophe that left 'modern man in search of a soul' (Jung, 1957).

Primary and secondary processes revisited

As we have seen throughout this study, Jung as a depth psychologist believed that it is in the womb of our personal subconscious and collective unconscious, our primary processes, that all of our conscious cognitive processes, our secondary processes, originate. Any idea is conceived in primary processes, gestates in the womb of those processes, and operates in the conscious world while constantly being coloured by them. Reason is a later stratum 'geologically' formed upon the primary process in the evolution of the psyche. It is a secondary process. The key to both individual mental health and social cultural health is to unite the primary and secondary processes so that they operate together. But that had not happened—at least, not yet, and time was running short.

This was not only a historical imperative. It was an ethical one. For, the archetypes and the collective unconscious were not only the *source* of our highest spiritual values by a classical Jungian view. They were also the *goal* of those values. They were not only primally alpha but also transcendentally omega. They were the archaeology *and* teleology of human values. That which threw us into the world and left us feeling stumped, stranded, and hopeless[4] was the very same Reality behind appearances that called us back—another paradox that lay at the heart of things. Finally, behind paradox after paradox there lay the conviction that the archetypes were nothing less than those nodal metaphysical 'formations' where the mind of God interlocked with the mind of man, insofar as the miniscule mind of man could 'take God in'—a conviction, even a confession of faith by Jung, that, he concluded, 'satisfies me completely' (Jung, 1977, p. 667). For Jung, it was the better part of wisdom to rest in that perspective since, ultimately, it is the one that puts things into the most felicitous focus and was itself a kind of grace to know, considering that 'a man can know even less about God than an ant can know of the contents of the British Museum' (Jung, 1967b, p. 235, fn. 6).

Dystopian prospects for education and therapy

Jung's diagnosis of therapy and education being the same, so was his prognosis. They were in the gravest possible risk of becoming tools in the hands of the State to blot out the individual's soul and prepare him for absorption into the high-tech degradation of the collective. If modern man was in search of a soul, it is because man was becoming increasingly 'desymbolized' and wouldn't know a genuine symbol from a fast-food logo.

Thus, of therapy he imagined in true dystopian fashion that

> The totalitarian state could not tolerate for a moment the right of psychotherapy to help man fulfill his natural destiny. On the contrary, it would be bound to insist that psychotherapy should be nothing but a tool for the production of manpower useful to the state. In this way it would become a mere technique tied to a single aim—that of increasing social efficiency.
>
> (1966b, p. 107)

Of the equally inglorious role of education in bringing this dystopia to pass, he wrote:

> [A] predominately scientific and technological education, such as is the usual thing nowadays, can ... bring about a spiritual regression and a considerable increase of psychic dissociation ... Loss of roots and lack of tradition neuroticize the masses and prepare them for collective hysteria.
>
> (1969c, p. 181)

For both of the patients in Jung's psychotherapy of culture—psychology and education— with their parallel historical developments (Jansz and van Drunen, 2004), the aetiology of the illness was the same. It lay in a rationalism that had overstepped its bounds. Not content to be an important way of knowing, it had in the last several centuries vaunted itself as the *only* important way of knowing. Jung was a physician and a scholar. It was not his intention to minimize our ratiocinative capacities. He understood the beauty of science. But he also understood how it could turn vicious in what it could bring to pass, when it cast off Spirit.

Setting things straight. The primacy of the symbol

Jung aimed to put science in its proper place and not let it run roughshod over other forms of knowing that were valid. And this was particularly true, Jung announced, when it came to that most insistent and consequential of all questions, the question of values: What should we most prize in this life and how should we best go about finding, celebrating, acting on, and preserving it? To separate those questions from the aims of therapy and education was a fool's errand.

Not only was the modern corporate state of mass men psychologically distressed; it was morally diseased too. We may pride ourselves on having outgrown the medieval notion that the devil has horns, but what we fail to see—Jung, the metaphysical dualist held—is that the devil has not gone away. The master of disguises and legerdemain, he has just traded in his horns for the political doctrines and state institutions that hypnotize the mass man, requiring him to relinquish his birthright as a unique being in search of the Divine for a mess of political pottage. 'Who would suspect [the devil] under those high-sounding names of his, such as public welfare, lifelong security, peace among the nations, etc.? He hides under idealisms, under -isms in general, and of these the most pernicious is doctrinairism' (1969c, p. 86).

It was high time we admitted that the knowledge we needed lay outside the scope of mere ratiocination. It eluded the syllogism, it transcended the merely empirical, and it was to be neither found nor created even in the world's most state-of-the-art laboratories or, worse still, states that had become laboratories of social engineering. 'The intellect is undeniably useful in its own field', Jung the physician immediately allowed, but quickly qualified it by proclaiming that it 'is a great cheat and illusionist outside of it whenever it tries to manipulate values' (1969c, p. 32). For, in issues of feelings and value, 'The concept is only a word, a counter, and it has meaning and use only because it stands for a certain sum of experience' (1969c, p. 33).

Indeed, if we looked at it straight on, apart from how invested we are in all of our 'rational' conclusions or political 'positions', would we not find that what we are pleased to call our rationality and proud to call our politics 'are in point of fact nothing more than the sum total of all [our] prejudices and myopic views' dressed up in impressive rhetoric, supported by carefully picked data no doubt but with us finding a way (subconsciously if all else failed) to dismiss data that did not suit our fancy?

From this it follows that any view of education that strives to be ethically viable and emotionally sustaining must begin there, in the collective unconscious and its archetypes. It is our poetic faculty that is 'the unacknowledged legislator of the world', Shelley proclaimed in his 'Defence of Poetry'. It is that same capability that should be the governing ethos of psychology and education.

Notes

1   In conversation with Evelyn Mayes, M.Ed. on the future of curriculum theory. 8/18/2019.

2   For particularly fine political studies from a Jungian perspective, see Samuels' (2001). *Politics on the couch: Citizenship and the internal life,* Gellert's (2001) *The fate of America: An inquiry into national character*, and Gray's (1996) *Archetypal explorations: An integrative approach to human behaviour.*

3   A hypothesis roundly challenged by the great sociologist of religion, Peter Berger (1967), and the eminent historian of religion, Martin Marty (1970).

4   A condition Heidegger (1965) called *Geworfenheit—or* 'thrown-ness'.

Chapter 8

Beyond theory

Towards psyche as symbol in archetypal pedagogy

Summary

Jung did not offer a model of psyche so much as a lexicon of it in all its ambiguity and contradictions. Concepts of enormous charm abound in *The Collected Works*. However, one looks in vain for a *theory of psyche*. Although there *are* types and degrees of systematicity in *The Collected Works*, Jung did not devise an endopsychic model. What he primarily offered were terms in a 'psychospiritual lexicon', grouped around certain types of experiences—inner and outer (although primarily inner), which he identified with key terms that encoded those experiences—archetypes, the transcendent function, *anima* and *animus*, the shadow, *puer* and *puella*, complexes, individuation, and so on. These overlapping terms were loosely contained definitionally. A systematic model of psyche would have defeated Jung's Gnostic purpose of encouraging each reader to find his own path to individuation. The pedagogical implications of this include fostering multiple perspectives on a single topic, the importance of polysemy, the privileging of individual processes over group dynamics, honouring ambiguity as a condition of creativity, a constant search for the personally sacred in subject matter. Crucially, it is made clear in this chapter that Jung saw psyche as ultimately a metaphysical reality, indeed as reality itself.

Introduction

In Jungian scholarship, there is the inevitable conversation about what concept or theory is most important in the 18 volumes of Jung's *Collected Works*.[1]

Concepts of enormous charm, open-ended and generative, abound in *The Collected Works*. However, one looks in vain for a *theory of psyche* within all those volumes. In fact, for decades one of the chief complaints against Jung has been that he does not offer us a clear-cut theory of mind (Eisendrath-Young and Hall, 1991; Glover, 1956). Let us consider the question of whether Jung had a 'theory' of psyche, and, if he did not, why he did not. To do so, we ought first to consider what is meant by a 'theory'.

There are many types of theories, ranging from theories about how the universe came into being to how best to govern a nation to how to interpret a poem. There are even theories about theories, called metatheories. In psychology most theories seem to share the following three features: 1) they are internally consistent; their constituent concepts do not contradict each other but fit; 2) they attempt to explain more or less agreed upon facts; it is the interpretation of the facts that is usually at stake, not their existence; and 3) they often aim to predict and control the behaviour of something or someone in settings and situations that the theory and the discipline of which it is a part purport to be covering.

Jung and theory

Internal consistency. Agreed upon facts

Regarding the first criterion, Jung is famous for making statements about a certain topic in one essay that it is hard to reconcile with statements about the same topic in another essay. For this reason, some readers simply throw up their hands in despair and declare him unreadable. He is not internally consistent.

Rowland (2005) brilliantly accounts for these inconsistencies in Jung by looking at him as primarily a literary writer, not a scientific one, and also as a trickster who is 'teasing' the reader into thinking for herself on matters that allow many interpretations, each of which Jung from time to time gives voice to as a 'writer' just as a novelist might offer different characters' perspectives on a single event.

I have suggested (2017a) that Jung's presentation of and conclusions about a certain topic may vary from essay to essay depending on several considerations.

First, who was his audience and how much were they willing and able to receive his complex, Gnostic view of things? We must not under-appreciate the role of Gnosticism in Jung's writings. Gnostic Christianity of the first two centuries ce, a religious perspective and a historical period that influenced Jung greatly (Ellenberger, 1970; Hoeller, 1982), addressed different groups of people differently, depending on what it judged to be their stage of spiritual advancement. They found part of their warrant to do so in the example of Paul; for, did not the Apostle himself proclaim: 'I have become all things to all men so that I may by all means save some. To the weak, I became weak ...' (1 *Corinthians* 9: 22)?

That Jung leaned markedly in the Gnostic direction is beyond controversy (Hoeller, 1982; see also Martin, 1985; Owens, 2010; Segal, 1995). In 1916, when Jung had just entered his 40s, he wrote a mystical piece called *Septem Sermones ad Mortuos, Seven Sermons to the Dead*—a consummately Gnostic text that Jung seems to have felt he 'channelled' for a 2nd-century Gnostic mystic and scholar, Basilides, who lived in Alexandria when it was the hub of learning in that century. Jung wished for it never to be published, but it saw the light of day eventually (Hoeller, 1982).

Jung the Gnostic understood the need to speak to different people in his audience at different levels simultaneously, just as the great Gnostic presenters like Basilides tailored their discourses to whether their audience was comprised mostly of *sarkikoi*, or those who insisted upon adhering to physical and moral laws in the explanation of things since they lived according to mere nature and the impulsions of the flesh; or *pneumatikoi*, those who lived according to the trans-legal, supra-empirical promptings of the Spirit owing to their advanced mystical development (Jonas, 1958). What would be required would be that the speaker present two different perspectives on complex spiritual matters, often in the same text to two very different audiences simultaneously. It was as if a politician managed to address a mixed group of radical Right and radical Left auditors about multiculturalism in terms that each group would agree with, feeling as if only it as a group was being addressed and affirmed. It is a delicate task for a speaker or writer, demanding a hefty measure of rhetorical finesse.

This is just the kind of thing that we find in St Paul's epistles, according to Gnostic scholar Elaine Pagels (1992), which she feels explains some of the tensions and apparent contradictions the letters of Paul (whom she believes to have been a Gnostic), especially around the topic of the life, death, and resurrection of Jesus. To the *sarkikoi* everything depended on whether the accounts of Jesus' life were consistent with each other and, above all, whether the physical resurrection of Christ was a historical fact or not. Their faith was based on the belief that it all happened pretty much as reported and that it implied certain absolute moral standards. For the *pneumatikoi* what mattered was not whether this or that thing was historically verisimilar in physical time and space, especially if that thing was the Resurrection. What mattered was what the symbolism of it all might mean for oneself internally. This was especially true for the *pneumatikoi* since the symbolism pointed to realities in other realms of existence that the *sarkikoi* were frankly clueless about.

Regarding not only the first but also the second criterion of what makes a good theory, Jung spoke about things and processes that many did not believe really existed, or at least that they doubted existed. To imagine a probably typical example:

> What is all this stuff and nonsense about these totally indescribable, so-called spiritual structures called 'archetypes' that somehow magically manifest themselves in different cultures over space and time in individual dreams and various cultures' religious myths? And this man claims to be a scientist? This is pure fantasy!

According to the ranking Gnostic Catholic archbishop in the U.S. and Jungian scholar Stephen Hoeller (1982), we see a similar thing going on in

Jung's writings as went on in the writings of the Gnostic masters. Jung is writing about complex, strange, and sometimes controversial matters that are not just conventionally 'psychological'; rather, they are 'psycho-*spiritual*'. These included things that 'exist' in a hazy land between inner and outer reality: synchronicity, reincarnation, telepathy, the paranormal, visions, and other 'events' and 'states of being' in the inner and outer world that not only get into spiritual matters but sometimes into *controversial* spiritual matters.

If Jung were to write of such things (and how could he not? They were the substance of his experience), it would necessarily be in veiled language. His statements would necessarily be ambiguous—now underplaying such phenomena for the scientists' sake, now affirming them for the believers' sake, both of whom were reading the same essay and to both of whom Jung wished to appeal. Some groups would doubt whether such things as he had experienced even existed at all. Other groups would receive what he had to say about complex psychospiritual matters in a wide variety of ways. Jung had to be careful, as did the Gnostic masters, to craft what he was saying to whatever group he was saying it to. It is little wonder that a reader unaware of this complex situation might think he is finding evidence of Jung contradicting himself when, in fact, Jung is trying to address differently oriented audiences about these supremely complex matters.

Among his readers would be those who did not credit the depth psychology agenda in the first place, from Freud to Jung and the whole bizarre depth-psychology crew. Then again, some of his readers were undoubtedly Freudians and more concerned, perhaps, with finding fault with him than considering insights he might have to offer. Additionally, there would be those who saw Jung as a sort of prophet of the New Age, his words almost scriptural in their authority (Noll, 1994). Finally, there would be groups of different orientations who supported his work in many ways but disagreed with each other about any interpretation of him but their own, each looking for passages to support their particular view of him while also looking for passages to discredit those who also saw him positively but from a very different angle. With such a multiple audience on such complex matters, one might well write in styles and convey ideas that 1) were not always perfectly consistent from essay to essay and 2) mentioned things one reader might just dismiss as sheer imagination at the same time as another reader might be rapt in fascination with.

A pedagogy that emerges directly from the writings of Jung will to some degree be shaped by the Gnostic vessel from which it came forth. In this instance, this means that different students in the classroom at different levels of cognitive and psychospiritual development must be approached differentially (although with equal care) by the teacher; for, each student will have different strengths and weaknesses across all the domains of her being, and all these domains will figure into how she learns, according to holistic theory,[2] from the sensori-motor to the psychosocial to the cognitive to the ethico-spiritual elements of her existential makeup (Mayes et al., 2016). From a Gnostic Jungian perspective, the holistic curriculum is thus the best kind because of its multidimensionality—a standard feature of Gnostic discourse and the ontology it rests upon (Jonas, 1958).

The evolving Jung

Second, where was Jung in his own evolving views of things, especially spiritual matters, when he wrote a particular essay? There were six decades from his first publications until his last. Changes in opinions are inevitable over even several decades, and we have cause for concern only when a person's views do *not* change over six decades.

Jung and complexity

Third, which aspect of something was Jung talking about? Jung believed that 'truth' was multifaceted and that only a zealot or opportunist would stress one aspect of the truth about something to the exclusion of other equally legitimate but contradictory aspects of it. Jung felt that he could hardly be blamed for the myriad of possibilities of interpretation and choice that greeted a person at virtually every turn in the maze of life. Regarding the nature of an archetype, for instance, Jung wrote in response to critics who said that his ideas were too complex and sometimes at odds with each other:

> I admit at once that [the idea of archetypes] is a controversial idea and more than a little perplexing. But I have always wondered what sort of ideas my critics would have used to characterize the empirical material in question.
>
> (1967b, p. 77 n15)

The educational philosopher Maxine Greene's notion of a 'Cubist Curriculum' answers to the kind of curriculum that a Jungian psychology would imply. In the 'Cubist Curriculum', as in Cubist art, one is looking at the same object from various angles simultaneously in order to not be tied into a single 'official' interpretation. The purpose is to defamiliarize consensual reality. Reality being multiple since we inhabit what William James (1977) called 'a pluralistic universe', our understanding of it must also be polyvalent.[3] This 'polysemous curriculum', as one might call it, not only encourages but requires students to take different and even contradictory perspectives on topics and to imagine answers which, although they may be negotiated as a collective process to some extent, must, at the end of the day, be appropriated individually by each student in a way that it provides her material that enriches her life-narrative biographically, world-historically and transcendentally. This notion is at the heart of archetypal pedagogy and any narratively generative curriculum.

Jung, paradox, and the transcendent function

Fourth, do we see the transcendent function at work regarding a particular issue that Jung is presently wrestling with? Are there contrarieties that Jung is trying to synthesize in order to arrive at a more nuanced understanding and reconciliation of the tension from a broader point of view and maybe even from higher ontological ground? And is he trying to exemplify it in a passage where an unsuspecting reader sees merely ambiguity or sheer inconsistency? As the wise therapist sometimes does in the consulting room, Jung sometimes 'models' processes for us in an essay to show how they work. In a sense, his life was an attempt to live out the principles of individuation in his own way and rhythm so that his readers might find their own paths to live it out in their own ways, too. 'Thank God I am Jung and not a Jungian!' Jung is rumoured to have said.

The transcendent function 'embraces but transcends' polar opposites in an ongoing dialectical process operating in the service of evolution (Wilber, 2000). An organism—whether it is a single organism or a member of a social organism—is stimulated to move to ever higher planes of vision and action. Miller (2004) reckons this concept the most important one in Jung's work. Kelly (1993) and Solomon (1994) have shown how indebted Jung was to Hegel in formulating the transcendent function.

The pedagogical possibilities of dialectics have been understood since Plato, of course. Here, they interface with Jung's views on education, establishing yet another link between Jung and Plato. This connection is not just a coincidence. Like Plato, Jung believed that essential knowledge resided at the individual's core, where her quintessential identity lay. It was a matter of reawakening a person, though dialogical means, to who they really were. This was good pedagogy and good therapy.

From a Jungian standpoint, curricular issues should thus not typically be treated as simple dichotomies—right or wrong, true or false, normal or deviant. Some issues do cry out to high heaven for judgement, of course. Beyond question is the moral depravity of such things as child abuse and genocide. Most curricular issues, however, are occasions for shuttling back and forth between poles in order to see the ethical legitimacy of each pole (at least, in its own terms) and the insights that lie in various shades of grey in between. Indeed, the philosopher of the social sciences Brian Fay (2000) has said this is a necessary strategy in any analysis that aims at looking sensitively at a range of worldviews regarding a specific issue. He calls it the 'the Principle of Charity'.

Shirley Bryce Heath (1983) in her sociolinguistic study of literacy practices among three different socioeconomic groups of students in Appalachia, *Ways with Words*, argued for turning students in a classroom into 'ethnographic detectives' of each other's cultures, their investigations of each other based on whatever curricular topic was up for analysis at that time.

The movie *Remember the Titans* (2000) masterfully shows these ideas being put into practice by a wise African American football coach with a team that suffers from a severe 'Black'/'White' division among its players. The coach assigns each member an opposite-race member of the team to 'buddy up' with throughout the season in order to research that dyadic partner's life. After a rocky start, each team member learns to honour the other's way of being and even to adopt some of its aspects into his own now-psychosocially enriched life.

Was Jung a 'theorist'?

By the first criterion of what constitutes a theory, internal consistency in the use of important terms that fit into the standard discourses of a discipline—in this case, psychology—Jung fails miserably. Or, depending upon how one looks at it, he succeeds marvellously in attending to the wisdom in Ralph Waldo Emerson's bold assertion in *Self Reliance* that 'A foolish consistency is the hobgoblin of little minds.' Jung was interested in psychospiritual experience; and experience often does not conform to our mental models of what it should be. Jung followed experiences wherever they led him—even if the journey took him to very different necks of the woods regarding a single issue.

It is worthwhile revisiting from Chapter 1 Jung's letter to a friend in 1929 in which he imagines a physicist who is speaking of atoms. This physicist understands that in saying the word 'atom', his use of it refers to 'merely his own abstractions', since what an atom really is, even *if* an atom really is, is not clear, even to a physicist for whom the term 'atom', although of great theoretical power and pragmatic usefulness, may not be referring to something really real. 'That would be my case', Jung readily confesses. 'I haven't the faintest idea what "psyche" is in itself'—a stunning enough admission from one of the leading psychologists in the history of the field. At this point, one could simply throw up one's hands, abandon the whole depth psychology enterprise, and take up coin collecting or antique car repair. The alternative, which Jung takes and so probably should we, is to carry on in this fascinating line of inquiry but all the while realizing that when we speak of 'facts' and 'models' to account for them, we are actually using 'abstractions, concepts, views, figures, knowing that they are our specific illusions'. It will be recalled that Jung called this approach one of 'non-concretization' (Jung, 1984, p. 11). It is hard to imagine anything more contrary to the second criterion of what a theory is—namely, that it works off of generally agreed upon facts—than Jung's characterization of them as 'specific illusions' and his doctrine of 'non-concretization'.

To the third criterion about whether something is a psychological theory—which is whether or not it can be used to predict and control human behaviour—Jung is the most adamantly adverse. Jung reserves his special ire for psychologies and pedagogies that render the individual no longer an individual but a predictable, controllable cog in a machine. We have seen throughout this study Jung's contempt for any corporate body that shapes individuals into conformity. Such corporate entities are evil in Jung's view. Evil is a strong word, but no other will do in light of Jung's suggestion that it is the devil himself who heads these unholy combinations.

Let us not mince words. We misread Jung here and do him an injustice if we patronizingly reduce his use of the term 'devil' to a mere rhetorical flourish. As a pastor's son, later as a Gnostic psychologist, a firm believer in God as comprised of both light and dark, and always pondering the ethical dimension of things, we may well imagine that Jung took very much to heart St Paul's notice in *Ephesians* 6: 12 that 'our struggle is not against flesh and blood but against ... spiritual forces of evil in the heavenly realms'. Indeed, it was because of his belief in the ontological reality of evil that Jung was so fervently against the Augustinian doctrine of the *privatio boni* as discussed in Chapter 3.

The Evil One's tactics are not new, Jung says. He camouflages himself to get the individual to hand over her agency and individuality to him, which has ever been his great plan, in exchange for some spurious comfort or security or pleasure. Now, however, in the age of corporatism, with its protestations of social benevolence and its tools of electronic surveillance and control, the devil, warns Jung, conceals himself under 'high-sounding names' and attractive causes ('public welfare, lifelong security, peace among the nations, etc.') to lull the only half-heartedly free human being into a soporific conformity as he stumbles his increasingly faceless way with the rest of the herd down the 'road to serfdom' (Hayek, 1944). To Jung, the growing focus on prediction and control of the individual in the social sciences was symptomatic of the times and too susceptible to governmental mischief to take it lightly.

> Jung found statistical approaches to psyche, the main means of prediction and control of the individual, especially antithetical to the spirit of psychology since they were antithetical to the spirit of man. Jung is reported to have said in a conversation that had just turned to the subject of statistics: 'Well, you know, as soon as you start talking about statistics, psychology goes out the window'.
>
> (Hart, 1997, p. 97)

Elsewhere, Jung put the case more emphatically.

> Under the influence of scientific assumptions, not only the psyche but the individual man, and, indeed, all individual events whatsoever suffer a levelling down and a process of blurring that distorts the picture of reality into a conceptual average *State policy decides what should be taught and studied.*
>
> (Jung, 1977, pp. 252–253; emphasis mine)

Statistical, norm-referenced, standardized approaches to education strip the student of her identity, unmask the State as not an instrument of democracy at the local level but a usurper and distorter of her nation's foundational stories at the federal level, and, worst of all, they turn the sky slate-grey and mute for those who now feel alienated from heaven by the excessively secularizing, stealthily encroaching State. Nothing is so antithetical to the felicitous blending of the three narratives—the personal, the world-historical, and the spiritual—as is their levelling into the uniform narrative of the statistical manipulation of the student in the service of the State.

The consequences for American schools

In 1961, President Eisenhower in his final address to the nation warned that the growth of a 'military-industrial complex' was beginning to pose a clear and present danger to American democracy. In 1988, Lawrence Cremin, the dean of American educational history, took it a step further than President Eisenhower and said that it was the newly emerging military-industrial-*educational* complex that now constituted the threat. Colleges of education have tripped over themselves running towards ever-bigger grants to research ever-more efficient means of training teachers to train children to become obedient and efficient 'worker-citizens' (Spring, 1976) through the instrumentalities of standardized education—the dystopian assault on democracy through (mis)education. Dewey is turning in his grave.

Jung apolitical, as his critics charge? To the contrary, Jung was highly political. Only, it is not the politics they want in his insistence upon the importance of tradition, the sanctity of the individual, and the dangers of corporatism and collectivism.

Experience and reason

'We miss the meaning of the individual psyche', Jung declared, 'if we interpret it on the basis of any fixed theory, however fond of it we may be' (1954, p. 93; cf. also p. 113). Elsewhere, he expands upon this idea: 'There is and can be no self-knowledge based on theoretical assumptions, for the object of this knowledge is an individual … He is not to be understood as a recurrent unit but as something unique and singular' (Jung, 1970a, p. 250).

These statements and others like them that proliferate in Jung regarding individual knowledge versus theoretical knowledge are key to understanding Jung personally, politically, culturally, and in terms of his vast scholarly output on topics that ranged from art criticism to medicine, cosmology to microphysics, and from the most sweeping world-historical dynamics to the subtlest psychodynamics. It is his total dedication to the notion of the individual that asserts itself, that indeed will allow nothing to silence it, and that Jung will not quibble or prevaricate about.

On this point, Jung was adamant: From epistemology to axiology, it was the celebration and defence of the individual that was both the cornerstone and capstone of his work. It was the individual, that 'delicate plant' to whom 'special attention' must be paid—especially in a day and age when it seemed that the individual was on the point of being 'completely smothered' by either capitalist corporatism or socialist collectivism—it was the individual who was the alpha and omega of his clinical and scholarly endeavours. And thus arose the especially pressing need in the 20th century to punctiliously nurture and jealously guard the individual as a moral agent (Jung, 1967b, p. 153).

For Jung, an individual's experience of something, her subjectivity, is irreducible. Experience cannot be peeled away to reveal something even more fundamental, something upon which experience rests. For, what would that be if not another experience? This makes sense when we consider that for Jung 'psyche' and 'subjectivity' are simply two ways of talking about the same thing—the former term having more the feel of a being and the latter a state of being. But for Jung they are very much the same. Everything we experience must be through psyche, or else how would it qualify as an experience? Similarly, everything that happens in the psyche is our experience, for what else could psyche be producing? And all of this happens before the primal data of an experience is transformed into that more processed noetic state called 'consciousness'.

And if it is true that our experience includes but is not the same thing as our conscious awareness of a situation, then psyche and subjectivity seem to be approaching some sort of superior epistemological status to simple conscious awareness. This is another way of making a point that has appeared frequently in these pages. It is that our secondary psychological processes grow out of our primary processes. We *make* our rationality but we *are* our subjectivity. As such, our psyche, our subjectivity, is also unconscious (Jung, 1969a, p. 200) and somatic (Jung, 1967b, p. 115). Subjectivity might be characterized as a type of holism. But even that does not extend the reach of psyche far enough.

For, psyche, although involving the entire organism, goes beyond the organism. This gives out onto the most extraordinary prospect—namely that psyche is not so much founded in the individual as the individual is founded in psyche. Indeed, Jung goes so far as to aver that our intuitions and experiences about not only this world but of a possible world or worlds beyond this world are necessarily products of psyche. 'Metaphysical statements are … statements of the psyche, and are therefore psychological' (Jung, 1978, pp. 61, 105). And there is more to it even than just the fact that psyche is the one that can make ontological and metaphysical statements. For finally, Jung takes this genealogy of psyche to the final degree and ascribes to it the right to make metaphysical assertions because psyche is but 'legitimately reporting its own actual metaphysical standing'; at least from a Vedantic and Buddhistic point of view: It is the psyche Jung proclaims, 'which, by the divine creative power inherent in it, makes the metaphysical assertion; it posits the distinctions between metaphysical entities. Not only is [psyche] the condition of all metaphysical reality, it is that reality' (Jung, 1978, p. 62). And then comes the climax of this ontological crescendo with the proclamation that 'Psyche is existent. It is even existence itself' (1938, p. 12).

As surprising as Jung's conclusion is here, perhaps we should not be quite so startled. After all, he is simply stating what the situation is in the Eastern religions with their extreme subjectivism: Each person's absolute centre is also one of the infinite sites of the Divine Centre, which the doctrine of 'Tat tvam asi' ('You are that [divine reality])' already implies. This declamation accords well with Jung's Gnostic perspective in which the individual's spiritual 'knowledge' (hence the term 'Gnosis,' Greek for 'knowledge') of the Divine is so refined that it is absorbed into that Divine just as the Divine takes up full residence in the spiritual adept—to formalize it in the mysterious 'ceremony of the bridal chamber' in Gnosticism (Jonas, 1958).

When all is said and done, we will probably not go too far afield in asserting that Jung's 'reporting' of Eastern spirituality is not only Jung's descriptive rendering of that spirituality but also is, in considerable measure, a confession of his own faith. Jung's aversion to 'theory' emerges as part and parcel of this faith.

Conscious thought (however instinctively we identify with it) and especially 'theory' operate many circles away from the epicentre and source, where subjectivity/experience, and, in a word, psyche, rule and reign as the universal truth. This is why a purely intellectual psychology—a strictly 'cognitive' one—is counterintuitive and even 'impractical', for 'the totality of the psyche can never be grasped by the intellect alone' (Jung, 1967b, p. 119). Indeed, how could it when 'there is no knowledge about the psyche, only in the psyche' (Jung, 1954, p. 87).

The problem with theory, despite its legitimate secondary uses, is that it is precisely that epiphenomenal form of mentation 'that satisfies intellect alone' and is thus not 'practical', for it does not bring one to oneself as the Divine and the Divine in oneself, which, in narratival terms, represents the melding of the biographical narrative and the Eternal narrative of the perpetual, sempiternal Now: the 'breaking through', the ongoing advent of the Ever Present Origin into the individual's particular life, which now also becomes the archetypal life, 'the mythic life' (Houston, 1996), and the full establishment of the ego-Self axis (Edinger, 1973).

Any archetypal pedagogy must have this breaking through of the Divine in the individual student along with the individual student's reaching out to the Divine as central to its curricular choices, pedagogical practices, and 'desired outcomes'. It need not be explicit and it certainly is not measurable. It is, however, everywhere the intention of an archetypal pedagogy to engage in the acts of education with such transcendent outcomes in mind and with the immeasurable consequences of such education radiating throughout the student's entire life—the deployment of the curriculum as an occasion for melding the individual's biographical narrative with the Eternal narrative of the ever-present 'Now' (Gebser, 1985; Tillich, 1963).

The least measurable approach to education, archetypal pedagogy is the potentially the most consequential. Not susceptible to being summarized in a PowerPoint presentation, it will endow the student with power at many points. Not associated with any particular 'style' of teaching or 'theory' of mind, it is the guiding light of the teacher whom the student will remember most fondly years later as the one who expanded his mind the most. For in the spirit of the archetypal and centred in psyche, such a teacher 'speaks with a thousand voices; he enthralls and overpowers, while at the same time he lifts the idea he is seeking to express out of the occasional and transitory into the realm of the ever-enduring' (Jung, 1966a, p. 82). The coextensive nature of the Archetypal and Eternal reveals itself in psyche.

When the matter under analysis in a classroom and the 'ever-enduring' intersect, a holy spirit descends upon a classroom, the discourses are tongued with fire, and pedagogy becomes a Pentecost.

On the particular and the universal

Looked at from another angle, we might begin by noting that theory is gen-eralizable but experience never can be. For, experience is the unique phenom-enological texture, different from person to person, of whatever presents itself to the individual from psychic moment to moment (Brooke, 2009). Consciousness knows itself as consciousness, indeed it comes into being, in its first barely articulable apperception that it is 'having' an experience. However, the truth of the matter, Jung argues, is not that consciousness is having the experience but that that experience is engendering consciousness.

Adam and Eve gain knowledge, 'become conscious', only after preexistent experiences lead them to the act of partaking of the Tree of Knowledge—that is, to the arrival at a state of conscious awareness that allows the formulation of theory. In other words, 'the psyche itself, in relation to consciousness, is preexistent ...' as *Genesis* also makes clear. As well, however, it is 'the psyche itself, in relation to consciousness, [that] is [also] transcendent' because it is the voice of Spirit that calls us beyond merely human awareness to transfigured consciousness in the Divine, as *John's* Gospel (17: 3) makes clear (Jung, 1954, p. 91). Before the apple and after the apocalypse, there is psyche, timeless but ever timely; before time and after time but making the events of time possible. What Jung says of a symbol may also be said of the psyche, pointing to the isomorphism between psyche and symbol—namely, that one cannot exist without the other (Jung, 1978, p. 30). Psyche ranges from the 'infrared' (that is, the feral core of human instincts) to the 'ultraviolet' (that is, the perfec-tion of spirit) on the spectrum of existential possibility (Jung, 1969a, pp. 211, 213) and may well be tantamount to what Jung means by his difficult but rewarding concept of the 'psychoid'.[4] The psychoid is that shared ontological space from which both matter and spirit originate. One, however, starting at the base, makes a half circle as it goes to the top. The other does the same thing on the other side. They meet to form the apex of that perfect symbol. This is the realm of the psychoid, which, wedding matter and spirit, is also the general headquarters for synchronicity.

At any rate, the Existentialist motto 'Existence precedes essence' finds its psychological correlative here insofar as 'Experience precedes theory'. Experience precedes whatever concepts we may then go on to devise about an event, outer or inner. Experience is the existential sense of an event, the kiln in which the building blocks of concepts are fired, formed, and then only later fitted together into rational structures, but structures that invisibly bear the signature of the subjectivity that produced them on every single stone.

Alchemy and theory

Concepts are made of the primordial material of experience. This is symbolized in what the alchemists called the *prima materia* that launched the alchemical process ultimately resulting in the production of gold. Of course, Jung saw alchemy not as proto-chemistry but as proto-psychology, each step of the alchemical process a symbol of the transformations of psyche from the *prima materia* of one's original, infrastructural psychic experiences, to the golden 'philosopher's stone' of the transformed, integral psyche after the alchemy of the analytical process in the consulting room (1968a, 1968b, 1970c).

Working the *prima materia* would always be the first step in creating the most lustrous philosopher's stone, or *lapis philosophorum*, the triumphant end-product of the entire alchemical process. In other words, theory, aptly called a *Philosopher's* Stone, begins in experience, the *prima materia*. And however rarefied the theory may grow, the Philosopher's Stone, also known as the spiritual alchemist's alchemical gold, will always be infused with those originary chemicals of experience that constitute it. An experience therefore can never be something that is defined by the rational reflecting on it or the discursive expression of it. An experience is that out of which rational analysis and discursive expression arise as secondary processes. Experience is the creator; the concept is the created. Experience is also the *prima materia*; theory is the alchemical gold.

Jung's point was simply but unyieldingly that the subjective precedes the objective as primordial origin. Yet it is equally true that the subjective calls the objective up to higher ground as the final realization of the rational ego coming into contact with, becoming subordinate to, and operating in harmony with the transrational Self; for, the temporal must finally serve the eternal and therein find its own realization. 'The psyche itself, in relation to consciousness, is preexistent and transcendent', Jung proclaimed (1954, p. 91).

Other mediators of 'objectivity'

There are other forces that impact the objective moment and render it less than objective. These are external forces, and thus not strictly speaking radically subjective, but potent enough forces, filled with emotional energy, to also impinge on and then make hash out of the idea that we *are* our rational consciousness—the premise of the cognitive sciences (Beck, 1995; Beck and Weishaar, 1995).

Consider that even that most objective of all things, a syllogism, is coloured not only so radically by subjectivity as such, as has just been discussed, but also by externally prompted events that trigger internally felt emotions.

Take the most famous syllogism of them all:

> Major premise: 'All men are mortal'.
> Minor premise: 'Socrates is a man'.
> Conclusion: 'Socrates is mortal'.

Where is the reader as he reads this? Is he sipping coffee at his favourite coffee house? Is it piping hot or has it gone tepid? What a bother! Now he has to go get it reheated. If only he could have a smoke in the shop where he sits as he rereads the syllogism. He wouldn't mind the tepid coffee so much. Is it peak hour, distracting him with all the noise? A slow hour? A bit sleepy as he reads the famous syllogistic lines, he drifts off for ten seconds of dazed dozing and a fitful flash of a dream of a raven picking at an old man's bones just after he reads the syllogistic conclusion, which grows from a blur to recognizable words again as he wakes up with a start, his eyes now refocusing as they tighten up and narrow into waking precision. Embarrassed and casting a furtive glance around the café, he wonders if he snored during his quicksilver nap.

At a deeper than merely environmental level but still in a subjectively strong fashion, maybe he has definite opinions about Plato one way or another. Do those come to bear on his assessment of the general argument I am making about Jung? If he studied logic in a philosophy class, did he do well or not, was the teacher agreeable or an arrogant power monger? Those emotions will also tinge how he interacts with me in our author-reader relationship right now as I, another teacher, bring up the issue of Plato. To what purposes does he, the reader, intend to put the knowledge he may gain in this book? Does he feel good about this or apprehensive? Are these purposes that he has chosen or that have been foisted on him?

And let us not forget that this is, after all, about our mortality, the spectre of the grim reaper always floating in the malevolent magic that seems to lurk in the ornate darkness of the baroque rafters, patient and grinning, casting the reaper's silent commentary over every scene and statement by his mere presence, darkening even the brightness of a syllogism, that luminescence of logic. For when it comes to premises and conclusions, death's premises are unassailable and he knows that 'all men are mortal' better than anyone. What is more: his conclusion is always the most final and irreversible of them all.

On and on the list goes of factors, internal and external, intrinsic to psyche or merely interactive with it, that will lend an absolute specificity to our coffee-house dweller's already-unique experience of the syllogism. Some of the factors cannot even be rendered in words, for they are entrenched in his neurological system and embedded in the attitudes of his community-of-origin, which he may never entirely shake, may not even ever become entirely conscious of, no matter how hard he may try (Fay, 1987). Therapy has its limits.

No one will think the same way about that syllogism as he does in that moment. Not even he will ever feel the same way the next time he encounters it, for the feeling-tone permeating his fungible thoughts at that later reading will differ from those of someone sitting next to him, reading the syllogism in a conceptually similar manner but experiencing the syllogism in a phenomenologically idiosyncratic manner; for, his reading is founded on primary processes that are entirely his own. To try to communicate what they are, exactly, is like trying to explain the colour turquoise to a non-sighted person. One's experience is fundamental. It is incommunicable in itself but the basis upon which all one's conceptualizations and communications arise.

Everything rests upon this basis, even something very objective. Perform a differential equation, for instance, and it is still an experience that is entirely one's own for reasons that are embedded in and encrusted with one's associations, imaginings, hopes, and fears that surround him. For he is still someone who is doing advanced maths for certain reasons that are tied into larger and deeper purposes that are inextricable from his lifeworld and his life-story.

Other circumstances and conditions, in this case, world-historical, affect the performance of the mathematical operation, too. For instance, if the person doing the differential equation had been a woman 70 years ago, she would have been thought a very strange creature indeed since it was considered unfeminine to do advanced mathematics. Most men would have avoided her, been intimidated by her, and possibly even laughed at her to her face for being such a 'freak'. Had she chosen maths as a career and taken it to the professorial level, hers would probably have been a lonely life indeed.

Now, if something as objective as a syllogism or a differential equation already places one squarely in a subjective universe, how much more, *a fortiori*, does an emotionally, politically, ethically, or spiritually mercurial or incendiary idea invite, if not incite, all sorts of experiential tidal waves? All knowledge is had—every shred of it—only insofar as it is primarily processed by psyche. As noted above, Jung insisted 'there is no knowledge about the psyche, only knowledge in the psyche' (1954, p. 87).

Jung v. Freud on theory

This attitude stands in stark contrast to Freud's attempt at scientific explanations of what the psyche 'is' and how it 'really' operates. Jung's tentativeness about the enigma of the psyche was one of the major reasons for his break with Freud around 1912 (Bair, 2003). For, Freud, a product of 18th-century scientism and 19th-century naturalism, believed that there were laws of psyche that governed human behaviour (Becker, 1966; Rieff, 1961). This had to be the case, Freud felt, if psychoanalysis were to survive academic politics to become a scientific theory (Ellenberger, 1970). But building a theory was precisely not what Jung was aiming at and this tension contributed to their falling out.

In his 'scientism', Freud was a product of 18th-century Enlightenment rationalism and 19th-century naturalism, which clung to the fond hope that reason could discover ultimate ethical and ontological truths in natural laws—or at least that it could find those ultimate truths by using the same investigative procedures that had been used to discover those natural laws (Becker, 1966; Foucault, 1975; Rieff, 1961). Freud did what Jung refused to do—concretize his terms and constructs.

Jung takes a humbler approach, noting throughout his writings that it is *hubris* to fancy that such an evolutionarily-late-and-limited an organ as the human brain could understand things, much less control them, in any great measure of wisdom or security. If we must theorize and make models, then let us do so with a large grain of salt, understanding that these are mental pictures that we fashion out of our own inner need, not necessarily because they are a 'mirror of nature', reflecting how things 'really are' (Rorty, 1981).

Theorizing psyche

The challenges to the mind in trying to construct models or theories of nature increased exponentially, Jung pointed out, when the natural phenomenon that one was theorizing or modelling was the mind itself. For, theorizing requires standing apart from the thing one is theorizing about in order to get a detached purchase on it. How in the world could mind ever stand apart from itself to theorize itself? How could it 'take out' and subject to 'analysis' the very thing that made analysis possible in the first place? The answer to that question, of course, is that it couldn't—at least, not without some sort of metaphysical self-division that takes us well beyond the realm of theorizing and into esoteric spiritual practices, about which I am not competent to speculate.[5]

Apart from such yogic feats, the self-theorizing mind would simply sink under the unbearable epistemological weight of having to understand something by using the very thing one does not understand to accomplish the understanding of it. One would need to know the mystery to solve the mystery.

Thus, it is important that the reader of Jung keep in mind that Jung, in his confrontation with psyche and the terms and constructs he devised to engage in that ontological meeting, was not positing a model of mind. Different interpreters of Jung are perfectly free, of course, to do so from his writings. What I am arguing is that this is not what Jung was doing. I am taking seriously his statement that 'we miss the meaning of the individual psyche if we interpret it on the basis of any fixed theory'.

So, if Jung was not theorizing in his writing, what was he doing? I would like to suggest here, as I did in a previous study of Jung (Mayes, 2017a), that he was offering a lexicon of terms and constructs that each represented an aspect of his studies, personal explorations, and decades of clinical experiences regarding the mystery of psyche. What is more, these different aspects are so interwoven in such complex permutations that it is often difficult to tell exactly where one starts and the other leaves off. One does not come to rest in theories and final definitions in reading Jung. One arrives at constant possibilities for further conceptualization, action, and transformation.

I am proposing that the reader of Jung's 'lexicon' is finally called upon to deploy each item, each 'node', in such a way that it opens up a range of the other thickly interconnected nodes of psychospiritual experience to explore and weave together in her own ways and for her own purposes. The resulting energic tapestries will be mutable and mobile, always in process of transformation, and may, *Deus concedente*, represent varied moments and movements of her journey to her own centre, itself in movement—a centre, or series of transforming centres, that are quite unique to her but universal in that, as in the medieval theologian's definition of God, the Self is 'a centre whose circle is everywhere'.

Jung thus encourages, indeed requires, the individual to find herself in freedom and as psyche—precisely because she is unhampered by a static model—and, through acts of psychospiritual and ethical courage, to preserve the emphasis on the individual that was so key to Jung. At the same time, she does this in order to commune with the Divine that takes up residence within her. She tabernacles in the Divine as It tabernacles in her. She establishes the link with the perennial Presence that has ever been the One Narrative of Heaven. It reclaims her narrative as she affirms Its. And this dual dance of the Divine and the individual takes place on a symbol-strewn stage, designed by the cultural unconscious (Henderson, 1990) to suit her cultural contexts and commitments. Conservatively rooted in the past and its images and narratives, she is also being progressively trajected towards the future in her innovative deployment of them. The universal narrative thereby finds what Shakespeare called 'a local habitation and a name' in the individual, while, like Mary in the *Magnificat*, the individual is exalted and finds her true identity in being filled with the Universal Spirit (*A Midsummer Night's Dream*, Act V, 1, l. 1847; *Luke* 1: 46–55).

In archetypal pedagogy, these same purposes underlie what a teacher chooses to teach and how she teaches it. The idea is for the curriculum to be not only an occasion for the expansion of specific knowledge but also for the general operation of Spirit in the revelation of perennial truths. This consists of the realization of the individual student's life-story through being touched by the Universal, on one hand, and the reaffirmation of the Universal narrative by the student's receptive act of free will in sacramentally 'taking it in', on the other hand.

When the Eternal breaks through into this classroom at this time while the temporal individual breaks out into the Eternal through this classroom at this time, then the curriculum has become an instance of 'realized eschatology', the classroom a conduit between heaven and earth, and salvation a known experience in the here and now. Pedagogy thereby rises to its highest purpose: the transformation of the classroom into an educationally devotional space—a *temenos* where the language spoken is symbols. Accordingly, it is to Jung's view of the supreme importance of the symbol psychologically, politically, culturally, and ontologically, that we now return to mine it for its significance educationally, and therewith to conclude this study.

Notes

1 There are 20 volumes in *The Collected Works*. The last volumes, however, are a general bibliography and a general index to all the preceding volumes.
2 See Forbes, 2003; Mayes, 2020; 2005b; Miller, 1988 on both the theory and practice of holistic education.
3 In his essay on Picasso, Jung entirely misses these epistemological and curricular implication of Picasso's work. Jung, 1966a, pp. 135–141.
4 For more on the important and in some ways summative idea of the psychoid in Jung's work as the point of origin and point of reunion of the physical and material realms of existence, within whose circular divergence from and then reunion with each other synchronicities are ontologically founded, see Frey-Rohn, 1974, pp. 117, 121, 174; Gray, 1996, p. 58; Jacobi, 1968, p. 64;, pp. 21, 25; Pauson, 1988, pp. 35, 42; Peat, 1988, pp. 115, 154; Ulanov, 1999, p. 137.
5 For the interested reader, these matters have been approached from an archetypal perspective in two volumes edited by Joseph Campbell (1960, 1955).

Chapter 9

Archetypal pedagogy as meta-symbol

Although Jung did not hammer out a theory of psyche, his statements about symbols were literally voluminous since no topic concerned Jung more deeply in every volume of his *Collected Works* than that of the nature of a symbol (Savickas, 1979). Jung deserves a great deal more attention than he gets in the fields of semantics and aesthetics for his insights into what a symbol is. It is arguably his central theme—specifically, how catastrophic to human functioning it is at not only the cognitive level but also the psychodynamic, cultural, and ethical levels when an individual and her culture become 'de-symbolized'. For, more than just a cognitive capacity that sets us apart from other primates, the making and processing of living symbols is an existential necessity. Flowers need water. People need symbols.

What was now lacking in the 20th century were robust symbols to live by—symbols that had proven themselves to be durable historically, despite their current descent into desuetude; symbols that could be rehabilitated by being redefined by the individual in compelling new ways, which would require of her painstaking and often painful acts of self-examination. The task was enormous, historically unprecedented, and it was far from given that humanity could accomplish it and find a way to sidestep planetary annihilation.

But then again, Jung never minimized the colossal collective scope of this work, nor did he sugarcoat what it would cost the individual—at least a critical mass of them—to purposefully evolve psychospiritually. This would, he said, be an *opus contra naturam*, 'a work against [human] nature' since it would be the individual striving against the complacency of 'the natural man' to transcend himself in a Promethean courage coupled with an almost monastic humility. Only here was there hope. It was to raise human consciousness enough that the species might survive, if only by the skin of its teeth.

Lest we be lulled into a shallow New Age optimism, we must always remember that Jung's 'hermeneutics of hope' was always shadowed by Johannine premonitions of disaster, some of them, indeed, perhaps from the *Book of Revelation*, which in any case must have deeply impressed the extraordinarily sensitive pastor's son and imprinted themselves on his soul, rebellious but also susceptible, as he grew up hearing them from the pulpit and reading them in catechesis and obligatory scripture study in a home that was not only Protestant, where such study was widespread, but a rectory, where it was obligatory (Jung, 1965).

Throughout his life, Jung had had visions—some of them open ones—of cultural collapse, global conflagrations, and all manner of apocalyptic finales to the human drama. But as he saw it, these would usher in not a New Jerusalem; rather, a nuclear fire licking the surface of the entire globe. We had all been given a brief but horrifying preview of what was possible at Hiroshima and Nagasaki. It was enough.

This ending, all too possible, would, Jung said, be preceded by an era of feeble cynicism or dissociation at the individual level and either docile apathy or fanatical commitment to murderous political ideologies at the collective level. It was already upon us. If the 'modern man' now found himself 'in search of a soul', the aetiology of this psychosocial and ethico-spiritual pathology which had individuals rushing to therapy in large numbers or subscribing to vile political ideologies in dangerous droves was all too easy to diagnose, according to Jung the physician and cultural critic (1970a). It lay in the deep 'asymbolic' ditch into which we had fallen, a ditch that seemed to stretch down to Hades itself. Time was short. The end was nigh. Not since the Plague of the calamitous 14th century had Europe felt its destiny so terrifyingly (Tuchman, 1978).

Jung said we are all in need of a life imbued with ethically and ontologically relevant and credible symbols but that most of us no longer have this. We have only 'an awful, grinding, banal life' in which we have been reduced to our social identity and utilitarian function in the society. But this will never do, Jung insists, for we are creatures who need to feel that we are part a 'divine drama' and that without that feeling we will one day simply wither and die psychospiritually (1977, pp. 274).

A world-historical rift, perhaps even a gaping ontological laceration, between the now-fled Transcendental Narrative ('the divine drama') and the eviscerated personal narratives of the ordinary citizen (just 'awful, grinding, banal' stories at this point) was festering with a suppurating meaninglessness that was infecting the whole world. As mentioned in Chapter 1 and discussed in more depth in Chapter 7, Jung, the cultural epidemiologist, traced back to the Enlightenment philosophers the origin of our disease: the demythologizing of life that had landed us today in the throes of asymbolism.

Somehow (God alone knew how, but then again, man is weak) these intellectual adepts had entirely dazzled us, and we quickly turned our back on our better angels (Becker, 1966). With their deductive methodologies, coupled with the closest of inductive procedures that led to breathtaking and truly important results (such mighty improvements in man's physical life over the last three centuries!), the Enlightenment philosophers promised, just as their descendants in the sciences continue to promise, to correspondingly perfect man's social and ethical life using those same scientific means.

But this, Jung insisted, was a category error—a mistaken application of the perspectives and procedures of one field of thought and action to another. And what several centuries of such faulty philosophical parallelism had shown was that the rules of conquering tuberculosis, constructing particle-accelerators, or building vehicles that take human beings into space had little relevance, if any, to expunging evil from the human breast, building a just and compassionate society, or bringing individuals closer to a sense of the holy in inner space.

Drastic times call for drastic measures. Never had the times been more drastic than now. The drastic measure to save the day? Treaties were written on paper; paper burns. International leagues were comprised of nations; nations betray. 'Mutually assured destruction' through opposite but equal arsenals simply proliferated, upped the ante, and hastened the day of reckoning. No external answer would do the trick, for all had been tried in one form or another and had been found wanting in the balance. Man must now do that thing that he had most avoided. He must look squarely *at* himself by looking deeply *into* himself with a fierce honesty that would inevitably be excruciating (1969b, p. 208). Here was the true and final *Imitatio Christi*; our historical period, our cross. It was the Passion of Western Culture and the *Via Dolorosa* of the last three centuries that had led us to this historical Golgotha.

However, here, in the 'undiscovered self' (1958) would the human being find the wellsprings of the symbols that had previously supported humanity culturally and had invested life, however physically harsh, with meaning … but now did not. From those springs the individual could draw. We could, through inner pilgrimage, go to the source, the font of the collective uncon-scious, invest the old symbols with new life, individual by individual, as the individual appropriated those symbols in her own singular fashion, along with new symbols that would emerge in individuals in their dreams, thera-peutic processes, creative products, and simply in their deeper imaginings. These they could bring to bear in ways of seeing and being that, finally, would set a Renaissance in motion.

The biographical narrative, the cultural narrative, and the Eternal narrative would thus be revived and brought into sync again. It would be the narratival correlative of the new epoch that astrology was announcing in the shift of the Platonic month from the Age of Pisces to the Age of Aquarius (Jung, 1970a, 1969c). That the odds against it were great did not matter in light of the prac-tical fact that humanity had no choice at this point. Humanity would either find a way to re-symbolize life in each individual's and culture's connection with the heavens, or else the planet was on a collision course with nuclear extinction.

It all revolved around the symbol. Understanding the nature of a symbol according to Jung thus becomes a matter of first importance in reading him. Its importance in educational matters is equally great.

We will look at this in more depth in this chapter, primarily in order to mine Jung's writings for some of their subtler educational implications regarding the cruciality of the symbolic domain in deep educational processes. The contrary view in education, the view that the student and knowledge are things to be quantified and manipulated for socioeconomic purposes, the one that this present book has in part been written to resist, was established by Edward Thorndike.

He set the asymbolic, doggedly empirical tone for a great deal of educational research and practice with his famous proclamation in the opening years of the 20th century that 'All that exists, exists in some amount, and can be measured'. This sign-based approach to educational processes and goals is anathema to archetypal pedagogy when it is made the most important thing in educational processes as is presently the case in American education. Therefore, equally important as understanding a symbol in this educational controversy is understanding a sign.

The sign and the symbol in educational processes

The words 'symbol' and 'sign' are often used interchangeably, as if they meant more or less the same thing. And in sentences like 'This ring is a sign of our love for each other' and 'This ring is a symbol of our love for each other', the two words are occasionally functionally equivalent. But generally, the word 'sign' carries quite a different 'semantic load', as linguists put it, than does the word 'symbol'.

Sign and behaviour

To be a good sign requires that that sign mean one thing, one thing only, so that the connection between the sign and that which is signified is clear, linear, unobstructed, and efficient. The more precise and invariant the connection between the sign and the signified, the better the sign has done its job and the more smoothly has the linear path from A directly to B been accomplished— with no ifs, ands, or buts about it. A sign is unambiguous. A stop *sign* means to bring your car or bike to a halt before proceeding—nothing else. How you feel about the matter is irrelevant, and the response to the officer who stops you and asks for your identification that you don't *feel* like it just like you didn't *feel* like stopping at the sign will win you the invitation to step out of the car, now with various new problems and penalties because you failed to respond to another unambiguous, sign-related imperative: 'Please show me your driver's licence and title to the car.'

A sign is thus not only direct but *directive*. It requires a certain behaviour, B, as a congruous response to it. It can even compel that action and, as in the case of a stop sign, lead to a fine if that action, B, is not performed—or worse in this case, in which two sign-based directives were ordered and blithely ignored. It may even be the case in a sign-based communication that disobedience will call the action of the State into play to ensure compliance. As John Locke (1689/1962) reminds us in his *Two Treatises of Civil Government,* behind every sign-based directive of the State ultimately stands poised the full force of the State—its 'instruments of terror'—to police and impose it. Signs are no joking matter.

Although no fine is levied if a mistake is made in maths in a school assignment, there are still consequences that are just as bad, even worse than a one-time fee. In the student's school life, some of those repercussions of inadequately responding to a sign in either its explicit or implicit demand for a certain response (and no other) include low-track placement, marginalization in the academic culture of the school, possible ridicule, and diminished college opportunities (if any). After one's school years, the shock waves continue to spread in terms of truncated life-opportunities after one's school years and, worst of all, the general miasma that seems to seep through one's life-narrative—a story that is now stained and stymied by the sense of oneself as intellectually inadequate and perhaps even unlovable on that account. Schools have their own 'instruments of terror' to enforce their will, which is, after all, increasingly the will of the State in academic form as Cremin's (1988) military-industrial-*educational* complex metastasizes.

In general, therefore, the clearer the connection between the sign as the indicated procedure and B as the signified result, the better the sign has done its job and the more smoothly has gone the linear function of A leading directly to B. *An effective sign leaves no room for interpretation by the person who is processing it.* For, there *is* no interpretation. There is only the command and obedience, stimulus and response. Behaviourism is clearly a psychology of 'signification' (although not necessarily of 'significance', one hastens to add).

Emotion and intuition as 'static' and 'noise'

There is no room for emotion in the world of signs. Indeed, feelings are procedural *static*. A technical term for such static in systems theory is 'noise'. In addition to barring the emotional and ethical valuation of a situation, there is also but scant room for intuition in a world strictly constituted by signs. Intuition is messy because, as the soul of creativity, it entails spontaneity and the ability, even the willingness, to err. But these may too easily lead in a world of signs to procedural missteps, violations of algorithms, and so they are relegated to the category of 'noise', too.

All of these variations on 'noise' obscure the algorithms of the sign and may gum things up—sometimes fatally if the task is high-stakes, where violating instructions on a hunch or failing to complete a task because emotions spook or seduce you into ill-advised action or deflated inaction that can put a task or mission and the lives engaged in it at risk. Signs serve many necessary and even healthful functions in a wide range of circumstances so that, although we must be sensible of the politics of signification and its potentially oppressive nature, we must equally understand that signs are an integral part of our lives that it is well for us to grasp and act responsibly on. Imprecise math in calculating the angle of descent for a jumbo jet carrying 400 passengers would bring with it costs that are incalculable. Less catastrophically, anyone who has ever been stumped trying to perform a procedure in maths in some daily matter knows that the more exasperated one becomes, the more difficult it grows to solve the problem. Emotions are a fast-track to failure in the world of signs. Emotions and intuitions are in-*sign*-ificant to the situation.

On the objective and the subjective

Looked at from the cold eye of objectivity, emotions generally represent procedural static of the worst kind. They are the most glaring instances of introducing the element of personal response *to* a situation *into* the situation. That empirical static may be so great that it is impossible to 'hear' what the sign is saying—like sirens warning of a danger so loudly and incessantly that one cannot hear what the emergency rescue person is saying about how to rectify the situation.

The larger point is this: Emotional responses are expressions of how a person, a *subject,* feels about what is happening. They come directly from the person, the subject, and thus they are *subject*-ive. And in the examples just given, subjectivity may be fatal if it makes it difficult or impossible to know what must be done *object*-ively about the *objects* that are malfunctioning, or the signs that have failed to tell one how to handle those objects properly. For here, handling objects with maximum efficiency—*object*-ive knowledge— is paramount and providing such knowledge is what signs are all about. Subjectivity is forbidden in the world of signs; subjectivity, indeed, is what signs must keep in check, even eliminate, if things are not to get out of hand with, finally, hell to pay.

The primacy of the symbol

The problem, of course, is that the most important things about life are not simple binaries about objects: on/off, opened/closed, yes/no, positive reinforcement/negative reinforcement. In fact, life is generally very *unlike* that. To be sure, in the *practical* realm of keeping life moving along in physical safety and material adequacy, signs are of tremendous importance. They make life *possible.* They are, as Heidegger (1964) reminds us in *Being and Time,* 'ontic' considerations in evaluating a situation in terms of its *practical* import. They are necessary but emphatically secondary considerations, except when life and limb are at stake, and sometimes even then they are secondary, as when a soldier chooses to be tortured to death instead of revealing his comrades' present location to the enemy.

Ontic factors, although they may make life possible, do not make life *worth-while*. Only our *values* do that, and we have access to the *ontological* realm of values primarily through our emotion and intuition—an idea that runs throughout modern ethics from Kierkegaard to Camus.

Values are those feeling-saturated apperceptions that have to do with relationships with others and with the Divine; with beauty, inspiration, and wisdom; and with what makes a society good and compassionate and worth living in and dying for. In short, the most important things in life are *subjective*. Objective knowledge will not take you very far at all in arriving at ethical conclusions. As the old philosophical saw goes, 'You can't get to "ought" from "is".'

Values are matters of the heart and soul. To find them, there are no theorems; to live them out in the complexity of human experience, there are no simple algorithms (or complex algorithms either, for that matter). No equations identify or guarantee them. We arrive at them, know them, embrace them, express them, and live them as compassionately, gracefully, and honestly as we can, not through the rigid *information* imposed on us by signs but by virtue of the *wisdom* we discover through symbols.

Signs make life institutionally efficient, physically comfortable, and materially adequate. Symbols make life ethically rich, emotionally nuanced, and existentially abundant. A society that has mastered how to turn its signs to profitability but forgotten how to live in symbols prophetically is vacuous at best and will presently turn vicious, and its efficiency will turn to evil. Few things have ever been as efficient as the concentration camps of World War Two. Technical superiority without moral bearings in a nation is a world-historical catastrophe waiting to happen—and it usually does.

Signs are excellent servants but tyrannical masters, for they allow no room for individual interpretation, which, of course, rules them out, from a Jungian perspective, of possessing any authority or ability to determine what the goals of education should be, which must be precisely that which *maximizes* the possibility of interpretation—within, of course, stabilizing traditional parameters that keep a social body from being blown away by any prevailing ideological wind.

The primacy of symbols in educational policies and processes

The governing spirit of education must be 'symbolic' because the discovery of ethical values in multifaceted explorations of a topic in conversations, in which many symbolic universes have a chance to be seriously heard and deeply considered, is the greatest of educational virtues in a democracy. Indeed, Dewey felt it was the *sine qua non* of a democracy that different 'symbolic worlds' (Blumer, 1969; Hewitt, 1984) get refreshed and enlarged in each other—not that such richly various systems get sucked into a single, anti-narratival black-hole of the State's Uni-Narrative. Without such diversely flowering discourse in the classroom, a democracy would soon become a wasteland and perish, Dewey warned. It is in such discourse alone that a pluralistic vision may form around a particular issue or topic—a socially constructed one, to be sure, but also one in which individual and different cultural worldviews have been duly considered, and one in which each individual may continue to interpret the collective view in his own way. On one hand, this lively and many-faceted dialogue honours the individual's primacy while, on the other hand, such dialogue operates on the strength of a radical interdependence of all the dialogists. Such conversation must not be suffocated to death-by-boredom in classrooms that are scholastic jail cells whose bars are made of rigid, state-imposed signs and whose walls consist of the drab concrete of the intellectually eviscerating standardized curriculum. Nothing is more antithetical to a 'pedagogy of freedom' than the standardized curriculum and a pedagogy of signs (Freire, 2001).

A sign-based approach to education—and a standardized curriculum is the most extreme instance of it—disallows interpretation by the student. Under the banner of the sign, standardized testing renders education inert in an utter, abject objectivity. It is *education for signification*—conformity that prepares the student to become a 'worker-citizen' (Spring, 1976) who will perform a prescribed function in the 'the sorting machine' of the political economy after psychometric and standardized academic testing has determined what that function will be (Jones, Jones, and Hargrove, 2003; Spring, 2006).

We should, therefore, not be surprised that one half of those who become teachers have left the profession within five years. Low pay is certainly a factor. However, the teacher knew about this long before she entered teaching. Another factor in her disillusionment with the field is how teachers are, on one hand, held up high as noble, self-sacrificing servants of the nation while, on the other hand, they are daily torn down in the media as incompetent, permissive, and the source of all our social woes. Teachers suffer greatly because they know that this is how they are seen. They feel the weight of that great American pastime of exporting all of its intractable social problems to the schools. The injustice of it, the exhaustion it causes in the teachers' rent hearts, forces them to leave. And who can blame them?

But a third factor in the flight from teaching, and perhaps the main one, is the increasing corporatization of the work, the rigidity of the curricula that the teacher is compelled to deliver, and the decreasing degrees of freedom the teacher has in how she teaches 'her children' given that she is monitored by both physical and symbolic means. There are fewer and fewer safe-zones where 'subjectivity', the teacher's and the student's, may roam to resolve dialectical tensions that are the necessary fuel of any creative educational process. However, when this does happen, then the classroom discourse becomes truly democratic and the classroom becomes what Dewey called 'a laboratory of democracy' (1916).

The archetypal symbol

Since Part I of this study focused on archetypes and archetypal symbols, I will quickly review some of the major points made there to continue exploring what a pedagogy in the spirit of the symbol would look like from a Jungian perspective and juxtaposed against training in the service of the sign.

I have characterized the collective unconscious as the dynamic psychic matrix from which all our other psychic functioning—conscious, subconscious, and unconscious—emerges. It is composed of archetypes. As the source of all human symbolizing, they are best pictured poetically, in this case as constantly interacting, occasionally overlapping, and subtly transforming 'patterns of energy'—again, using the word 'energy' metaphorically, not literally, although archetypes quite possibly do leave actual energic *signatures*, a point of central concern in Jungian approaches to physics and somatics (Cambray, 2009; Meier, 1986; Spiegelman and Mansfeld, 1996).

I pointed out that it is through the archetypes that we interpret and shape our subjective and objective worlds in a distinctly human manner that has, in the most essential ways, remained fairly constant throughout history and across cultures although man's material circumstances have changed and technical knowledge has grown with a wild exponentiality.

I made the unpopular point that, in addition to celebrating diversity, it is also necessary to recognize and honour certain timeless, archetypal truths that do not change or go away. They are key to the survival of cultures, whether dominant or subdominant ones. Jung the conservative understood this well (Jung, 1967b, p. 27). For Jung, like his favourite philosopher, Kant, the most important questions are ethical ones (Stevens, 2006, p. 254). This ethical universality has vast implications for multicultural education, which I and my colleagues (2016) discussed in a preliminary fashion in *Understanding the Whole Student: Holistic Multicultural Education*. This remains a wide-open field for further theoretical and practical work in order to resist the ethical relativism that besets multicultural education, entangled as it is with some of the most ethically corrosive notions in postmodern theory, notions which finally prove to be destabilizing for subdominant cultures, not empowering, seeing as it is often its foundational myths and religious practices that are what a subdominant culture principally still has to hold onto as a source of strength in the face of the onslaught of colonialism (Geo-JaJa, 2019; Geo-JaJa and Mangum, 2003).

Although it is impossible to experience an archetype directly, it is possible to access, work with, and be worked upon by archetypes in an indirect but still impressive manner because archetypal energy manifests itself in the form of archetypal images and symbols, and these we *can* know and work with. Archetypal symbols are manifestations of the ultimately inscrutable archetypes. They are the core mysteries of life, which is another way of 'defining' an archetype. Said Jung, 'the unconscious is not this thing or that;

it is the Unknown as it immediately affects us' (1968a, p. 68). The collective unconscious is nothing other than the enigma of existence itself as it beckons human consciousness, which responds by reaching out to it. Archetypes are the 'categories' of that engagement.

The symbol is 'the best possible expression', as Jung put it, 'for something that cannot be expressed otherwise than by a more or less close analogy' (1971, p. 63, fn. 44). Jung strongly intimates that symbols point to realms of reality that go beyond mere ego-consciousness and propositional reasoning by portraying a symbol as 'the best possible expression for a complex fact not yet clearly apprehended by consciousness' (1969a, p. 75).

We can catch a vision of the tremendous range of the symbol and what it can both create and reflect by considering that it moves easily at levels stretching from the pre-rational, to and through the rational mind, and then, escaping the gravity of mere reason, the symbol crosses over that barrier of transcendence, and takes on its transrational form.

In short, having passed through all semiotic realms, the symbol is able to assume its full power as, paradoxically, 'the primitive exponent of the unconscious, but at the same time an idea that corresponds to the highest intuition of the conscious mind' (1978, p. 30).

Training in the service of the sign, education in the spirit of the symbol

As both theorists and teachers, we must carefully distinguish between 'training' (a technical project) and 'education' (a moral endeavour) and to be vigilant in preserving the great traditions of the latter before pedagogy quite succumbs to the former and becomes a mechanical exercise, not an ethical commitment (Palmer, 1998); uninspired obedience, not a theatrical art (Sarason, 1999); and a job, not a calling (Pinnegar, 2017). These differences boil down to this all-important distinction I am endeavouring to draw between Training in the Service of the Sign and Education in the Spirit of the Symbol.

Training in the service of the sign

In training in the service of the sign, the teacher's role is as logistically simple as it is existentially problematic. By being restricted only to delivering a standardized curriculum, the teacher becomes a prime means of inculcating the official version of reality, 'consensual reality' and the closely related State version of reality, in children, who unquestioningly look up to her as a reliable source, especially in the K-3 years (Crain, 2010). The teacher then becomes an agent of maintaining consensual reality through scholastic means. This is not surprising since the curricula of most State-sponsored schools are naturally designed to preserve the norms and narratives of the sponsoring culture (Pai and Adler, 2010). Several potential problems arise here, however.

Political problems for the teacher and student in sign-based training

The teacher may not fully subscribe to the norms of the sponsoring culture. Or she may see a serious discrepancy between the culture's ideals and its actual performance. Or the hidden and null curricula may contain ideological biases and skewed information that she finds politically and ethically odious and possibly damaging to her children—especially a dilemma for her when some of those biases and that misinformation may militate against the well-being of the very groups from which her students come. In these instances, the teacher is in a bind—caught between the devil and the deep blue sea. To what extent does she teach the curriculum as it is *forced* upon her and which her students will be judged by, depending on the scores they get on standardized assessments? To what extent does she resist the existentially corrosive, even ethically corrupt messages contained in the curriculum and encourage her students to do the same, thereby becoming an agent of ideological and political resistance and disruption—teaching then becoming 'a subversive activity'? (Postman and Weingartner, 1969)

Psychospiritual problems for the teacher and student in sign-based training

Meaning comes into being only when subjectivity comes into play. A classroom under the sway of training in the sign is a world of objects merely, objects among objects, the ultimate objects being the teacher and the students themselves. For to the degree that an educational system erases the teacher's and student's subjectivity and 'gives in' to the goose-stepping sign, to that very degree does the classroom become a site of alienation from self and others. When this happens, then, as Buber wrote, 'the continuing growing world of It overruns [a person] and robs him of the reality of his own I, till the incubus over him and the ghost within him whisper to one another the confession of their non-salvation' (1965, p. 46).

What Buber here cries out against from a theological position is what the pedagogical psychoanalysts have inveighed about for a century, with very little effect, from a deep psychodynamic position—namely, that the objectification of the student atrophies his 'learning ego', causes him to condemn himself as a learner, and leads him to a final judgement on himself as not only academically inept but existentially deficient (Anthony, 1989). This is a lament that has been the constant theme of the psychoanalytic literature on education for the last century (Mayes, 2009).

The other abuse of the learner is harder to spot because it is camouflaged in praise, recognition, ribbons, and medals. It is the student who learns the invidious lesson that she is important because (and *only* because) she dances so well to a corporate educational drumbeat, choreographed by the mostly hidden dance-masters of a military-industrial-educational ballet (Cremin, 1988). The price of that toxic success is that she is caught in the crazy-making conundrum of 'learning for love, not the liberating pursuit of the love of learning' (Ekstein and Motto, 1968). It is a form of child abuse by educational means (Block, 1997). Only, now the child is tied to her classroom chair with chains of satin.

The corporate occupation of the child's soul

The basic difference between training in the service of the sign and education in the service of the symbol has to do with narratives.

In training in the service of the sign, there is essentially only one narrative, just as in schooling there is by this view only the standardized, norm-referenced, 'one best system', and for the same reason (Tyack, 1974). It is that there is one criterion in terms of which all specific narratives are examined to judge the goodness of fit of the individual's biographical narrative to the overarching systemic narrative. Let us call the latter the 'uni-narrative', and it revolves around the question: 'How effectively and efficiently can this future worker-citizen called a "student" in his present developmental stages fill his function in the mechanism of the State and what must be done to maximize that?' (Spring, 1976)

It is not as if the individual's biographical narrative does not count. To the contrary, the individual's specific biography may be studied very closely, even using qualitative methodologies to do so although not for the reason many of those methodologies were originally devised—to identify, safeguard, and even enshrine human variability. Unlike in the dystopian literature of the mid-20th century, personal variations in narratives are not necessarily scrutinized in order to find ways to eradicate them. It is rather to put those differences to work for the State.

Thus, radical political slogans about guerilla warfare may become the motto of an advertising campaign for a sporting company, or a meditative technique from Theravada Buddhism intended to promote detachment from the empirical world may be packaged by a corporate education firm to use with middle-management to enhance its efficiency. Denise Gelberg (1997) has shown how Progressive educational principles and their liberating effects on children are still alive and well in schools today—but only in teaching wealthy children at upper SES schools to prepare them for a satisfying life of creativity and leadership. Lower SES children still labour under older pedagogies, 'drill and kill' methods, that prepare them for a life of social servitude and emotional diminishment.

The 'Movement'—and the coopting of the symbol

As the Movement of the 1960s disassembled into its component causes in the 1970s—health, environmentalism, sexual liberation/identity, economic justice, alternative spirituality, popular art, appropriate technology, nutritional purity, and so on—each part became the site for corporate enterprise to move in, in what proved to be, after all, a 'divide and conquer' gambit to monetize that aspect of what had purported to be a total revolutionary ideology. The 'politics of liberation' morphed into a 'politics of self-identity' (Giddens, 1991, 1990), with each aspect of the Movement representing a certain emphasis in identity that appealed differentially to different groups, which then became not sites of resistance to the prevailing culture, but adornments to different aspects of it, a culture which itself remained ideologically unchanged and structurally very similar.

Thus it is that since the tumultuous decade of the 1960s, 'difference' has become the new norm, which the State is only too willing to embrace since the State is not typically immoral as much as it is amoral. Virtually anything is permissible since that brief but consequential epoch of cultural dislocation—nothing is too distasteful, nothing too self-indulgent—as long as it contributes to the smooth operation of the slightly repositioned but still hegemonic State—or at least, as long as it does not interfere with it; and ideally as long as it maximizes profit.

Indeed, difference, when thus canalized, can be turned to the advantage of the State in the energy and flexibility it lends to the social machine while still allowing the machine to go on its world-historical way on ever greater fields of profitability and conquest (Friedman, 2000). Thus, universities have in crescendo increasingly become bastions of business-related fields always with an eye to profitability coupled with an excessive, counterintuitive, and ultimately anti-democratic indulgence of 'difference' as long as that difference may ultimately become the site of another market, which it invariably does become (Best and Kellner, 2001; Giroux and Merciades, 2001).

When difference does pose a problem to the smooth functioning of the new surveillance State, however, there are two lines of response by the military-industrial-educational complex to deal with it (Cremin, 1988). The first is to develop a therapeutic and/or educational 'treatment' to eliminate the difference. Failing that, legal measures will be put into place to punish it and prisons will be expanded (recently by private firms) to physically remove and contain the threat of difference that remains defiant.

The therapeutic and educational intervention will come in the form of treatments and curricula that, as just mentioned, do not approach personal details as unimportant. In fact, such differences are examined closely but always with an eye to the formulation of psychosocial theories and models that will be rendered mathematically, tested through lavish governmental grants in a wide variety of academic venues to assess their efficacy, and finally, if they make the grade, used as instrumentalities to enforce the will of the State. In extreme cases, the new 'instruments of terror' are not loaded muskets with bayonets affixed as in Locke's day, but electrodes affixed to the frontal lobes of enemies of the State and negative reinforcement schedules devised to neurologically guarantee obedience as in Kubrick's 1970 classic *A Clockwork Orange*.

Archetypal pedagogy as cultural resistance

The situation is reversed in archetypal pedagogy's idea of education in the spirit of the symbol. What is the spirit of the symbol in this deployment of it?

First and foremost, it fashions the goals of education in the very terms we use to describe a symbol. It is multifaceted, organically forming, and organically expanding, seeking out as many associations and implications as possible that emanate from a certain curricular issue and aiming at Dewey's Social Reconstructionist ideal of speaking truth to power, not toadying to it.

Unlike a sign, which wants a simple answer and eschews ambiguity as either error or weakness, a symbol causes us to consider a question in its moral and ontological polysemy, and to approach the question in its existential ornateness, and thus to approach moral questions in compassion, not judgement. Indeed, it requires that we hone our intellects in order to see a question for what it is, not for what our fantasizing would have it be. In this sense, symbolic ways of knowing are more realistic than sign-based ways, for symbolic knowing lets knowledge take on the complex contours that probably characterize reality much more faithfully than the simple right angles and Y-shapes of a conceptually comfortable but existentially naïve flowchart.

Empirical facts matter. Ignore them for even a day and watch the bother that accrues that must then be attended to in double measure the next day to clean up the mess. Ignore them in education and all sorts of crackbrain theories can arise that can engender Hydra-headed beasts of personal and political mischief that it takes a lifetime to rectify—and even to atone for. *The point is not that signs do not matter. They matter greatly. But they also matter secondarily.* It is a question of not putting the cart before the horse, which is what we do when we fixate on instrumentalities and lose the spirit that inspires us about how to handle signs wisely, not wickedly or wantonly.

I once read a high school maths text from a curriculum in a *Hitlerschule*—a Hitler School—from 1940. It asked students to use an algebraic formula that had just been explained to calculate whether it was more cost-effective to eliminate a group of Jews, black people, and 'mentally retarded' on the spot or to relocate them to a camp and use them for labour and human experimentation before gassing them. Any system that places the instrumental over the ethical, the sign over the symbol, is headed in that direction and may soon enough reach it, to its historical shame and to our collective horror.

To found a curriculum on signs to the exclusion of symbols is a pedagogical catastrophe. It turns a blind eye and deaf ear to the emotional nuances and ethical worth of what is being studied, how students and teachers are interacting in the process of studying it, how it all figures into the student's life-narrative, and what it might mean for democracy. In ignoring all of this—even in just giving it short shrift—and disregarding both the teacher's and the student's subjectivity, the spirit is barred from the classroom, the subjective curriculum is declared null and void, education becomes training, and the classroom will soon enough grow into a space of either apathy or resentment—two profoundly anti-narratival emotions.

Apathy is the dull dread that there is no story to be told, just random events. Resentment is the suspicion that if there is a story, it is one that is rigged against oneself. In both apathy and resentment, the past seems to have proven to be a lie; for, it has led one to this paltry present. And where the past and the present are now seen as such trivial or vexing illusions, where is there any basis for imagining, much less working to build, a significant future? It is the paralysis of time, and the paralysis of time is the essence of neurosis. Such education is thus ultimately 'training for neurosis'.

The individual wanes, denarrativized, in a curriculum built only of signs. With the past a deception, the present a calamity, and the future an impossibility, the individual freezes phenomenologically. Time stops. And the classroom—what should be a sanctuary of fellowship in a building abuzz with discourses that matter—becomes a theatre of despair, where merely memorized scripts are delivered emotionlessly and it is the actors, not the surveilling audience, who are captive. This death of hope (the crucifixion of the spirit on a corporate cross since Spirit *is* hope) becomes the real lesson that the student then carries with him for the rest of his life. A pedagogy of signs, trivializing knowledge, minimizing the learner, alienating him from others and himself, and finally preparing him only to fit into the total machinery of the State—what could be farther from the psychologically, politically, and spiritually salvific narrative of oneself 'as one or the actors in the divine drama of life', a pedagogy of the symbol best offers and which a pedagogy of *archetypal* symbolisms offers most poetically, passionately, and purposefully of all (Jung, 1977, p. 275)?

Education in the spirit of the symbol: creativity across the curriculum

The objection may understandably be raised that education taking place primarily in the symbolic mode, not in the signifying mode, is all very well and good in the study of poetry, for example, which will invariably be in the symbolic mode and not the signifying one. But what about other fields, economics or engineering, for instance, where signification is key, and where getting signs wrong can have grave consequences?

First, it is important to bear in mind that archetypal pedagogy deploys symbols as such in order to clarify and place in historical context certain roles and issues that are central to educational settings and processes: for instance, the classroom as a *temenos*, the teacher as the wise elder and the student as the hero or heroine of a heroic quest, knowledge as a philosopher's stone, and getting knowledge as an alchemical process or an odyssey through a dark forest of adventure.

However, *archetypal pedagogy uses the term 'symbol' in a manner that is itself symbolic*. The adjectival 'symbol' in archetypal pedagogy generally refers to any pedagogy in any field of study when it 1) draws on emotion and intuition; 2) is dedicated to exploring the complexity of an issue, multiple ways of seeing it and approaching its resolution; 3) uses the transcendent function to identify opposite positions on a topic, honouring both when possible, and then transcending both in a manner that brings the student to a higher plane of processing, a new vision of things; 4) understands the centrality of a student's narrative of herself as a learner in her total life-narrative and that therefore is dedicated to building her up in the 'emotional experience of teaching and learning', not tearing her down (Salzberger-Wittenberg, 1989); 5) employs archetypal reflectivity for teachers to see their work against the backdrop of the Eternal; and thus 6) encourages, indeed will not rest content with anything less than, I-Thou interactions in class that help the student identify herself as an autonomous being but one whose identity is largely formed through compassionate conversation in the company of her fellow beings. For I cannot know myself apart from how others register my presence and either bloom or wither under it in direct proportion as they either bloom or wither under mine.

There is thus nothing that is so inherently symbolic in one field that it will guarantee a 'symbolic pedagogy' in teaching that field, just as there is nothing so sign based in another field that it precludes a 'symbolic presentation'. As I have written elsewhere:

> The trigonometry teacher whose passion for the dance of a sine wave makes the brain waves of his students also dance is teaching in the spirit of the ever-expanding symbol. Such a teacher gives his students a glimpse of a landscape strewn with the sinuous blossoming of numeric functions. The English teacher who cynically deconstructs one of John Donne's Holy Sonnets and trashes its noble intent just to make a fashionable political point has sullied something of tremendous archetypal worth, turning the poem into a mere sign of an ideological agenda, one that is here today but will be gone tomorrow with the next literary-critical fad.
>
> (Mayes, 2017b, p. 89)

Education in the spirit of the symbol applies to teaching maths as much as it does to teaching literature when the teacher approaches her subject in a way that both invokes and evokes the mystery of the universe and invites her students to dance with her in a celebration of it; conversely, one can teach literature in a rote and anti-symbolic fashion when all that matters is memorizing facts about historical epochs and genres in literary criticism that may impress your guests at a dinner party but that does nothing to make you a person who has become more emotionally and morally attuned to the human condition. *Spiritus est qui vivificat!* It is the Spirit that gives life! And it gives life as easily in a chemistry classes as in the history of music if it is being taught in a fresh archetypal spirit.

In terms of the politics of pedagogy, training in the service of the sign generally winds up requiring of teachers that they be complicitous—indeed, that they be key—in a programme of socially engineering their students into objects of the State. A pedagogy of the symbol invites the teacher to find her Self in exploring her field and in sharing those discoveries with her students in compassion and creativity as subjects. She thereby sets her students moving—each in his or her own way yet also collectively in faith—toward that same Spirit whose sweet enticing invests our personal and political narratives with a goodness and a purpose that exiles cynicism and disperses despair.

Helping the student find her own sacred core, however she conceives it, however it evolves, and doing so through both 'archetypal reflectivity' and the medium of educational processes that are infused with the symbolic and are mindful of the student *sub specie aeternitatis*—this is the alpha and the omega of archetypal pedagogy.

A pedagogy of life

These, then, are finally the stakes in a classroom. Will it be a site of life or death?

Will the classroom be a temple of archetypal incarnation and resurrection; or will it be a Golgotha, where what is divine in the child is nailed to a statistical cross and tortured to despair by the edicts of a colonizing corporate army in fiscal phalanxes?

Will the student be invited into it in the sacred spirit of intellectual adventure, in psychospiritual ardency, in communion with teacher and fellow students? Will the curriculum itself serve as a vehicle for psychic expansion, ideological refining on the whetstone of democratic dialectics, and the reconfiguring of the past into a reclamation project in the service of a spiritualized future of sovereign, individuated individuals? Or will it be a grave, the death of dialogue, a dearth of community, the creeping imposition of a motionless present, paralysed and paralysing, in the stasis of state-generated 'facts' that one rejects at one's academic and professional peril but that one yields to in an act of ethical capitulation and even narratival suicide?

At the beginning of John's Gospel, we read that the Light shines in the darkness and the darkness will never overcome it. Now, at what may prove to be the apocalyptic juncture in human history that Jung foresaw and thus foretold, how we choose to educate our children—whether in that narratival Light that liberates them as individuals becoming divinized as a people or in the darkness that divides and conquers—will put John's promise to the test.

References

Adams, M. (1995). *The multicultural imagination: 'Race,' colour, and the unconscious.* London: Routledge.

Aichhorn, A. (1951 [1925]) *Wayward youth: A psychoanalytic study of delinquent children, illustrated by Actual Case Histories.* New York: Viking Press.

Ajaya, S. (1985). *Psychotherapy east and west: A unifying paradigm.* Honesdale: Himalayan International Institute.

Alter, R. (1981). *The art of biblical narrative.* New York: Basic Books.

Anthony, E. (1989). The psychoanalytic approach to learning theory (with more than a passing reference to Piaget). In K. Field, B. Cohler, and G. Wool (Eds), *Learning and education: Psychoanalytic perspectives* (pp. 99–126). Madison: International Universities Press.

Apple, M. (1990). *Ideology and curriculum.* London: Routledge.

Apple, M. (1987). Gendered teaching, gendered labor. In T. Popkewitz (Ed.), *Critical studies in teacher education* (pp. 57–83). London: Falmer Press.

Arendt, H. (1951). *The origins of totalitarianism.* New York: World Book Publishing Company.

Aristotle. (2000). *The metaphysics.* Oxford: Oxford University Press.

Assagioli, R. (1965). *Psychosynthesis: A manual of principles and techniques.* New York: Penguin Group.

Auerbach, E. (1968). *Mimesis: The representation of reality in western literature.* Princeton: Princeton University Press.

Bair, D. (2003). *Jung: A biography.* Boston, MA: Little, Brown.

Bandura, R. (1986). *Social foundations of thought and action.* Englewood Cliffs: Prentice-Hall.

Banks, J. and Banks, C. (Eds) (2001). *Multicultural education: Issues and perspectives* (4th edition). New York: Wiley.

Barford, D. (Ed.). (2002). *The ship of thought: Essays on psychoanalysis and learning.* London: Karnac Books.

Barnaby, P. and D'Acierno, P. (Eds) (1990). *C. G. Jung and the humanities: Toward a hermeneutics of culture.* Princeton: Princeton University Press.

Basch, M. (1989) The teacher, the transference, and development. In K. Field, B. Cohler, and G. Wool (Eds), *Learning and education: Psychoanalytic perspectives* (pp. 771–788). Madison: International Universities Press.

Barzun, J. (2000). *From dawn to decadence: Five hundred years of Western cultural life.* New York: HarperCollins.

Bateson, G. (1972). *Steps to an ecology of mind.* New York: Ballantine Books.

Beck, A. and Weishaar, M. (1995). Cognitive psychotherapy. In R. Corsini and D. Wedding (Eds), *Current psychotherapies* (pp. 229–261). Itasca: Peacock Publishers.

Beck, J. (1995). *Cognitive therapy: Basics and beyond*. New York: Guilford Press.

Becker, C. (1966). *The heavenly city of the eighteenth-century philosophers*. New Haven: Yale University Press.

Bell, D. (1976). *The cultural contradictions of capitalism*. New York: Basic Books.

Bellah, R., Madsen, R., Sullivan, W., Swidler, A., and Tipton, S. (1996). *Habits of the heart*. Berkeley: University of California Press.

Berger, P. (1967). *The sacred canopy: Elements of a sociological theory of religion*. New York: Doubleday and Company.

Bergson, H. (1902). *Creative evolution*. New York: Modern Library.

Berliner, D. and Biddle, B. (1995). *The manufactured crisis: Myths, fraud, and the attack upon America's public schools*. Reading, MA: Addison Wesley.

Bernstein, B. (1996). *Pedagogy, symbolic control, and identity: Theory, research, critique*. London: Taylor and Francis.

Bernstein, H. (1989). Self-organization as a fundamental psychological need. In K. Field, B. Cohler, and G. Wool (Eds), *Learning and education: Psychoanalytic perspectives* (pp. 143–158). Madison: International Universities Press.

Best, S. and Kellner, D. (1991). *Postmodern theory*. New York: Guilford Press.

Block, A. (1997) *I'm only bleeding: Education as the practice of social violence against children*. New York: Peter Lang.

Bloom, H. (1994). *The Western Canon: The books and school of the ages*. New York: Harcourt Brace.

Blos, P. (1940). *The adolescent personality: A study of individual behavior for the Commission on Secondary School Curriculum*. New York: D. Appleton-Century.

Blumer, H. (1969). *Symbolic interactionism*. Englewood Cliffs: Prentice-Hall.

Bohm, D. (1986). Time, the implicate order, and pre-space. In D. Griffin (Ed.), *Physics and the ultimate significance of time* (pp. 177–208). Albany: State University of New York Press.

Bonhoffer, D. (1963). *The cost of discipleship*. New York: Collier Books.

Boorstein, S. (Ed.) (1996). *Transpersonal psychotherapy*. Albany: SUNY Press.

Booth, W. (1961). *The rhetoric of fiction*. Chicago: University of Chicago Press.

Borrowman, M. (1965). *Teacher education in America: A documentary history*. New York: Teachers College Press.

Bourdieu, P. (1977). Cultural reproduction. In J. Karabel and A. Halsey (Eds), *Power and ideology in education* (pp. 487–507). New York: Oxford Press.

Bowles, S. and Gintis, H. (1976). *Schooling in capitalist America*. New York: Basic Books.

Bradford, S. (1982). *Disraeli: A biography*. New York: Stein and Day.

Britzman, D. (2003) *After-Education: Anna Freud, Melanie Klein, and Psychoanalytic Histories of Learning*. Albany: State University of New York Press.

Britzman, D. (2001). *Freud and education*. London: Routledge.

Britzman, D. (1999). Between 'lifting' and 'accepting': Observations on the work of Angst in learning. In S. Appel (Ed.), *Psychoanalysis and pedagogy* (pp. 1–16). London: Bergin and Garvey.

Brooke, R. (2009). *Jung and phenomenology*. London: Routledge.

Brophy, J. (1994). *Motivating students to learn*. Boston, MA: McGraw-Hill.

Brown, N. O. (1970). *Life against death: The psychoanalytic meaning of history. Middletown*. Middletown: Wesleyan University Press.

Brown, R. (1979). *The community of the Beloved Disciple*. New York: Paulist Press.

Bruner, J. (1996). *The culture of education*. Cambridge, MA: Harvard University Press.

Buber, M. (1985). *Between man and man*. New York: Vintage.

Buber, M. (1965). *I and thou*. New York: Vintage.

Bullough, R. (2001). *Uncertain lives: Children of hope, teachers of promise*. New York: Teachers College, Columbia University.

Bullough, R., Jr. (1991). Exploring personal teaching metaphors in preservice teacher education. *Journal of Teacher Education, 42(1)*, 43–51.

Bullough, R. (1988). *The forgotten dream of American public education*. Ames: Iowa State University Press.

Bullough, R. V., Jr., Patterson, R. S., and Mayes, C. (2002). Teaching as prophecy. *Curriculum Inquiry, 32(3)*, 341–348.

Bullough, R., Jr. and Gitlin, A. (1995). *Becoming a student of teaching: Methodologies for exploring self and school context*. New York: Garland Publishing.

Bunyan, J. (1678/2003). *The pilgrim's progress*. Oxford: Oxford University Press.

Burke, K. (1989). *On symbols and society* (J. Gusfield, Ed.). Chicago: University of Chicago Press.

Cambray, J. (2009). *Synchronicity: Nature and psyche in an interconnected universe*. College Station: Texas A&M University Press.

Campbell, J. (Ed.). (1960). *Spiritual disciplines: Papers from the Eranos yearbooks*. Princeton: Princeton University Press.

Campbell, J. (Ed.). (1955). *The mysteries: Papers from the Eranos yearbooks*. Princeton: Princeton University Press.

Campbell, J. (1949). *The hero with a thousand faces*. Princeton: Princeton University Press.

Carnot, S. (1824/1986). *Reflections on the motive power of fire*. Manchester: Manchester University Press.

Carotenuto, A. (1994). *The call of the daimon*. Wilmette: Chiron Publications.

Chapman, J. (1988). *Jung's three theories of religious experience*. Lewiston: Edwin Mellen Press.

Chardin, T. de. (1975). *The phenomenon of man*. New York: Perennial Library.

Charet, F. X. (1993). *Spiritualism and the foundations of C. G. Jung's philosophy*. Albany: State University of New York Press.

Chinen, A. (1989). *In the ever after: Fairy tales and the second half of life*. Wilmette: Chiron Publications.

Clifford, G. and Guthrie, J. (1988). *Ed school: A brief for professional development*. Chicago: University of Chicago Press.

Clift, R. and Houston, W. (1990). The potential for research contributions to reflective practice. In W. Clift and M. Pugach (Eds), *Encouraging reflective practice in Education: An analysis of issues and programmes* (pp. 208–222). New York: Teachers College Press.

Clandinin, J. and Connelly, M. (2000). *Narrative inquiry: Experience and story in qualitative research*. San Francisco: Jossey Bass.

Cohler, B. (1989). Psychoanalysis and education: Motive, meaning, and self. In K. Field, B. Cohler, and G. Wool (Eds), *Learning and education: Psychoanalytic perspectives* (pp. 11–84). Madison: International Universities Press.

Conforti, M. (1999). *Field, form, and fate: Patterns in mind, nature, and psyche.* Woodstock: Spring Publications.

Conger, J. and Galambos, J. (1997). *Adolescence and youth: Psychological development in a changing world.* New York: Longman.

Cortright, B. (2017). *Psychotherapy and spirit: Theory and practice in transpersonal Psychotherapy.* Albany: State University of New York Press.

Crain, W. (2010). *Theories of development: Concepts and applications* (6th edition). New York: Pearson.

Cremin, L. (1988). *American education: The metropolitan experience: 1876–1980.* New York: Harper and Row.

Cremin, L. (1964). *The transformation of the school: Progressivism in American education, 1876–1957.* New York: Vintage Press.

Croce, B. (1953). The primacy of the symbol. In E. Vivas and M. Krieger (Eds), *Theories of aesthetics* (pp. 234–256). New York: Reinhart.

Cuban, L. (1993). *How teachers taught: Constancy and change in American classrooms, 1890–1990.* New York: Teachers College Press.

Cuban, L. (1989). The persistence of reform in American schools. In D. Warren (Ed.), *American teachers: Histories of a profession at work* (pp. 370–392). New York: Macmillan Publishing.

Deleuze, G. and Guattari, F. (1987). *A thousand plateaus.* Minneapolis: University of Minnesota Press.

Devall, B. (1985). *Deep ecology.* Salt Lake City: G. M. Smith.

Devine, D. (1995). Prejudice and out-group perception. In A. Tesser (Ed.), *Advanced social psychology* (pp. 467–524). New York: McGraw-Hill.

Dewey, J. (1916). Democracy and education. New York: Macmillan.

Diekman, H. (1999). *Complexes: Diagnosis and therapy in analytical psychology.* Wilmette: Chiron Publications.

Douglas, C. (1997). The historical context of analytical psychology. In P. Young-Eisendrath and T. Dawson (Eds), *The Cambridge companion to Jung* (pp. 17–34). Cambridge: Cambridge University Press.

Dourley, J. (1984). *The illness that we are: A Jungian critique of Christianity.* Toronto: Inner City Books.

Dourley, J. (1981). *C. G. Jung and Paul Tillich: Psyche as sacrament.* Toronto: Inner City Books.

Dunne, J. (1973). *Time and myth.* Garden City: Doubleday.

Durkheim, E. (1912/1995). *The elementary forms of religious life.* New York: Free Press.

Edinger, E. (1985). *Anatomy of the psyche: Alchemical symbolism in psychotherapy.* La Salle: Open Court.

Edinger, E. (1973). *Ego and archetype: Individuation and the religious function of the psyche.* Baltimore: Penguin Press.

Eisendrath-Young, P. and Hall, J. (1991). *Jung's self-psychology: A constructivist perspective.* New York: Guilford Press.

Eisner, E. and Vallance, E. (1985). *The educational imagination: On the design and evaluation of school programs.* New York: Macmillan.

Ekstein, R. and Motto, R. (1968) *From learning for love to love of learning: Essays on psychoanalysis and education.* New York: Brunner/Mazel Publishers.

Eliade, M. (1959). *The sacred and the profane: The nature of religion.* New York: Harcourt Brace Jovanovich.

Eliade, M. (1954). *The myth of the eternal return, or, Cosmos and history.* Princeton: Princeton University Press.

Eliade, M. (1951/1974). *Shamanism: Archaic techniques of ecstasy.* Princeton: Princeton University Press.

Eliot, T. S. (1971). *The complete poems and plays.* New York: Harcourt, Brace, Jovanovich.

Eliot, T. S. (1949). *Notes towards the definition of culture.* New York: Harcourt, Brace, Jovanovich.

Ellenberger, H. (1970). *The discovery of the unconscious: The history and evolution of dynamic psychiatry.* New York: Basic Books.

Ellis, Anita J. (2001). *An expression of the community: Cincinnati Public Schools' legacy of art and architecture.* Cincinnati: Art League Press.

Epstein, M. (1995). *Thoughts without a thinker: Psychotherapy from a Buddhist perspective.* New York: Basic Books.

Erikson, E. (1997). *The life cycle completed.* New York: W. W. Norton.

Fairbairn, W. R. D. (1992). *Psychoanalytic studies of the personality.* London: Routledge.

Fay, B. (2000). *Contemporary philosophy of social science: A multicultural approach.* Oxford: Blackwell Publishers.

Fay, B. (1987). *Critical social science: Liberation and its limits.* Ithaca: Cornell University Press.

Feige, D. (1999). The legacy of Gregory Bateson: Envisioning aesthetic epistemologies and praxis. In J. Kane (Ed.), *Education, information, and transformation* (pp. 77–109). Columbus: Merrill/Prentice Hall.

Fenichel, O. (1945). *The psychoanalytic theory of neurosis.* New York: W. W. Norton.

Ferrer, J. (2002). *Revisioning transpersonal theory: A participatory vision of human spirituality.* Albany: State University of New York Press.

Ferrucci, P. (1982) *What we may be: Techniques for psychological and spiritual growth through Psychosynthesis.* Los Angeles: Jeremy Tarcher.

Field, K. (1989) Some reflections on the teacher-student dialogue: A psychoanalytic perspective. In K. Field, B. Cohler, and G. Wool (Eds), *Learning and education: Psychoanalytic perspectives* (pp. 851–926). Madison: International Universities Press.

Field, K., Cohler, B., and Wool, G. (Eds) (1989). *Learning and education: psychoanalytic perspectives.* Madison: International Universities Press.

Fielder, L. (1969). *Love and death in the American novel.* New York: Stein and Day.

Firman, J. and Vargiu, J. (1996). *Personal and transpersonal growth. In transpersonal psychotherapy* (S. Boorstein, Ed.) (pp. 117–142). Albany: SUNY Press.

Fish, S. (1980). *Is there a text in this class? The authority of interpretive communities.* Cambridge, MA: Harvard University Press.

Forbes, S. (2003). *Holistic education: An analysis of its nature and ideas.* Brandon: Foundation for Educational Renewal Press.

Foucault, M. (1980). *Power/knowledge: Selected interviews and other writings, 1972–1977.* New York: Pantheon Books.

Foucault, M. (1979). *Discipline and punish.* New York: Vintage Books.

Foucault, M. (1975). *The birth of the clinic.* New York: Vintage Books.

Foucault, M. (1972). *The archaeology of knowledge.* New York: Pantheon Books.

Fordham, M. (1994). *Children as individuals.* London: Free Association Books.

Frankl, V. (1967). *Man's search for meaning.* New York: Washington Square Press.

Freire, P. (2001). *Pedagogy and freedom: Ethics, democracy, and civic courage.* New York: Rowman and Littlefield.

Freire, P. (1970). *The pedagogy of the oppressed.* New York: Seabury Press.

Freud, S. (1957). *A general selection from the works of Sigmund Freud* (J. Rickman, Ed.). Garden City: Doubleday and Company.

Freud, A. (1930). *Introduction to psychoanalysis: Lectures for child analysts and teachers, 1922–1935.* New York: International Universities Press.

Frey-Rohn, L. (1974). *From Freud to Jung: A comparative study of the psychology of the unconscious.* New York: G. P. Putnam's Sons.

Friedman, T. (2000). *The Lexus and the olive tree.* New York: Anchor Books.

Frye, N. (1957). *Anatomy of criticism: Four essays by Northrop Frye.* Princeton: Princeton University Press.

Gadamer, H. (1993). *Truth and method.* New York: Continuum.

Gardner, J. (1978). *On moral fiction.* New York: Basic Books.

Gay, P. (1998). *Freud: A life for our time.* New York: W. W. Norton.

Gebser, J. (1985). *The ever-present origin.* Athens: Ohio University Press.

Gelberg, D. (1997). *The 'business' of reforming American schools.* Albany: State University of New York Press.

Gellert, M. (2001). *The fate of America: An inquiry into national character.* Washington, DC: Brassey's.

Geo-JaJa, M. A. (2019). Human rights undermined and development denied: Neoliberalism and the imperialism of aid on culture. *Development and Change Journal, 37*(3): 78–94.

Geo-JaJa, M. A. and Mangum, G. (2003). Economic adjustment, education and human resource development in Africa: The case of Nigeria. *International Review of Education, 49(3–4),* 293–318.

Giddens, A. (2002). *Runaway world: How globalization is reshaping our lives.* London: Profile.

Giddens, A. (1991). *Modernity and self-identity: Self and society in the late modern age.* Stanford: Stanford University Press.

Giddens, A. (1990). *The consequences of modernity.* Stanford: Stanford University Press.

Giroux, H. and Myrciades, K. (Eds) (2001). *Beyond the corporate university: Culture and pedagogy in the new millennium.* Lanham: Rowman and Littlefield.

Gitlin, A. (1992). *Teachers' voices for school change: An introduction to educative research.* New York: Teachers College Press.

Glover, E. (1956). *Freud or Jung?* New York: Basic Books.

Goffman, E. (1997). *The Goffman reader* (C. Lemert and A. Branaman, Eds). London: Blackwell.

Goldbrunner, J. (1965). *Individuation: A study of the depth psychology of Carl Gustav Jung.* Indiana: University of Notre Dame Press.

Gramsci, A. (1971). *Selections from the prison notebooks.* New York: New International Publishers.

Graves, R. (1959). *The white goddess: A historical grammar of poetic myth.* New York: Farrar, Straus, and Giroux.

Gray, R. (1996). *Archetypal explorations: An integrative approach to human behavior.* London: Routledge.

Greene, M. (1974). Cognition, consciousness, and curriculum. In W. Pinar (Ed.), *Heightened consciousness, cultural revolution, and curriculum theory* (pp. 69–83). Berkeley: McCutchan Publishing.

Grof, S. and Grof, C. (Eds) (1989). *Spiritual emergency: When personal transformation becomes a crisis.* Los Angeles: Jeremy P. Tarcher.

Grossman, B. (1975). Freud and the classroom. In T. Roberts (Ed.), *Four psychologies applied to education: Freudian, behavioral, humanistic, transpersonal* (pp. 63–69). Cambridge, MA: Schenkman.

Guenther, H. and Kawamura, L. (1975). *Mind in Buddhist psychology.* Berkeley: Dharma Publishing.

Habermas, J. (1975). *Legitimation crisis.* New York: Beacon Press.

Halliday, M. (1978). *Language as social semiotic.* London: Edward Arnold.

Harding, E. (1963). *Psychic energy: Its source and its transformation.* New York: Putnam Publishing.

Hart, D. (1997). The classical Jungian school. In P. Young-Eisendrath and T. Dawson (Eds), *The Cambridge companion to Jung* (pp. 89–100). Cambridge: Cambridge University Press.

Hartshorne, C. (1984). *Omnipotence and other theological mistakes.* Albany: State University of New York Press.

Hauke, C. (2000). *Jung and the postmodern: The interpretation of realities.* London: Routledge.

Hayek, F. (1944). *The road to serfdom.* London: Routledge.

Heath, S. (1983). *Ways with words: Language, life, and work in communities and classrooms.* Cambridge: Cambridge University Press.

Heidegger, M. (1964). *Being and time* (E. Robinson, Trans.). New York: Harper and Row.

Heisig, J. (1979). *Imago Dei: A study of C. G. Jung's psychology of religion.* Lewisburg: Bucknell University Press.

Henderson, J. (1990). *Shadow and self: Selected papers in Analytical Psychology.* Wilmette: Chiron Publications.

Herzog, E. (1967). *Psyche and death.* New York: C. G. Jung Foundation for Analytical Studies.

Hewitt, J. (1984). *Self and society: A symbolic interactionist social psychology.* Boston, MA: Allyn and Bacon.

Hilgard, E. (1987). *Psychology in America: A historical survey.* San Diego: Harcourt Brace Jovanovich.

Hillman, J. (2004). *Archetypal psychology.* Putnam: Spring Publication.

Hoeller, S. (1982). *The gnostic Jung and the seven sermons to the dead.* Wheaton: Theosophical Publishing House.

Hollis, J. (2000). *The archeytpal imagination.* Texas: A&M Press.

Homans, P. (1995). *Jung in context: Modernity and the making of a psychology.* Chicago: University of Chicago Press.

Horowitz, I. (1993). *The decomposition of sociology.* New York: Oxford University Press.

Houston, J. (1996). *A mythic life: Learning to live our greater story.* San Francisco: Harper Collins Publishers.

Huebner, D. (1999). *The lure of the transcendent: Collected essays by Dwayne E. Huebner.* London: Lawrence Erlbaum Associates.

Huxley, J. (1945). *The perennial philosophy.* New York: Harper.

Hyde, L. (1998). *Trickster makes this world: Mischief, myth and art.* New York: North Point Press.

Jacobi, J. (1974). *Complex/archetype/symbol in the psychology of C. G. Jung.* Princeton: Princeton University Press.

Jacobi, J. (1968). *The psychology of C. G. Jung: An introduction with illustrations.* New Haven: Yale University Press.

James, W. (1977). *A pluralistic universe.* Cambridge, MA: Harvard University Press.

Jansz, J. and van Drunen, P. (2004). *A social history of psychology.* Oxford: Blackwell Publishing.

Jaspers, K. (1986). *Basic philosophical writings: A selection.* Athens: Ohio State University Press.

Jonas, H. (1958). *The gnostic god: The message of the alien God and the beginnings of Christianity.* Boston, MA: Beacon Press.

Jones, R. (Ed.) (1966) *Contemporary educational psychology: Selected readings.* New York: Harper and Row.

Jones, R. (1968) *Fantasy and feeling in education.* New York: New York University Press.

Jones, M., Jones, B., and Hargrove, T. (2003). *The unintended consequences of high-stakes testing.* Lanham: Rowman and Littlefield.

Joseph, P. and Burnaford, G. (1994). *Images of schoolteachers in twentieth-century America: Paragons, polarities, complexities.* New York: St Martin's Press.

Jung, C. G. (1984). *Psychology and western religion* (R. F. C. Hull, Trans.). Princeton: Princeton University Press.

Jung, C. G. (1978). *Psychology and the East* (R. F. C. Hull, Trans.). Princeton: Princeton University Press.

Jung, C. G. (1977). *The symbolic life* (Volume 18 in *The Collected Works*) (R. F. C. Hull, Trans.). Princeton: Princeton University Press.

Jung, C. G. (1973). *Letters* (Volume 1). (R. F. C. Hull, Trans.). Princeton: Princeton University Press.

Jung, C. G. (1971). *Psychological types* (Volume 6 in *The Collected Works*) (R. F. C. Hull, Trans.). Princeton: Princeton University Press.

Jung, C. G. (1970a). *Civilization in transition* (Volume 10 in *The Collected Works*) (R. F. C. Hull, Trans.). Princeton: Princeton University Press.

Jung, C. G. (1970b). *Psychology and religion: West and East* (Volume 11 in *The Collected Works*) (R. F. C. Hull, Trans.). Princeton: Princeton University Press.

Jung, C. G. (1969a). *The structure and dynamics of the psyche* (Volume 8 in *The Collected Works*) (R. F. C. Hull, Trans.). Princeton: Princeton University Press.

Jung, C. G. (1969b). *The archetypes and the collective unconscious* (Volume 9.1 in *The Collected Works*) (R. F. C. Hull, Trans.). Princeton: Princeton University Press.

Jung, C. G. (1969c). *Aion: Researches into the phenomenology of the self* (Volume 9.2 in *The Collected Works*) (R. F. C. Hull, Trans.). Princeton: Princeton University Press.

Jung, C. G. (1968a). *Psychology and alchemy* (Volume 12 in *The Collected Works*) (R. F. C. Hull, Trans.). Princeton: Princeton University Press.

Jung, C. G. (1968b). *Alchemical studies* (Volume 13 in *The Collected Works*) (R. F. C. Hull, Trans.). Princeton: Princeton University Press.

Jung, C. G. (1970c). *Mysterium coniunctionis* (Volume 14 in *The Collected Works*) (R. F. C. Hull, Trans.). Princeton: Princeton University Press.

Jung, C. G. (1967a). *Symbols of transformation: Analysis of the prelude to a case of schizophrenia* (Volume 5 in *The Collected Works*) (R. F. C. Hull, Trans.). Princeton: Princeton University Press.

Jung, C. G. (1967b). *Two essays on analytical psychology* (Volume 7 in *The Collected Works*) (R. F. C. Hull, Trans.). Princeton: Princeton University Press.

Jung, C. G. (1966a). *The spirit in man, art, and literature* (Volume 15 in the *Collected Works*) (R. F. C. Hull, Trans.). Princeton: Princeton University Press.

Jung, C. G. (1966b). *Psychology and Western religion* (Volumes 11 and 18 in *The Collected Works*) (R. F. C. Hull, Trans.). Princeton: Princeton University Press.

Jung, C. G. (1965). *Memories, dreams, reflections.* New York: Vintage.

Jung, C. G. (1958). *The undiscovered self.* Boston, MA: Little, Brown.

Jung, C. G. (1957). *Modern man in search of a soul.* New York: Harcourt, Brace and World.

Jung, C. G. (1954). *The development of personality: Papers on child psychology, education, and related subjects* (Volume 17 in *The Collected Works*) (R. F. C. Hull, Trans.). Princeton: Princeton University Press.

Jung, C. G. (1938). *Psychology and religion.* New Haven: Yale University Press.

Kalsched, D. (1996). *The inner world of trauma: Archetypal defences of the personal spirit.* London: Routledge.

Kant, I. (1781/1997). *The critique of pure reason.* Chicago: Hackett Publishing.

Kelly, S. (1993). *Individuation and the absolute: Hegel, Jung and the path towards wholeness.* Mahwah: Paulist Press.

Kelsey, M. (1984). Jung as philosopher and theologian. In R. Papadopoulos and G. Saayman (Eds), *Jung in modern perspective: The master and his legacy* (pp. 182–192). Lindfield: Unity Press.

Kermode, F. (2000). *The sense of an ending: Studies in the theory of fiction.* Oxford: Oxford University Press.

Kierkegaard, S. (1969). *A Kierkegaard Anthology* (R. Bretall, Ed.). Princeton: Princeton University Press.

Kierkegaard, S. (2003). *Fear and trembling* (A. Hannay, Trans.). New York: Penguin Books.

Kirschner, S. (1996). *The religious and romantic origins of psychoanalysis: Individuation and integration in post-Freudian theory.* New York: Cambridge University Press.

Klein, M. (1932/1975). *The psychoanalysis of children* (A. Strachey, Trans.). New York: Delacorte Press.

Kliebard, H. (1986). *The struggle for the American curriculum: 1893–1958.* New York: Routledge.

Kniker, C. (1990). Teacher education and religion: The role of foundations courses in preparing students to teach about religions. *Religion and Public Education, 17(2),* 203–222.

Kniker, C. (1985). *Teaching about religion in the public schools.* Bloomington: Phi Delta Kappa.

Knox, J. (2004). Developmental aspects of analytical psychology: New perspectives from cognitive neuroscience and attachment theory. In J. Cambray and L. Carter (Eds), *Analytical psychology: Contemporary perspectives in Jungian analysis* (pp. 56–82). London: Brunner Routledge.

Kohut, H. (1978). *The search for self: Selected writings of Heinz Kohut: 1950–1978.* P. Ornstein (Ed.). Madison: International Universities Press.

Kopp, S. (1972). *If you meet the Buddha on the road, kill him: The pilgrimage of psychotherapy patients.* New York: Bantam.

Kozol, J. (1991). *Savage inequalities: Children in American schools.* New York: Harper.

Kristeva, J. (1989). *Language—The unknown: An invitation to linguistics.* New York: Columbia University Press.

Kubie, L. (1967) The forgotten man of education. In R. Jones (Ed.), *Contemporary educational psychology: Selected readings* (pp. 61–71). New York: Harper and Row.

Lacan, J. (1977). *Ecrits*. New York: W. W. Norton.

Lauter, E. and Rupprecht, C. (Eds) (1985). *Feminist archetypal theory: Interdisciplinary revisions of Jungian thought*. Knoxville: University of Tennessee Press.

Laux, D. (1968) A new role for teachers? In R. Jones (Ed.), *Contemporary educational psychology: Selected readings* (pp. 187–195). New York: Harper and Row.

Levinas, E. (1996). *Basic philosophical writings*. Bloomington: Indiana University Press.

Levi-Strauss, C. (1987). *Anthropology and myth*. New York: Blackwell.

Levi-Strauss, C. (1963). *Structural anthropology*. New York.

Linde, C. (1993). *Life stories: The creation of coherence*. New York: Oxford University Press.

Locke, J. (1689/1962). *Two treatises of civil government*. New York: Dutton.

López-Pedraza, R. (2012). *Hermes and his children*. Einsiedeln: Daimon Verlag.

Lyotard, J. (1984). *The postmodern condition*. Minneapolis: University of Minnesota Press.

Macias, J. (1987). The hidden curriculum of Papago teachers: American Indian strategies for mitigating cultural discontinuity in early schooling. In G. Spindler and L. Spindler (Eds), *Interpretive ethnography of education: At home and abroad* (pp. 363–380). London: Psychology Press.

Mailer, N. (1972). *Existential errands*. New York: Little, Brown.

Main, R. (2006). Religion. In R. K. Papodapoulos (Ed.), *The handbook of Jungian psychology: Theory, practice and applications* (pp. 296–303). London: Routledge Press.

Main, R. (2004). *The rupture of time: Synchronicity and Jung's critique of modern Western culture*. New York: Brunner-Routledge.

Martin, L. (1985). Jung as gnostic. In L. Martin and J. Goss (Eds), *Essays on the study of Jung and religion*. Lanham: University Press of America.

Marty, M. (1970). *Righteous empire: The Protestant experience in America*. New York: Dial Press.

Marx, K. (1843,1844/1978). *The Marx-Engels reader* (R. Tucker, Ed.). New York: W. W. Norton.

Matlin, M. (2012). *Cognition* (8th edition). New York: Wiley.

Matoon, M. (1985). *Jungian psychology in perspective*. New York: Free Press.

May, R. and Yalom, I. (1995). Existential psychotherapy. In R. Corsini and D. Wedding (Eds), *Current psychotherapies* (pp. 262–292). Itasca: F. E. Peacock.

Mayes, C. (2020). *Developing the whole student: New horizons in holistic educational theory and practice*. Lanham: Rowman and Littlefield.

Mayes, C. (2019b). *Reclaiming the fire: Depth psychology in teacher renewal*. Lanham: Rowman and Littlefield.

Mayes, C. (2017a). *An introduction to The Collected Works of C. G. Jung: Psyche as spirit*. Lanham: Rowman and Littlefield.

Mayes, C. (2017b). *Teaching and learning for wholeness: The role of archetypes in educational processes*. Lanham: Rowman and Littlefield.

Mayes, C. (2017c). Art as Individuation, individuation as art. *Quadrant: Journal of the C. G. Jung Society for Analytical Psychology, 46(2)*, 69–81.

Mayes, C. (2017d). Jung's view of the symbol and the sign in education. *Psychological Perspectives: A Semi-Annual Journal of Jungian Thought, 59(2)*, 191–201.

Mayes, C. (2015). *The archetypal hero's journey in teaching and learning: A study in Jungian pedagogy*. Madison: Atwood Educational Press.

Mayes, C. (2012). *Inside education: Depth psychology in teaching and learning*. Madison: Atwood Publishing.

Mayes, C. (2011). *After the apocalypse*. Provo: Onyx Press.

Mayes, C. (2010). *Nurturing the whole student. Five dimensions of holistic pedagogy*. Lanham: Rowman and Littlefield.

Mayes, C. (2009). The psychoanalysts' view of teaching and learning: 1922–2002. *Journal of Curriculum Studies, 40(2)*, 121–143.

Mayes, C. (2005a). *Jung and education: Elements of an archetypal pedagogy*. Lanham: Rowman and Littlefield.

Mayes, C. (2005b). *Seven curricular landscapes: An approach to the holistic curriculum*. Lanham: University Press of America.

Mayes, C. (2005c). Teaching and time: Foundations of a temporal pedagogy. *Teaching Education Quarterly, 32(2)*, 143–160.

Mayes, C. (2004). *Teaching mysteries: Foundations of a spiritual pedagogy*. Lanham: University Press of America.

Mayes, C. (2002). The teacher as an archetype of spirit. *Journal of Curriculum Studies, 34(6)*, 699–718.

Mayes, C. (2001). A transpersonal model for teacher reflectivity. *Journal of Curriculum Studies, 35(2)*, 56–70.

Mayes, C. (1999). Reflecting on the archetypes of teaching. *Teaching Education, 10(2)*, 3–16.

Mayes, C. (1998). The use of contemplative practices in teacher education. *Encounter: Education for Meaning and Social Justice, 11(3)*, 17–31.

Mayes, C. (1997). *Teacher education reform at the University of Utah: Problems and prospects. A dissertation*. University of Utah College of Education. Salt Lake City, UT.

Mayes, C. (1996). *The Holmes Reports: Perils and possibilities*. An unpublished dissertation. The University of Utah College of Education, Department of Language, Literacy and Culture. Salt Lake City, UT.

Mayes, C., Grandstaff, M., and Fidyk, A. (2019). *Reclaiming the fire: Depth Psychology in teacher renewal*. Lanham: Rowman and Littlefield.

Mayes, C., Cutri, R., Goslin, N., and Montero, F. (2016). *Understanding the whole student: Holistic multicultural education* (2nd edition). Lanham: Rowman and Littlefield.

Mayes, C. and Williams, E. (2010). *Nurturing the whole student: Five dimensions of the curriculum*. Lanham: Rowman and Littlefield.

McLaren, P. (1998). *Life in schools: An introduction to critical pedagogy in the foundations of education* (3rd edition). New York: Longman.

McMillan, S. (2013). *A pedagogy of liminality: Kierkegaard's challenge to corporate education*. A dissertation. Department of Educational Leadership and Foundations: Brigham Young University. Provo, Utah. USA.

Meier, C. A. (1986). *Soul and body: Essays on the theories of C. G. Jung*. Santa Monica: Lapis Press.

Meissner, W. (1984). *Psychoanalysis and religious experience*. New Haven: Yale University Press.

Merton, T. (1977). *The collected poems of Thomas Merton*. New York: New Directions.

Merton, T. (1967). *Mystics and Zen masters*. New York: Dell Publishing.

Merzel, D. (2007). *Big mind: Finding your way*. Boulder. Big Mind Press.

Messerli, J. (1972). *Horace Mann: A biography*. New York: Knopf.

Miller, J. (2004). *The transcendent function: Jung's model of psychological growth through dialogue with the unconscious*. Albany: State University of New York Press.

Miller, J. (1988). *The holistic curriculum*. Toronto: Ontario Institute for Studies in Education.

Mocanin, R. (1986). *Jung's psychology and Tibetan Buddhism: Western and Eastern paths to the heart*. London: Wisdom Publications.

Moe, T. and Chubb, J. (2009). *Liberating learning: Technology, politics and the future of American education*. San Francisco: Jossey Bass.

Moffett, J. (1994). *The universal schoolhouse: Spiritual awakening through education*. San Francisco: Jossey Bass.

Morrow, R. and Torres, C. (1995). *Social theory and education: A critique of theories of social and cultural reproduction*. Albany: State University of New York Press.

Nagy, M. (1991). *Philosophical issues in the psychology of C. G. Jung*. Albany: State University of New York Press.

Niebuhr, R. (1944). *The children of light and the children of darkness: A vindication of democracy and a critique of its traditional defenders*. Chicago: University of Chicago Press.

Nielsen, I. (2002). *Cultic theatres and ritual drama: A study in regional development and religious interchange between East and West in antiquity*. Aarhaus: Aarhaus University Press.

Nieto, S. (2000). *Affirming diversity: The sociopolitical context of multicultural education*. New York: Addison, Wesley, Longman.

Noddings, N. (1995). Care and moral education. In W. Kohli (Ed.), *Critical conversations in the philosophy of education* (pp. 137–148). New York: Routledge.

Noddings, N. (1992). *The challenge to care in schools: An alternative approach to education*. New York: Teachers College Press.

Noll, R. (1994). *The Jung cult: Origins of a charismatic movement*. Princeton: Princeton University Press.

Nord, W. (1995). *Religion and American education: Rethinking a national dilemma*. Chapel Hill: University of North Carolina Press.

Nord, W. (1994). Ten suggestions for teaching about religion. In C. Haynes and O. Thomas (Eds), *Finding common ground: A first amendment guide to religion and public education*. Vanderbilt University: Freedom Forum First Amendment Center.

Nowotny, H. (1989). Mind, technologies, and collective time consciousness: From the future to an extended present. In J. G. Fraser (Ed.), *Time and mind: Interdisciplinary issues* (pp. 197–216). Madison: International Universities Press.

Odajnyk, V. (1976). *Jung and politics: The political and social ideas of C. G. Jung*. New York: Harper Colophon Publications.

Otto, R. (1960). *The idea of the holy*. Middlesex: Penguin Books.

Owens, L. (2010). The hermeneutics of vision: C. G. Jung and Liber novus. *The Gnostic: A Journal of Gnosticism, Western Esotericism and Spirituality*, *3*, 23–46.

Pagels, E. (1992). *The gnostic Paul: Gnostic exegeses of the Pauline letters*. Philadelphia: Trinity Press International.

Pai, Y. and Adler, S. (2010). *Cultural foundations of education* (3rd edition). New York: Merrill, Prentice Hall.

Palmer, M. (1995). *Freud and Jung on religion*. New York: Routledge.

Palmer, P. (1998). *The courage to teach: Exploring the inner landscape of a teacher's life*. San Francisco: Jossey Bass.

Pauson, M. (1988). *Jung the philosopher: Essays in Jungian thought*. New York: Peter Lang.

Pearson, G. (1954). *Psychoanalysis and the education of the child*. New York: W. W. Norton.

Peat, F. D. (1988). *Synchronicity: The bridge between mind and matter*. New York: Bantam.

Peller, L. (1967/1978). Psychoanalysis in public education. In E. Plank (Ed.), *On development and education of young children: Selected papers* (pp. 108–118). New York: Philosophical Library.

Peller, L. (1945/1978). Educational remarks. In E. Plank (Ed.), *On development and education of young children: Selected papers* (pp. 11–18). New York: Philosophical Library.

Perls, F. (1957). *Gestalt therapy*. New York: Bantam Books.

Pfister, O. (1922). *Psycho-analysis in the service of education, being an introduction to psycho-analysis*. London: Henry Kimpton.

Phenix, P. (1964). *Realms of meaning: A philosophy of the curriculum for general education*. New York: McGraw-Hill.

Philipson, M. (1963). *Outline of a Jungian aesthetic*. Evanston: Northwest University Press.

Piers, M. (1969). Play and mastery. In R. Ekstein and R. Motto (Eds), *From learning for love to love of learning: Essays on psychoanalysis and education* (pp. 99–106). New York: Brunner/Mazel Publishers.

Piers, G. and Piers, M. (1989). Modes of learning and the analytic process. In K. Field, B. Cohler, and G. Wool (Eds), *Learning and education: Psychoanalytic perspectives* (pp. 199–208). Madison: International Universities Press.

Pinnegar, S. (2017). Understanding field experience: The zone of maximal contact and the conundrums and sacred stories in teacher education. *Studying Teacher Education, 13*, 210–215. DOI: 10.1080/17425964.2017.1341259.

Pintrich, P., Marx, R., and Boyle, R. (1993). Beyond cold conceptual change: 'The role of motivational beliefs and classroom contextual factors in the process of conceptual change'. *Review of Educational Research, 63*, 167–199.

Plato. (1968). *The republic*. New York: Basic Books.

Popkewitz, T. (1987) *Critical studies in teacher education*. London: Falmer Press.

Postman, N. and Weingartner, C. (1969). *Teaching as a subversive activity*. New York: Free Press.

Progoff, I. (1959). *Depth psychology and modern man: A new view of the magnitude of human personality, its dimensions and resources*. New York: Julian Press.

Ravitch, D. (2000). *Left back: A century of failed school reforms*. New York: Simon and Schuster.

Ravitch, D. (1983). *The troubled crusade: American education, 1945–1980*. New York: Basic Books.

Redl, F. and Wattenberg, W. (1951). *Mental hygiene in teaching*. New York: Harcourt, Brace and Company.

Remen, R. (1999). Educating for mission, meaning and compassion. In S. Glazer (Ed.), *The heart of learning: Spirituality in education* (pp. 33–49). New York: Jeremy P. Tarcher.

Ricoeur, P. (1991). *Freud and philosophy: An essay in interpretation*. New Haven: Yale University Press.

Ricoeur, P. (1985). *Time and narrative*. Chicago: University of Chicago Press.

Rieff, P. (1987) *The triumph of the therapeutic: Uses of faith after Freud*. Chicago: University of Chicago Press.

Rieff, P. (1961). *Freud: The mind of the moralist*. Garden City: Doubleday and Company.

Rizzuto, A-M. (1979). *The birth of the living God: A psychoanalytic study*. Chicago: University of Chicago Press.

Robertson, R. (1995). *Jungian archetypes: Jung, Godel, and the history of archetypes*. York Beach: Nicolas-Hays.

Rogoff, B. (2003). *The cultural nature of human development*. New York: Oxford University Press.

Rogoff, B. (1990). *Apprenticeship in thinking: Cognitive development in social context*. New York: Oxford University Press.

Rohr, R. (2016). *The divine dance: The Trinity and your transformation*. London: SPK.

Rorty, R. (1981). *Philosophy and the mirror of nature*. Princeton: Princeton University Press.

Rowland, S. (2012). *C. G. Jung in the humanities: Taking the soul's path*. Dallas: Fdx Spring.

Rowland, S. (2008). *Psyche and the arts: Jungian approaches to music, architecture, literature and painting*. London: Routledge.

Rowland, S. (2005). *Jung as a writer*. London: Routledge.

Rowland, S. (2002). *Jung: A feminist revision*. New York: Wiley.

Rowland, S. (1999). *C. G. Jung and literary theory: The challenge from fiction*. New York: St Martin's Press.

Salzberger-Wittenberg, I. (1989). *The emotional experience of learning and teaching*. London: Routledge and Kegan Paul.

Samuels, A. (2001). *Politics on the couch: Citizenship and the internal life*. London: Routledge.

Samuels, A. (1997). *Jung and the post-Jungians*. London: Routledge.

Sandner, D. (1991). *Navaho symbols of healing: A Jungian exploration of ritual, image, and medicine*. Rochester: Healing Arts Press.

Sanford, J. (1993). *Mystical Christianity: A psychological commentary on the Gospel of John*. New York: Crossroads.

Sarason, S. (1999). *Teaching as a performing art*. New York: Teachers College Press.

Sartre, J. (1956). *Being and nothingness: An essay on phenomenological ontology*. New York: Philosophical Library.

Savickas, A. (1979). *The concept of symbol in the psychology of C. G. Jung*. Innsbruck: Resch Verlag.

Schafer, R. (1980). Narration in the psychoanalytic dialogue. *Critical Inquiry, 7(1)*, 29–54.

Scholes, R. (1980). Language, narrative, and anti-narrative. *Critical Inquiry, 7(1)*, 209–223.

Schön, D. (1987). *Educating the reflective practitioner*. San Francisco: Jossey Bass.

Schwartz-Salant, N. (1995). Archetypal factors underlying sexual acting-out in the transference/countertransference process. In N. Schwartz-Salant and M. Stein (Eds), *Transference/countertransference* (pp. 1–30). Wilmette, IL: Chiron Publications.

Scott, P. D. (2007). *The road to 9/11: Wealth, empire, and the future of America.* Berkeley: University of California Press.

Scotton, B., Chinen, A., and Battista, J. (Eds) (1996). *Textbook of transpersonal psychiatry and psychology.* New York: Basic Books.

Segal, R. (1995). *The allure of Gnosticism: The Gnostic experience in Jungian psychology and contemporary culture.* Chicago: Open Court.

Shamdasani, S. (2005). *Jung stripped bare by his biographers, even.* London: Karnac Books.

Shamdasani, S. (2003). *Jung and the making of modern psychology: The dream of a science.* Cambridge: Cambridge University Press.

Sheldrake, R. (1981). *A new science of life: The hypothesis of formative causation.* Los Angeles: Jeremy P. Tarcher.

Singer, J. (1988). Foreword. In D. Feinstein and S. Krippner (Eds), *Personal mythology: Using rituals, dreams, and imagination to discover your inner story.* Los Angeles: Jeremy P. Tarcher. Skinner.

Singer, T. (Ed.) (2000). *The vision thing: Myth, politics and psyche in the world.* London: Routledge.

Sklar, K. (1973). *Catherine Beecher: A study in American domesticity.* New Haven: Yale University Press.

Slife, B. (1993). *Time and psychological explanation.* Albany: State University of New York Press.

Snider, C. (1991). *The stuff that dreams are made on: A Jungian interpretation of literature.* Wilmette: Chiron Press.

Solomon, H. (1994). The transcendent function and Hegel's dialectical vision. *Journal of Analytical Psychology, 39(1),* 77–100.

Sommerville, M. and Rappaport, D. (Eds) (2000). *Transdisciplinarity: Recreating integrated knowledge.* Oxford: Oxford University Press.

Sourvinou-Inwood, S. (2003). *Tragedy and Athenian religion.* Lanham: Lexington Books.

Sovatsky, S. (1998). *Words from the soul: Time, East/West spirituality, and the psychotherapeutic narrative.* Albany: State University of New York Press.

Spiegelman, J. M. and Mansfeld, V. (1996). On the physics and psychology of the transference as an interactive field. In J. Spiegelman (Ed.), *Psychotherapy as a mutual process* (pp. 183–206). Tempe: New Falcon Publications.

Spring, J. (2006). *American education* (12th edition). New York: McGraw Hill.

Spring, J. (1976a). *The sorting machine: National educational policy since 1945.* New York: David McKay.

Spring, J. (1976b). *Educating the worker-citizen.* New York: McGraw Hill.

Stein, M. (2006). *The principle of individuation: Toward the development of human consciousness.* Wilmette: Chiron Publications.

Stein, M. (1995). Power, shamanism, and maieutics in the countertransference. In N. Schwartz- Salant and M. Stein (Eds), *Transference/countertransference* (pp. 67–88). Wilmette: Chiron Publications.

Stein, M. (1990). C. G. Jung: Psychologist and theologian. In R. Moore and D. Meckel (Eds), *Jung and Christianity in dialogue: Faith, feminism, and hermeneutics* (pp. 3–20). New York: Paulist Press.

Stein, M. (1984). Jung's Green Christ: Jung's challenge to contemporary religion. In M. Stein and R. Moore (Eds), *Jungian analysis*. Wilmette: Chiron Publications.

Stein, M. (Ed.) (1982). *Jungian analysis*. Boulder: Shambhala Publications.

Stevens, A. (2006). The archetypes. In R. K. Papodapoulos (Ed.), *The handbook of Jungian psychology: Theory, practice and applications* (pp. 74–93). London: Routledge Press.

Stevens, A. (2003). *Archetype revisited: An Updated natural history of the self*. Toronto: Inner City Books.

Stokes, D. (1997). *Called to teach: Exploring the worldview of called prospective teachers During Their preservice teacher education experience*. An unpublished dissertation. Salt Lake City: University of Utah.

Sugg, R. (Ed.) (1992). *Jungian literary criticism*. Evanston: Northwestern University Press.

Suzuki, D. T. (1964) *An Introduction to Zen Buddhism*. New York: Grove Press.

Symonds, P. (1951). *The ego and the self*. New York: Appleton-Century-Croft.

Tacey, D. (2001). *Jung and the New Age*. Philadelphia: Brunner Routledge.

Taylor, F. W. (1911). *The principles of scientific management*. New York: Harper and Brothers.

Thompson, J. and Mayes, C. (2020). Healing cultural divides: A Jungian approach. In *Psychological perspectives: A semiannual journey of Jungian thought*. C. G. Jung Institute of Los Angeles.

Thoreau, H. D. (1966). *Walden and Civil disobedience: Authoritative texts, background, reviews, and essays in criticism*. New York: W. W. Norton.

Tillich, P. (1972). *A history of Christian thought: From its Judaic and Hellenistic origins to Existentialism*. New York: Touchstone.

Tillich, P. (1963). *The eternal now: University sermons*. New York: Charles Scribner and Sons.

Tillich, P. (1956). *The essential Tillich*. New York: Macmillan Publishing.

Tillich, P. (1959). *Theology of culture*. New York: Oxford University Press.

Tillich, P. (1952). *The courage to be*. New Haven: Yale University Press.

Tomkins, S. (1979). *Script theory: Differential magnification of affects*. Nebraska Symposium on Motivation (R. A. Deinstbier, Ed.). Lincoln, NE: University of Nebraska Press.

Tuchman, B. (1978). *A distant mirror: The calamitous 14th century*. New York: Knopf.

Tyack, D. (1974). *The one best system: A history of American urban education*. Cambridge, MA: Harvard University Press.

Tyler, L. (1975). Curriculum development from a psychoanalytic perspective. In T. Roberts (Ed.), *Four psychologies applied to education: Freudian, behavioral, humanistic, transpersonal* (pp. 55–62). Cambridge, MA: Schenkman.

Ulanov, A. (2001). *Finding space: Winnicott, God, and psychic reality*. Louisville: Westminster John Knox Press.

Ulanov, A. (1999). *Religion and the spiritual in Carl Jung*. New York: Paulist Press.

Vanauken, S. (1980). *A severe mercy*. New York: Harper Collins.

Van der Post, L. (1975). *Jung and the story of our time*. New York: Vintage Classics.

Vedfelt, O. (2001). *The dimensions of dreams: From Freud and Jung to Boss, Perls, and R. E. M.—a comprehensive sourcebook*. New York: Fromm International.

Vinovskis, M. (1985). *The origin of public high schools: A reexamination of the Beverly high school controversy*. Madison: University of Wisconsin Press.

Violas, P. (1978). *Training of the urban working class: A history of twentieth-century American education*. Chicago: Rand McNally.

Von Franz, M-L. (1991). Meeting and Order: Concerning Meeting Points and Differences between Depth Psychology and Physics. In R. Papadopoulos and G. Saayman (Eds), *Jung in modern perspective: The master and his legacy* (pp. 268–286). Dorset: Prism Press.

Von Franz, M.-L. (1974). *Number and time: Reflections leading toward a unification of depth psychology and physics*. Evanston: Northwestern University Press.

Vygotsky, L. (1986). *Mind in society: The development of psychological functions*. Cambridge, MA: Harvard University Press.

Walsh, R. and Vaughan, F. (Eds) (1980). *Paths beyond ego: The transpersonal vision*. Los Angeles: Jeremy P. Tarcher.

Warshaw, T. (1986). Preparation for teaching about religions in public schools. *Religious Education, 81(1)*, 79–92.

Washburne, M. (1994). *Transpersonal psychology in psychoanalytic perspective*. Albany: State University of New York Press.

Watras, J. (2002). *The foundations of educational curriculum and diversity: 1565 to the Present*. Boston, MA: Allyn and Bacon.

Watson, L. and Watson-Franke, B.-M. (1985). *Interpreting life histories*. New Brunswick: Rutgers University Press.

Wertsch, J. (1995). *Vygotsky and the social formation of mind*. Cambridge, MA: Harvard University Press.

Wheelwright, P. (1974). Poetry, myth, and reality. In W. Handy and M. Westbrook (Eds), *Twentieth century criticism: The major statements* (pp. 252–266). New York: Macmillan.

White, H. (1980). The value of narrativity in the representation of reality. *Critical Inquiry, 7(1)*, 6–30.

White, V. (1982). *God and the unconscious*. Dallas: Spring Publications.

White, M. and Epston, D. (1990). *Narrative means to therapeutic ends*. New York: W. W. Norton.

Whitehead, A. (1929). *Process and reality: An essay in cosmology*. New York: Macmillan.

Whitehead, A. (1964). *The Aims of Education: And Other Essays*. New York: New American Library.

Wickes, F. (1927/1966). *The inner world of childhood*. Englewood Cliffs: Prentice Hall.

Wiedemann, F. (1995). Mother, father, teacher, sister: Transference/ countertransference with women in the first stage of animus development. In N. Schwartz-Salant and M. Stein (Eds). *Transference/countertransference* (pp. 175–190). Wilmette, IL: Chiron Publications.

Wilber, K. (2001). *Sex, ecology and spirituality: The spirit of evolution*. Boston, MA: Shambhala.

Wilber, K. (2000). *Integral psychology: Consciousness, spirit, psychology, therapy*. London: Shambhala.

Wilber, K. 1983. *A sociable God: A brief introduction to a transcendental sociology*. New York: McGraw-Hill Book Company.

Winnicott, D. W. (1992). *Psychoanalytic explorations* (C. Winnicott, R. Shepherd, and M. Davis, Eds). Cambridge, MA: Harvard University Press.

Zachry, C. (1940). *Emotion and conduct in adolescence. For the Commission on Secondary School Curriculum.* New York: Appleton-Century.

Zachry, C. (1929). *Personality adjustments of school children, with an introduction by William Heard Kilpatrick.* New York: C. Scribner's Sons.

Zinn, H. (1990). *A people's history of the United States.* New York: Harper Perennial.

Zoja, L. (1998). Analysis and tragedy. In A. Casement (Ed.), *Post-Jungians today: Key papers in contemporary analytical psychology* (pp. 33–49), London: Routledge.

Index